The Illustrated Encyclopedia of
THE EARTH'S RESOURCES

Marshall Cavendish

Academic Advisors:
Doctor Ray Hall,
Lecturer in Geography,
Queen Mary College, University of London.

Doctor P. F. Rawson, B.Sc., Ph.D., F.G.S.,
Queen Mary College, University of London.

Editors:
Michael Bisacre
Richard Carlisle
Deborah Robertson
John Ruck

Published by Marshall Cavendish Books Limited
58 Old Compton Street,
London W1V 5PA.

© Marshall Cavendish Limited 1975—84

Printed and bound in Italy by New Interlitho SpA.

ISBN 0 86307 198 8

Contents

The Planet Earth

The Land

The Oceans

The
Planet Earth

Earthquakes

Earthquakes are movements within the earth caused by natural or man-made stresses. Many are so slight that they can barely be detected but others can be violent and catastrophic. In 1960 the Agadir earthquake in Morocco killed 12,000 people and nearly 50,000 died as a result of the Peruvian earthquake of 1970.

There are some parts of the world, *seismic* regions, where earthquakes are common occurrences. These lie along relatively narrow and unstable sections of the earth's crust which are also often areas of volcanic activity.

At these points a constant build-up of stress is released by sections of rock shifting along fault planes—cracks in the earth. These movements, known as *tectonic* events, are usually felt over a wide area and can be prolonged. In the San Fernando earthquake in 1971 small aftershocks went on for more than three days after the main shock.

Sometimes old fault areas can be briefly reactivated, causing minor earthquakes in *aseismic* regions such as Britain where they do not normally occur. The stresses which cause major earthquakes, however, build up along the edges of the plates or layers which form the earth's outer crust.

When rocks yield under stress a series of shocks radiate in all directions. If they are strong enough to reach the earth's surface the ground trembles, and ripples may be produced so that cracks, or fissures, open and close.

At the beginning of an earthquake there will be minor shocks which may be barely felt, then several more violent tremors spaced from a few seconds to a few hours apart. These are followed by small aftershocks, which can continue for several days or even weeks, while the disturbed rocks in the region of origin readjust and settle down.

Earthquakes quite frequently accompany or anticipate volcanic eruptions. Although they may have disastrous effects in the immediate vicinity, these die out rapidly away from the eruption.

Apart from the immediate effects of collapsed buildings, the earthquake can create havoc by burying settlements under landslides, destroying coastal regions with tidal waves, and causing fires from damaged cables, gas mains and petrol storage tanks. It is these secondary effects that most often cause the appalling loss of life associated with an earthquake. In the San Francisco earthquake of 1906 fire caused 400 million dollars worth of damage, and destroyed 700,000 homes in the Tokyo earthquake of 1923. The destruction of sewage systems and water supplies also tends to lead to epidemics breaking out in the disaster area.

Many earthquakes occur in coastal regions or under the ocean floor, resulting in a sudden shift in the level of the sea bed. Huge waves or *tsunami* are created by the water displacement and their effect may be felt for hundreds of miles. In the open ocean these waves are hardly noticeable and make no impression on passing vessels. As the wave nears shore and reaches shallower water, however, it gets larger and larger and travels at great speed. The 'tidal' wave may surge far

Above: Movement of the San Andreas fault in 1906 produced an earthquake which destroyed large areas of San Francisco. Much of the damage was caused by fires that broke out as gas mains fractured. The seismograph tracing of the vibrations was recorded in Albany, New York, 4,830 km (3,000 miles) away.

Left: These two views of the Peruvian village of Yungay show how it looked before and after an earthquake in 1970. The shock dislodged snow and ice from Nevados Huascarán, highest peak in Peru. A massive avalanche careered along the Santa valley at 480 km (298 miles) per hour, devastating Yungay.

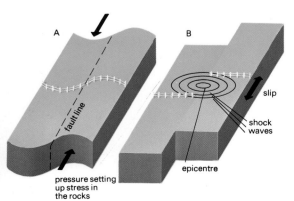

Left: The two sides of a fault have bonded since the last earthquake. As stress builds up around the bond, rocks bend to accommodate it in A. In B the bond fails and the rocks fracture. The stress is relieved and the rocks spring back causing vibrations from the spot, or focus, where the bond failed.

Right: Earth movements caused by earthquakes. A road in Hachinohe, Japan, has been partially destroyed by vertical subsidence. All the railway lines in Niigata, Japan (far right) were buckled by an earthquake in 1964. Undulatory features of this type are characteristic of earthquake damage and are often caused by soil liquefaction.

A

fault line

pressure setting up stress in the rocks

B

slip

shock waves

epicentre

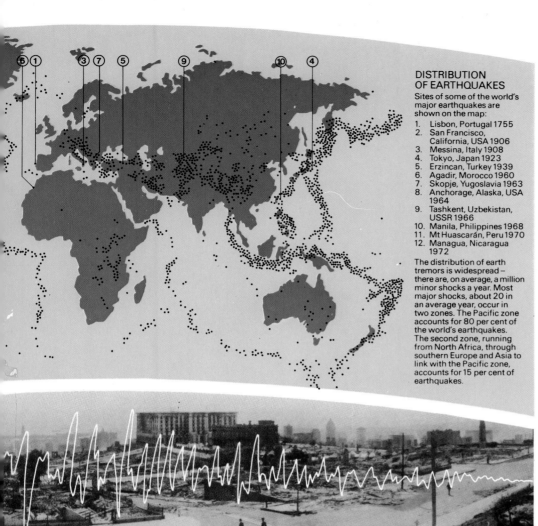

DISTRIBUTION OF EARTHQUAKES

Sites of some of the world's major earthquakes are shown on the map:

1. Lisbon, Portugal 1755
2. San Francisco, California, USA 1906
3. Messina, Italy 1908
4. Tokyo, Japan 1923
5. Erzincan, Turkey 1939
6. Agadir, Morocco 1960
7. Skopje, Yugoslavia 1963
8. Anchorage, Alaska, USA 1964
9. Tashkent, Uzbekistan, USSR 1966
10. Manila, Philippines 1968
11. Mt Huascarán, Peru 1970
12. Managua, Nicaragua 1972

The distribution of earth tremors is widespread – there are, on average, a million minor shocks a year. Most major shocks, about 20 in an average year, occur in two zones. The Pacific zone accounts for 80 per cent of the world's earthquakes. The second zone, running from North Africa, through southern Europe and Asia to link with the Pacific zone, accounts for 15 per cent of earthquakes.

of the continental shelf around land, however, the water piles up while continuing to move at a great speed. The result is a tidal wave or *tsunami* which sometimes surges far inland, especially along coasts with long narrow inlets. A tsunami can affect a region far removed from an earthquake. People have been drowned in Hawaii as a result of an earthquake in the Aleutian trench, over 3,000 km (1,900 miles) away in the North Pacific Ocean.

One of the most disastrous earthquakes in history, and one which first excited some scientific curiosity, was the Lisbon earthquake of 1 November 1755 in Portugal. This was felt over a wide area as witnessed by the account in *Gentleman's Magazine* of March 1756 by Mr Stoqueler, the Hamburg consul in Lisbon, who was about 30 km (19 miles) to the west-north-west of the city that day. 'The day broke with a serene sky, the wind continuing east; but at 9 o'clock the sun began to grow dim, and about half an hour after 9, we heard a rumbling like that of carriages, which increased so much as to resemble the noise of the loudest cannon; and immediately we felt the first shock, which was succeeded by a second, third and fourth.' In Lisbon itself, the first shock brought down many buildings while worshippers were at church—thousands were crushed. Many more were killed by the fires and tsunami which then swept parts of the city. The effects were felt, with diminishing intensity, as far away as Switzerland and Scotland where water levels in various lakes oscillated slightly. The resultant tsunami created noticeable waves in the North Sea and reached Martinique in the Caribbean.

While many in Europe found evidence

Left: Earthquakes under the sea or in coastal regions set up great waves, or tsunami, which can cause devastation far away from the earthquake site. Boats were flung inland at Kodiak by waves created by the Alaskan earthquake of 1964. A Pacific early warning system is now in operation.

Right: 'The Great Wave of Kanagawa', a Japanese print, shows a tsunami. Tsunamis are caused by rapid rise or fall of the sea floor during an earthquake. In open sea tsunami, often hundreds of miles long, may pass unnoticed. When they reach the continental shelf close to land, water piles up to heights of 12m (40ft).

Left: Another example of earth movement can be seen in this orange grove which was offset along the San Jacinto fault in California during the Imperial Valley earthquake of 1940. The photograph was taken 19 years later.

Right: The intensity of an earthquake diminishes from a zone of maximum effect, the *epicentre*, which is directly over its origin or *focus*, to areas where its effects can no longer be felt. The lines of equal intensity or *isoseismic* lines are arranged concentrically around the epicentre. The numerals show the intensity and the arrows show the movements of P and S waves and the two types of surface waves.

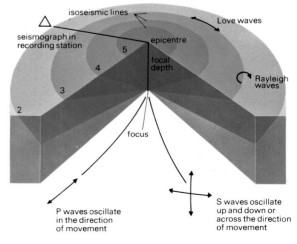

isoseismic lines

Love waves

seismograph in recording station

epicentre

focal depth

Rayleigh waves

5

4

3

2

focus

P waves oscillate in the direction of movement

S waves oscillate up and down or across the direction of movement

of God's or the Devil's work in these events, a small number of scientists pursued their own investigations. Thus Mr Stoqueler noted some of the local effects away from the city, such as springs drying up and new ones appearing, a swampy lake uplifted to form dry land, and the sea retreating so that 'you walk almost dry to places where before you could not wade'.

More importantly, as a result of collecting as many observations on the effect of the earthquake as possible, John Mitchell (1724-1793) suggested that an initial explosive shock could have given rise to waves spreading out through the rocks in all directions. This fundamental realization heralded an increasingly scientific approach to the study of earthquakes, or seismology.

Measurement of earthquakes

There are two main methods of measuring the strength of earthquakes—the Mercalli scale which relies on the comparison of eye-witness accounts of the effects of the earthquake and the Richter scale. In 1935 C. F. Richter, an American seismologist, devised a formula for calculating the strength of an earthquake from instrumental recordings of its magnitude. This is related to the total amount of energy stored in the rock under stress and released during an earthquake shock by the initial rock fractures at the point of origin, or *focus*.

The depth of the focus can be calculated. Shallow earthquakes have a focus above the boundary between the earth's crust and the deeper mantle. This boundary, known as the Moho after the Yugoslav seismologist Mohorovicic who discovered it, is 35 km (22 miles) deep. Intermediate

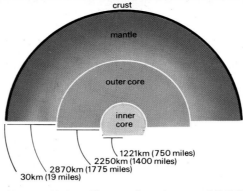

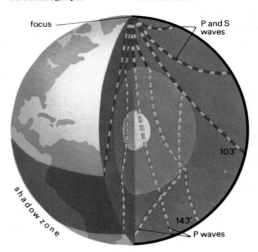

Above and below: The course of earthquake waves as they pass through the earth indicates its structure. The progress of the waves suggests a change in density and composition between the *crust* and the *mantle*. P and S waves that have travelled through the earth are registered on seismographs through an arc of 0°-103° from the epicentre. Both then disappear into the *shadow zone*. P waves alone, noticeably bent, reappear at 143°. This suggests a liquid outer core, since S waves cannot travel through liquids. Increased speed of P waves through the central part of the core suggests that the inner core is solid.

earthquakes have a focus between the Moho and a depth of 300 km (190 miles). Deep earthquakes have a focus below this, usually between 500 and 700 km (310 to 435 miles) from the surface.

A single earthquake produces three main types of shock wave, referred to as P, S and L waves. P or 'Primae' or 'Push and Pull' waves are analogous to sound waves in which each particle of rock vibrates longitudinally or parallel to the direction of the wave. S or 'Secundae' or 'Shear' waves are more like light waves in that each particle of rock has a shear motion, across the direction of movement of the wave. While P waves can pass through solids, liquids and gases, S waves pass through solids only. P waves also travel more quickly than S waves and therefore are picked up first by a distant seismograph.

A third, even slower set of waves are L or 'Long' waves which pass only through the earth's crust and are the last to be picked up by a seismograph. Conversely they are more easily detected than P and S waves at great distances from the source as they lose their energy more slowly. Surface waves set up by very large earthquakes have been recorded after they have travelled around the earth six times. There are two main types of L waves: Rayleigh waves and Love waves, which oscillate rather like P and S waves respectively.

A global network of seismological stations coupled with rapid exchange of information means that the focus, magnitude and *epicentre*, or the area of maximum effect, of an earthquake are quickly calculated. It also allows the study of the internal structure of the earth, using the

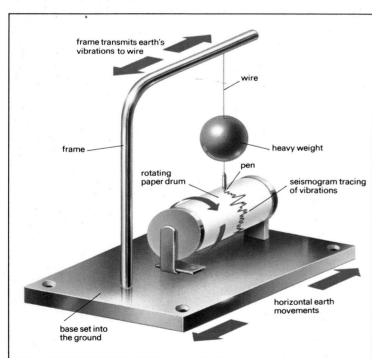

Above: A seismograph is a device for detecting and recording seismic waves. It consists of a spring suspended weight or pendulum and a clockwork-operated rotating drum. The frame of the device is set in bedrock. Seismic waves set up a horizontal motion which moves the frame backwards and forwards. The pen attached to the pendulum moves in the same way, marking the movements on the rotating drum. This produces a seismogram which indicates the duration and severity of the earth tremors. The record of an earthquake is a wavy line; when there is no movement the seismogram shows a straight line.

Right: The Mercalli scale uses observations of an earthquake's effect at a point on the earth's surface to assess its intensity. The scale is subjective and a reading can be exaggerated, for example, by the collapse of badly constructed buildings. However, it has given much useful information on the nature of earthquakes.

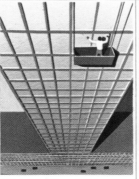

Point 2: Very slight. Felt by people on the upper floors of buildings and others favourably placed to sense tremors, such as those at rest.

Point 5: Quite strong. Small articles fall, liquids spill, sleepers wake, bells tinkle, doors swing open and closed. Noticed out of doors.

Point 7: Very strong. General alarm. Fall of loose plaster and tiles. Some buildings crack. Noticed by people driving vehicles.

various shock waves to 'X-ray' the structure. The behaviour of the various types of wave can be used, for example, to study the nature and relative thickness of the earth's crust in different regions. A natural progression from this is the creation of small, man-made seismic shocks to study the structures within the crust when looking for oil.

Earthquake distribution

The overall pattern of distribution of earthquake epicentres follows closely the regions of the last two major periods of mountain building during the Tertiary (between ten and 70 million years ago) and Recent (the last 11,000 years) eras, the rift valleys of Central and East Africa and the submarine mid-oceanic ridges. The distribution of active and recently extinct volcanoes is very similar. The pattern fits well with the arrangement of crustal plates which cover the surface of the globe. Such a distribution indicates stresses build up at the places where the crustal material is being formed at the mid-oceanic ridges and where the plate edges are moving against one another or plunging back down into the mantle.

The distribution of earthquake focusses is even more instructive. The deeper focus earthquakes, over 200 km (120 miles) deep, are limited to the ocean trench and island arc systems, such as the Japanese islands. They appear to originate in the zones where one crustal plate is being forced beneath another. The pattern of focusses indicates that the inclination of these zones is about 45°. The zones were discovered by the American seismologist, Hugo Benioff, and are known as Benioff zones or subduction zones.

Man-made earthquakes

Significant man-made earthquakes are created by nuclear explosions, major constructions such as dams and reservoirs, and by liquid injection into undergound reservoirs. The energy released by a nuclear explosion can equal that of a moderately strong earthquake, although the pattern of shock waves is different and can be distinguished from that of natural earthquakes. In regions of structural instability sudden changes in water level of a reservoir may lead to earthquakes. The pumping of liquid waste into deep wells near Denver, Colorado, and of water under pressure in the Rangely oil-field, Colorado, have both triggered off earthquakes in previously quiet areas.

Earthquake prediction and control

It is unlikely that inhabitants of the major earthquake zones could ever be moved out permanently, especially in view of the fertility and wealth of some regions, but it may prove possible to protect people from major disasters. Attempts have been made to recognize physical changes prior to a major earthquake. This work is still in its infancy, but several lines are possibly worth pursuing.

In Japan and the Soviet Union slight changes in the inclination of the ground have been detected prior to an earthquake. Changes in the pattern of microearthquakes, which form the normal background seismic activity have sometimes been observed before a major shock. Possibly the most important observation is the local change in the earth's magnetic field which has sometimes been detected prior to an earthquake.

Another recent discovery suggests that there is a marked variation in the velocity of P waves recorded from microquakes during quite long periods prior to major earthquakes. According to this theory, observations suggest that San Francisco and central California will remain free from major earthquakes for at least the next 25 years.

The modification of earthquake patterns to avoid a major disaster may soon prove scientifically possible. Small earthquakes have been induced by injecting fluids into faulted areas. From this it has been inferred that strains built up along faults such as the San Andreas fault in California could be released in a relatively controlled manner by artificially triggering small earthquakes. This could prevent a major natural earthquake which would otherwise appear to be unavoidable along the Californian fault.

The reduction of loss of life is already being tackled in other ways. Specially designed modern buildings can withstand significant tremors. In the Tokyo earthquake of 1923, for example, the Imperial Hotel designed by Frank Lloyd Wright suffered little damage. Further research is being conducted on building resistance in Tashkent in the Soviet Union where there are empty apartment blocks with machines on their roofs to induce vibrations and thus test resistance of the buildings to stresses and strains. Populations are also slowly being educated to take sensible shelter indoors instead of running into the open streets where debris from collapsing buildings may cause them injury. By taking such precautions it may be possible to minimize the devastation and loss of life caused by earthquakes in the future.

Far left: The earthquake that hit Anchorage in Alaska in 1964 caused relatively little damage to timber buildings. The brick building on the left has suffered considerable damage; in the timber house even the windows are intact.

Left: These buildings in Niigata, Japan were built to withstand earthquakes. When strong tremors shook the city in 1964 the structures survived— there was not even a hair line crack in the walls. They toppled because certain soils lose their rigidity and 'liquefy' as a result of repeated seismic shocks. Few structures can survive this process— the ground simply slides away beneath them.

Point 8. Destructive. High chimneys and bell towers collapse, statues move. Most buildings crack and branches are torn from trees.

Point 10: Disastrous. Most buildings destroyed. Landslides and large cracks in the ground. Tsunami flood coastal regions.

Point 12: Catastrophic. Near total destruction. Major distortions and changes of ground level. Loose objects are hurled into the air.

Above: The earthquake that struck Alaska in March 1964 was one of the most severe ever recorded and caused hundreds of millions of dollars-worth of damage. Landslides wrecked buildings, roads and railway lines. The houses shown here were smashed by a landslide with a front 2.4 km (1½ miles) long.

Right: Chang Heng, a Chinese astronomer, first recorded distant earth tremors in 132AD. His seismoscope contained a pendulum which moved in a particular direction when an earthquake set up vibrations in the casing. This tipped one of the metal balls from the side of the seismoscope.

Volcanoes

A volcano behaves like a giant chimney, conducting material from shallow depths in the earth up to the surface. When a volcano erupts, hot liquid rock, called *lava,* gases and rock fragments are spewed on to the surface through its opening. This 'chimney' may take the form of a tall mountain *cone.* Volcanoes, however, may also appear as gently-sloping domes, or even as long, low-lying slits through which lava oozes out to produce a flat lava field.

A volcanic eruption starts deep down in the earth's *crust* or in the upper *mantle*—the thicker under-lying layer. Here rocks melt to form *magma,* essentially a mixture of volcanic gases dissolved in liquid lava. Underground pressure from the weight of the surrounding rocks forces the magma towards the surface.

As the magma wells up, sometimes into an underground reservoir, or *magma chamber,* under the volcano, the pressure drops and the gases start to bubble out of the liquid. The gases consist mainly of steam, most of which comes from water seeping through the rocks of the upper crust to meet the rising magma. They also contain carbon dioxide, nitrogen, sulphur dioxide and small quantities of such noxious gases as hydrogen sulphide and hydrogen chloride.

Eventually magma finds its way to the surface in a volcanic eruption, either through an existing vent or fissure from a previous eruption, or by forcing its way up through new cracks in the crust. On the flanks and around the base of an existing cone, secondary vents often produce small 'pimples' known as *parasitic cones.* Mount Etna on Sicily, for example, has 200 such satellite cones.

Quiet eruptions

The thickness of the magma—whether it is thin and syrupy or tacky like toffee—depends on its temperature, pressure and chemical nature. This consistency determines how easily the volcanic gases will be able to escape into the atmosphere before or during an eruption.

In fluid, fairly flat magma—usually basaltic—that wells slowly up the central *vent* of a typical volcano, what little gas there is has plenty of time to separate peacefully from the magma. The gas-free lava collects in the funnel-shaped cup or *crater* at the summit of the volcano. When the crater is full, the lava spills over the edge and flows rapidly down the side of the cone in fiery rivers of *lava flows.*

When very liquid lava oozes out of a central vent or a big fissure it tends to spread out over a wide area, forming either huge plateaux or thin sheets of lava on the typically-gentle sloping dome of a *shield volcano.* Mauna Loa in Hawaii, the world's largest volcano with a base 100 km (62 miles) in diameter and rising 10,000 metres (32,820 feet) above the sea floor, is a perfect example of a shield volcano built up over the years.

When the lava first reaches the surface it is very hot and fluid at temperatures between 800°C and 1200°C. It quickly starts to cool and solidify into volcanic or *igneous* rock. As the molten lava cools, the different minerals it contains crystallize, just like ice crystals freezing in water.

Gordon Gahan, Photo Researchers

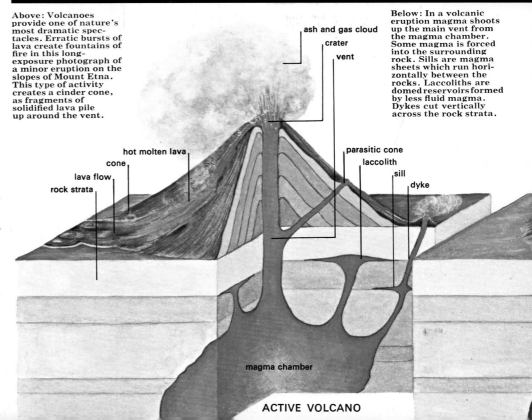

Above: Volcanoes provide one of nature's most dramatic spectacles. Erratic bursts of lava create fountains of fire in this long-exposure photograph of a minor eruption on the slopes of Mount Etna. This type of activity creates a cinder cone, as fragments of solidified lava pile up around the vent.

Below: In a volcanic eruption magma shoots up the main vent from the magma chamber. Some magma is forced into the surrounding rock. Sills are magma sheets which run horizontally between the rocks. Laccoliths are domed reservoirs formed by less fluid magma. Dykes cut vertically across the rock strata.

ash and gas cloud
crater
vent
hot molten lava
cone
parasitic cone
laccolith
lava flow
sill
rock strata
dyke

magma chamber

ACTIVE VOLCANO

Left: Mt Fuji, the highest mountain in Japan, is a dormant volcano which last erupted in 1707. It has a perfect conical shape, with a summit crater. Volcanic cones of this type, also seen at Etna, Vesuvius and Stromboli, are strato volcanoes, formed by alternating layers of lava and ash.

Right: Cerro Negro in Nicaragua, a cinder cone built up over an older terrace of lava flows. Vast dark clouds of ash are disgorged when gases escape carrying minute particles of cooled lava powder. Eventually a rain of ash falls from the spreading cloud, burying settlements and countryside.

Left: Fumaroles are small vents in the ground from which volcanic gases and steam escape.

Right: Cooler fumaroles are called solfataras. The steam they emit has a high sulphur content, and mineral deposits are formed as the water evaporates.

Left: Bird's eye view of a volcanic crater, surrounded by liquid basalt flows.

Above right: Molten lava sweeps down from an Icelandic volcano. Lava flows can reach speeds of up to 100 km (62 miles) per hour, but usually they move more sluggishly.

Below: A composite cone is built of layers of lava and pyroclasts. If the main vent grows too high or becomes plugged by lava, a parasitic cone forms. The vents of a dormant or extinct volcano are plugged by lava. Pressure may build under a dormant volcano causing it to erupt after a long period of inactivity.

Below: The lava plug may remain as a hill after the rest of the cone has been eroded. Edinburgh's Castle Rock, for example, is the plug of one vent of the Arthur's Seat volcano, active 325 million years ago. Erosion also reveals the existence of sills and dykes when ash and rock has worn away.

Right: Pahoehoe is highly fluid lava, spread in sheets, which drags the cooling surface layer into folds.

Below right: 500 million year-old pillow lavas formed underwater now lie above sea level. Rapid cooling creates bulbous shapes inside a glassy skin.

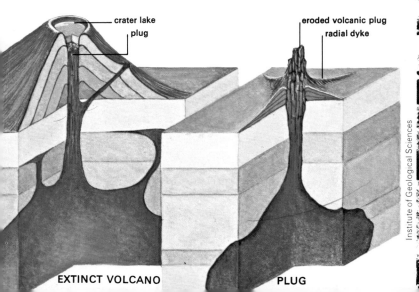

crater lake
plug

eroded volcanic plug
radial dyke

EXTINCT VOLCANO

PLUG

TYPES OF ERUPTIONS

Icelandic: Quiet eruption of lava from fissures builds up horizontal lava flows.

Hawaiian: Fluid lava erupts quietly and builds up huge shield volcanoes.

Strombolian: Minor explosions throw out lava which cools into pyroclasts.

Vulcanian: Explosive escape of gas from viscous magma. Clouds of volcanic ash form.

Vesuvian: Violent eruption produces huge quantities of ash. A vast cloud develops.

Pelean: Violent eruption of highly viscous magma. Hot gas cloud forms.

Plinean: Explosive outburst of gas sends ash several kilometres in to the air.

Thin sheets of lava cool quickly into fine grained rocks in which individual mineral crystals are invisible to the unaided eye. The more slowly the lava cools the larger the crystals grow before setting. Thicker blocks of lava take a long time to cool—they may still be too hot to touch several months after the eruption—and therefore form larger grained rocks. If the lava is chilled instantly, there is no time for this crystallization process to occur. Instead, it forms a volcanic glass called *obsidian*. This happens particularly in underwater eruptions, or where a stream of hot lava pours down into the sea.

Angry mountains

Where magma is of a slightly stickier consistency, the gas bubbles wind their way to the surface more slowly, growing as they climb and as more gas separates out of the rocky solution. These large bubbles burst when they reach the surface, splashing up a shower of lava spray that cascades over the sides of the vent in a spectacular natural fireworks display. The blobs of liquid lava clot quickly as they fly through the air, forming fragments of hard lava called *pyroclasts*. These missiles range in size from fine *dust* and *ash* to small pebble-sized particles called *lapilli* and large boulders or *bombs*. Bombs spin as they travel through the air, solidifying into characteristic shapes or spindle bombs. Breadcrust bombs on the other hand, have a zigzag pattern of cracks over the surface caused by the lava forming a solid skin which is broken by expansion and the escape of gas. Such bombs often shatter as they hit the ground.

A small pile of pyroclasts begins to form a *cinder cone* around the vent. The typical volcanic cone shape develops because most particles and all the larger, heavier fragments land near the vent, while smaller, lighter pieces are thrown further away. Consequently the volcanic mound grows more quickly nearer the vent, creating the classically rising slopes of a volcanic cone. Occasionally the globules of lava do not solidify in the air and form a *spatter cone* as they land.

In contrast to the fluid lavas, very tacky lavas barely flow at all but are squeezed out of the vent like toothpaste from a tube, forming steep-sided volcanic *domes* of hot lava in the crater. Sometimes a pocket of hotter, thinner lava forces its way through a crack in the dome creating a tall pinnacle of solid lava called a *spine* that towers over the vent. The spine of Mont Pelée on the island of Martinique in the Caribbean rose to the imposing height of 300m (984 ft) during its period of activity in 1902, before it cracked around the base and crumbled into the crater.

Thick lavas also tend to congeal in the vent and together with rubble from the crater form a plug that blocks the exit. Tremendous pressure builds up as gases are trapped under the plugged vent until the volcano literally 'blows its top' in a violent explosion.

Violent explosions, like the famous blast at Krakatoa in 1883, shoot vast quantities of rock, lava, gas and ash into the air. In the shock of the drop of pressure, the gases froth in the lava, but because of the thickness of the lava they are unable to burst free. If the lava drops back into the sea it sets very quickly, trapping the gas bubbles permanently into a petrified foam called *pumice*, which floats on water.

During a particularly violent eruption, the magma chamber may be completely emptied, leaving the central part of the cone unsupported. Often under such circumstances the crater and walls of the vent collapse into the hollow chamber, creating a large saucer-shaped depression known as a *caldera* across the summit of the volcano, which may be as much as several kilometres in diameter. An explosive eruption may cause the entire cone to fall into the magma chamber. After Krakatoa erupted, an underwater caldera 7 km (4.3 miles) in diameter was formed.

Life and death of a volcano

The sudden rise of a cinder cone called Parícutin on 20 February 1943—in the field of a surprised Mexican farmer—provided scientists with a rare opportunity to observe a volcano from its birth. In the first day of intense activity, it produced a huge glowing cloud of hot ash and a cone of pyroclasts 40 m (131 ft) high. After this astonishing effort, fissures opened around the base and lava seeped across the field. Eruptions continued with decreasing intensity until, when the volcano ceased eruption in 1952, the cone was 410 m (1,344 ft) high.

Library of Congress

The life-span of a volcano ranges from a few months to many thousands of years. Activity may vary greatly during that time. Of the 500 or so active volcanoes in the world today only a small number erupt each year. A few volcanoes, like Stromboli in the Lipari Islands off Italy, erupt continuously with successive bursts. The majority, however, erupt only irregularly and spend most of their time 'asleep'.

During these periods of inactivity, however, it is impossible to tell whether the volcano is really *extinct*—that is, stopped erupting for ever—or merely *dormant*, undergoing a temporary period of rest. Generally volcanoes are classified as extinct when no eruption has been noted in 'recorded history'.

Yet even then they may be potentially active, one day to wake up in a fresh eruption, with devastating results. Vesuvius, overlooking the Italian port of Naples, was thought to be extinct before its catastrophic eruption in 79AD which completely destroyed the Roman cities of Pompeii and Heraculaneum.

Causes of volcanic activity

Volcanoes are distributed in areas where conditions are suitable for the formation of magma. The concept of plate tectonics

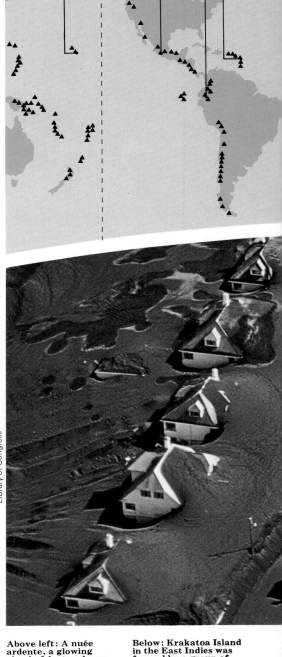

Above left: A nuée ardente, a glowing cloud of dust and gas, erupted from Mt Pelée in the island of Martinique at 7.50 am on 8 May 1902. The city of St Pierre, with its 30,000 inhabitants, was destroyed in seconds. The surge of gas that headed the cloud was hot enough to melt metal and glass.

Below: Krakatoa Island in the East Indies was formed by a group of volcanic cones built up from a prehistoric caldera. In 1883 a huge eruption destroyed most of the island and left a 300 m (1,000 ft) crater in the sea bed. The explosion, heard as far away as Australia, had worldwide effects. A tidal wave killed

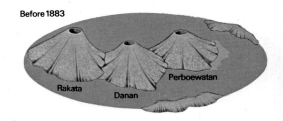

Before 1883

Rakata   Danan   Perboewatan

8

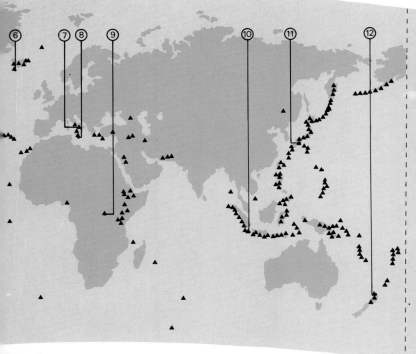

6 7 8 9   10   11   12

DISTRIBUTION OF VOLCANOES

Some of the world's major sites of volcanic activity are shown on the map:

1. Kilauea, Hawaii
2. Katmai, Alaska
3. Paricutin, Mexico
4. Cotopaxi, Ecuador
5. Pelée, Martinique
6. Surtsey, Iceland
7. Vesuvius, Italy
8. Etna, Italy
9. Nyamuragira, Zaire
10. Krakatoa, Indonesia
11. Sakurajima, Japan
12. White Island, New Zealand

Most active volcanoes are concentrated in a belt around the Pacific and one that extends through Indonesia and New Guinea. Indonesia has the greatest concentration of volcanoes with 29 actively emitting gases and 78 eruptions since records began.

provides an explanation of the distribution of active volcanoes. The earth has a cool rigid crust which consists of a dozen or so plates which are free to move in relation to each other and to glide relatively freely over the earth's surface.

The mantle of the earth, the layer below the crust, is solid and its temperature is normally not high enough to start the melting which forms magma. Pressure here also prevents melting. Heat from the earth's interior does, however, cause the slow circulation of the mantle, or *mantle convection*.

A constructive plate margin, such as the mid-Atlantic ridge, is one where new crustal material is formed by rising magma. Lower pressure in these places allows the hot mantle to melt and produce magma. This rises and forms new oceanic crust and volcanoes at the plate margins. Iceland is an area that experiences this process.

At destructive plate margins, usually at oceanic boundaries such as the trenches around the Pacific Ocean, the edge of one plate is forced beneath that of another, or *subducted*. Oceanic crust is carried down into the mantle and starts to melt. It then rises and heats the overlying continental material and may cause further independent melting. These various kinds of magma reach the surface and produce the different types of volcano found around the perimeter of the Pacific and in the island arcs of Indonesia, West Indies and Japan.

Hawaii, lying in the centre of the Pacific plate, does not fit this pattern. The islands are thought to overlie a 'hot spot' or *plume* of rising mantle which provides the magma for eruptions.

Effects of volcanic activity

Volcanic activity is the main process by which material from the interior of the earth reaches the surface, and it must have contributed to the formation of the atmosphere and the oceans. Volcanic gases, for example, include carbon dioxide which is vital to life on earth. Fertile soils develop from the weathering of volcanic ash and lava, and are extensively cultivated even on the lower slopes of active volcanoes.

Crushed lavas make suitable roadstone. Pumice is used industrially and domestically as an abrasive, and, along with perlite, volcanic glass which expands when heated, for insulation in buildings. Volcanic pipes of an unusual rock, called kimberlite, are the source of diamonds, and sulphur is exploited in the volcanic areas of Japan and Sicily. Volcanic activity provides hot water for central heating in Iceland and steam-generated electricity in New Zealand, Italy and the United States.

The death and destruction inflicted by some volcanic eruptions makes the task of predicting eruptions one of real concern. The start of an eruption can be forecast fairly accurately by monitoring the temperature, pressure and composition of the gases within a volcano. Minor earth tremors, caused by movement of magma within a volcano, are recorded by seismometers positioned at selected sites, and portable machines can determine the exact location of an expected eruption. Observatories have been established on many volcanoes but it is still not possible to predict the intensity or duration of an eruption.

Left: The eruption of Eldfjell on the Icelandic island of Heimay in 1973 partly buried the town of Vestmannaeyjar in dust and ash. Volcanic areas may be quiet for many years—the only known volcano on Heimay last erupted 5,000 years ago—and then come suddenly and violently to life.

Above: The volcanic island of Surtsey appeared off Iceland on 15 November 1963. First eruptions were explosive as sea water entered the vent. When the cone was large enough to prevent this, lava flows were erupted. Surtsey was 2.3 sq km (1 sq mile) in area and 410 m (1344 ft) high by 1965.

Below: Anak Krakatoa, meaning the 'child of Krakatoa', has emerged on the site of the old island in the Sunda Strait between Sumatra and Java. Pressures from a lava pocket in the old volcano threw up a new submarine cone which reached the surface in 1928. A year later a geyser began to spout steam.

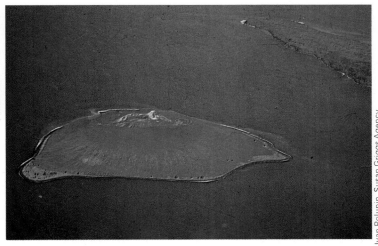

36,000 Indonesians and was recorded in the English Channel. For several years volcanic dust drifted around the earth in the upper atmosphere, causing brilliant red sunsets and reducing the earth's temperature by partly blocking the sun's rays. Recent volcanic activity has produced the tip of a new island.

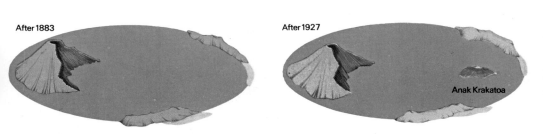

After 1883   After 1927   Anak Krakatoa

Continental Drift

A glance at a map of the Atlantic coasts of Europe, Africa and the Americas reveals a strikingly close match in their outline. With a little imagination, one could close the Atlantic and fit its western and eastern coastlines together, rather like matching up the pieces of a jig-saw puzzle. The startling conclusion this suggests is literally earth-shaking to scientists studying the history of planet earth. For the suggestion is that, sometime in the remote past, the distant continents were joined together, and have since drifted apart.

Early this century, an American geologist, Frank Taylor, became intrigued by the idea that the continents were once parts of a large land mass. In 1908 he put forward the imaginative theory that the continents may have been slowly drifting apart to reach their present-day arrangement. Meanwhile, working independently, the German meteorologist, astronomer and geophysicist, Alfred Wegener, was thinking along identical lines. His book, *Die Entstehung der Kontinente und Ozeane* — The Origin of Continents and Oceans — published in 1915, established him as a leading authority on the theory of continental drift.

For the next 40 years, however, the theory received little support. Critics pointed out that the reconstructions were based on flimsy evidence or were simply guess-work. Among the few who did believe in Wegener's idea was the South African geologist, Alexander du Toit. Working in South Africa and Brazil, he began to amass solid geological evidence in support of the theory.

Although some experts accepted du Toit's findings and those of other scientists, the majority discounted them on the basis that drift was impossible because there was no known mechanism which could cause whole continents to shift so dramatically. The breakthrough came, therefore, with the discovery of just such a mechanism — plate tectonics. .

The concept of *plate tectonics,* which sees the continents as being carried along on the top of slowly moving crustal plates, reversed general attitudes to continental drift. By the mid-1960s the theory had

Right: One of the first to attempt a pre-drift fit was the American Antonio Snider. In 1858 he published a map showing how he thought the Americas were joined to Africa some 300 million years ago.

NASA

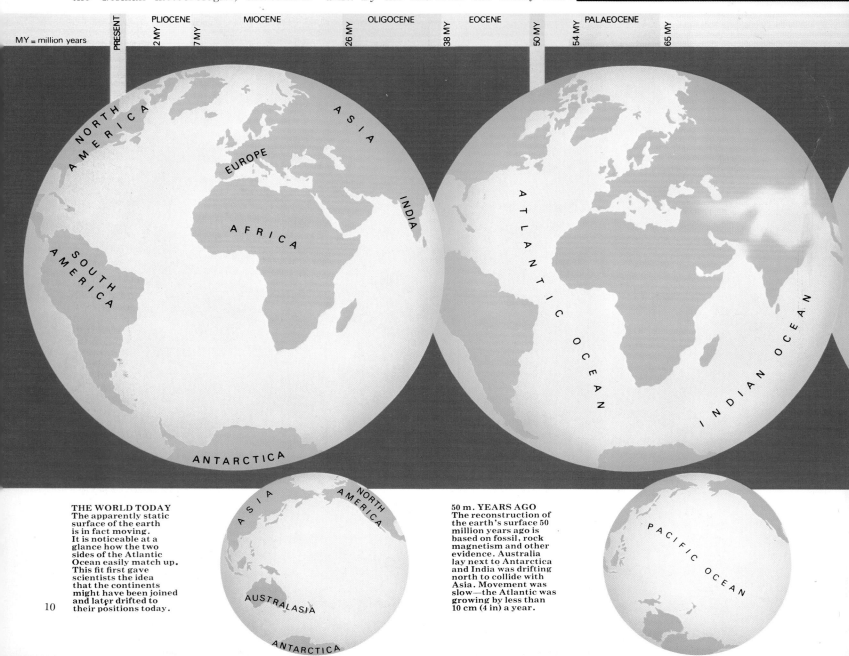

MY = million years

PRESENT | PLIOCENE | MIOCENE | OLIGOCENE | EOCENE | PALAEOCENE

2 MY | 7 MY | 26 MY | 38 MY | 50 MY | 54 MY | 65 MY

NORTH AMERICA

ASIA

EUROPE

SOUTH AMERICA

AFRICA

INDIA

ANTARCTICA

ATLANTIC OCEAN

INDIAN OCEAN

THE WORLD TODAY
The apparently static surface of the earth is in fact moving. It is noticeable at a glance how the two sides of the Atlantic Ocean easily match up. This fit first gave scientists the idea that the continents might have been joined and later drifted to their positions today.

ASIA

NORTH AMERICA

AUSTRALASIA

ANTARCTICA

50 m. YEARS AGO
The reconstruction of the earth's surface 50 million years ago is based on fossil, rock magnetism and other evidence. Australia lay next to Antarctica and India was drifting north to collide with Asia. Movement was slow—the Atlantic was growing by less than 10 cm (4 in) a year.

PACIFIC OCEAN

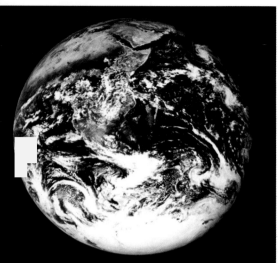

Below: South America (left) as seen from an orbiting NASA space-craft. Cloud-ringed North America and the western bulge of Africa are also clearly shown. (right) Most of Africa and Antarctica's polar ice-cap are visible.

NASA

been accepted and the very evidence which had previously been ignored or explained away is now used to assist in continental reconstruction.

The search for evidence

No one piece of evidence is enough to assess whether continental drift has occurred. Several lines must be pursued. Firstly, a pre-drift reconstruction of the arrangement of the continents should provide a reasonable geometric or outline fit. Early workers have been rightly criticized for fitting the present-day coastlines together and making no allowance for the submerged part of the continent, that is the *continental shelf* which juts out under the ocean.

Subsequent reconstructions have taken this factor into consideration. Computers have been used recently to construct a 'best fit' between the continents. Following the assumption that the edge of the continent lies on the continental slope, which descends steeply from the edge of the continental shelf to the deep ocean floor, reconstructions have been made for various depth contours. For most parts of the world, the 'best fit' is at about the 1,000 m (550 fathoms) depth contour, and provides striking geometrical evidence

that the continents were once joined together at the continental slope.

If the reconstructions are valid and drift has occurred, any two regions which formerly lay side by side, but are now far apart, should share common geological features. Ancient structural features such as the fold axes in mountain systems should match up. The detailed history of sedimentary rocks deposited in previously adjacent areas and the distribution of fossil animals and plants embedded in the rocks should likewise be almost identical.

This last line of evidence must be examined carefully. Geographically well-separated regions may have sedimentary and biological features in common just because they shared similar climates. The tropical rain forests of South America and Africa, for example, will both eventually produce the same type of coal bed deposits, but the plants enclosed within them may be very different.

Ancient climates also help in the work of reconstruction. Former climates leave their traces such as scratch marks where glaciers have dragged boulders over the land, and salt deposits which have developed in hot deserts. From such evidence a picture emerges of ancient climatic belts

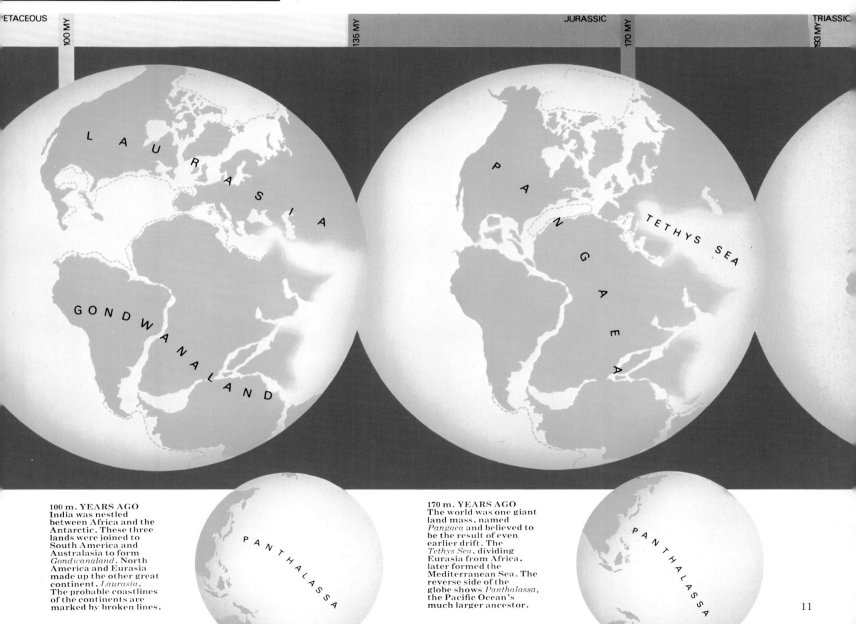

100 m. YEARS AGO India was nestled between Africa and the Antarctic. These three lands were joined to South America and Australasia to form *Gondwanaland*. North America and Eurasia made up the other great continent, *Laurasia*. The probable coastlines of the continents are marked by broken lines.

170 m. YEARS AGO The world was one giant land mass, named *Pangaea* and believed to be the result of even earlier drift. The *Tethys Sea*, dividing Eurasia from Africa, later formed the Mediterranean Sea. The reverse side of the globe shows *Panthalassa*, the Pacific Ocean's much larger ancestor.

which were in very different positions from those of today — hot deserts existed in modern polar regions and ice-caps invaded present equatorial zones. Presuming that the world's climatic pattern has always been basically similar to, though usually less extreme than, today's, the explanation must lie with the movement of the land masses which have drifted from one climatic zone to another. In a reconstruction, therefore, the original climatic belts, marked by rock and fossil clues, should line up and be roughly parallel to one another.

The most spectacular evidence for drift having taken place comes from palaeomagnetic work. *Palaeomagnetism* is the remnant of ancient magnetic traces preserved in rocks. Iron minerals crystallizing out from volcanic magma or molten rock generally become magnetized and line themselves up in the direction of the earth's magnetic field prevailing at that time. Even if, in the course of millions of years, magnetized iron mineral particles are eroded out of the parent rock and redeposited on the sea floor with other sediment, they will again orientate themselves exactly as a compass needle does in line with the earth's magnetic field.

Below: Continental drift explains the unexpected distribution of several fossils. Those of Cretaceous coral reefs and associated rudist bivalves (right) appear today in areas too cool for them to flourish. They could have grown further south, however, and been carried north by the drifting land.

Rudist bivalve

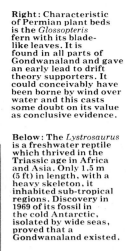

Right: Characteristic of Permian plant beds is the *Glossopteris* fern with its blade-like leaves. It is found in all parts of Gondwanaland and gave an early lead to drift theory supporters. It could conceivably have been borne by wind over water and this casts some doubt on its value as conclusive evidence.

Below: The *Lystrosaurus* is a freshwater reptile which thrived in the Triassic age in Africa and Asia. Only 1.5 m (5 ft) in length, with a heavy skeleton, it inhabited sub-tropical regions. Discovery in 1969 of its fossil in the cold Antarctic, isolated by wide seas, proved that a Gondwanaland existed.

Gordon Roberton

Coral

Lystrosaurus

CRETACEOUS | 135 MY | JURASSIC | 193 MY

In both cases, the magnetization is very stable and may be cemented within the rock to remain unaffected by subsequent changes in the earth's magnetic field. This means that the magnetism detected in a rock today can be used to fix the position of the earth's magnetic pole at the time when that rock was formed, though geological corrections may have to be made.

When there was no South Atlantic
The best examples of these various areas of evidence are found in South America and Africa. The fit of the Atlantic coastlines of these two continents shows an increasing gap north or south of a mid position. Much of that gap is filled in, however, if the continental shelf down to the 1,000 m (550 fathoms) depth contour is included in the fit. There are a few small areas of overlap, especially off the Niger River, but these are believed to date from after the break-up of the two continents.

There is ample data in support of the fit. Some was put forward by Wegener; much more was collected by du Toit and published in 1937. One aspect highlighted by both authorities was the distribution in Brazil and southwest Africa of glacial deposits from the Permo-Carboniferous age, some 300 million years ago.

These have since been intensively studied and tell a fascinating story. Southwest Africa was essentially an area of glacial erosion with material being moved from east to west towards the Atlantic. In contrast, the consolidated boulder clay, known as *tillite*, which covers Brazil was obviously deposited by extensive ice sheets moving in from the south east, from where the Atlantic now lies.

There are two conceivable sources for the tillite. Either this material was derived from the continental shelf — but this is unlikely considering the volume — or it came from southwest Africa.

Above: Places where evidence from ancient wildlife and glacial activity has been found are pin-pointed on a map of the world today. Until quite recently, some scientists argued that giant land-bridges, across which ancient animals and plants might have spread, connected the continents—located then in their present positions. Such talk had to be discounted as these bridges could not have sunk without trace. When Gondwanaland, where most evidence has been found, is reconstructed (right) there is a perfect match both in outline and in locations of recorded fossil finds. The spread of Carboniferous glaciation is marked by arrows.

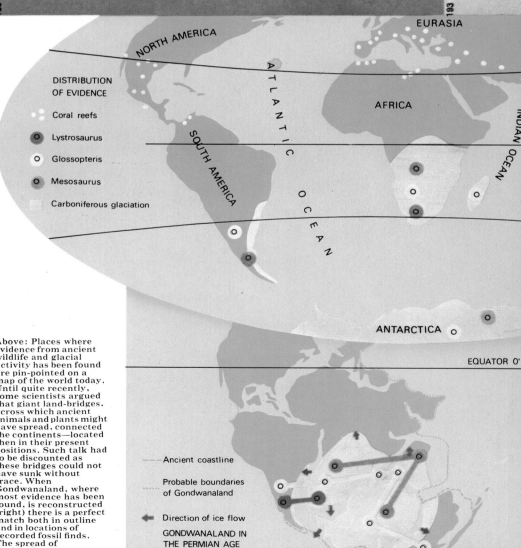

DISTRIBUTION OF EVIDENCE

∴ Coral reefs
◉ Lystrosaurus
○ Glossopteris
◉ Mesosaurus
▦ Carboniferous glaciation

NORTH AMERICA
EURASIA
ATLANTIC
AFRICA
SOUTH AMERICA
INDIAN OCEAN
ATLANTIC OCEAN
ANTARCTICA
EQUATOR 0°

- - - Ancient coastline

Probable boundaries of Gondwanaland

← Direction of ice flow

GONDWANALAND IN THE PERMIAN AGE

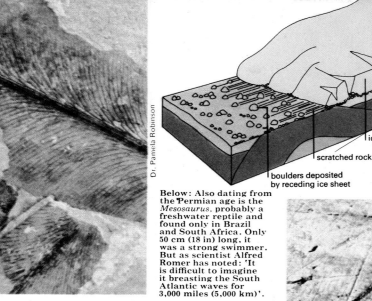

Left: In the late Carboniferous age, ice sheets swept over much of the southern continents. By dragging rocks over the land, they left scratch marks (below) and *erratic* boulders. Their distribution can be explained if parts of Gondwanaland then lay under the South Polar ice cap.

ice sheet

scratched rock

boulders deposited by receding ice sheet

Below: Also dating from the Permian age is the *Mesosaurus*, probably a freshwater reptile and found only in Brazil and South Africa. Only 50 cm (18 in) long, it was a strong swimmer. But as scientist Alfred Romer has noted: 'It is difficult to imagine it breasting the South Atlantic waves for 3,000 miles (5,000 km)'.

The sedimentary sequence on opposite sides of the Atlantic is remarkably similar, not only during Permo-Carboniferous times, but also from the Silurian age, some 400 million years ago, to the middle of the Cretaceous age, about 100 million years ago. Half-way through this 300 million year period, molten basalt rocks flooded parts of Brazil and South Africa and are overlain in both regions by red beds of desert origin which contain remains of similar vertebrate animals.

The sequence of sediments from the Cretaceous age along the coasts of Brazil and West Africa has recently attracted considerable attention. A series of freshwater sedimentary basins have the same rock sequences and contain identical fish and microscopic crustacean remains.

The sequence is of interest for another reason. The non-marine conditions were brought to an end by a sudden influx of salt water. As the water evaporated it left behind deposits of salt. After this, marine conditions remained but the sediments, and eventually the animal life, developed separately and uniquely on the opposite sides of the present-day South Atlantic. This gradual division of formerly united basins of marine deposits during the

lossopteris   Mesosaurus   Glaciation

TRIASSIC | 225 MY | PERMIAN | 280 MY | CARBONIFEROUS

Certain distinctive rock types enclosed within the Brazilian tillite can be matched with ones from southwest Africa. Moreover, palaeomagnetic observations confirm that the ice moving across southwest Africa was coming from the south polar region and that the pole at that time was lying to the southeast of South Africa.

Another outstanding piece of evidence has been established through the radioactive dating of rocks. Nearly all rocks contain minute amounts of radio-active elements which, in the course of time, decay to form other elements. As the various decay rates are known, it is possible to calculate the age of a rock by measuring the amount of the secondary element contained within it.

The Sahara shield was dated by this method and proved to be 2,000 million years old. Running alongside these ancient rocks is a group of younger rocks which are only 550 million years old. The dividing line between old and new is very clear and goes into the Atlantic near Accra, in Ghana. It reappears across the ocean at Sao Luis, in Brazil.

middle of the Cretaceous age provides an accurate date for the beginning of the opening of the South Atlantic.

Laurasia and Gondwanaland

By the end of the nineteenth century, it had been suggested that in Carboniferous times the present-day continental masses could be grouped into two supercontinents. The more southerly one was called *Gondwanaland,* and the more northerly one called *Laurasia.* These two supercontinents were separated by the *Tethys Ocean.* South America and Africa form part of Gondwanaland, but some of the other fragments of this enormous land mass are more difficult to piece together — the positioning of India is particularly problematic. The geometrical fit of the northern continents to form Laurasia is better, although the geological evidence to support the fit is not as firm as the evidence for joining South America to Africa.

Wegener proposed that, originally, Gondwanaland and Laurasia had been joined together and he called this gigantic continent *Pangaea,* from the Greek 'all the earth'. It is now realized that Pangaea not only pre-dates the most recent phase of continental drift, but also represents the culmination of an earlier period of drift. Before that, there were others, and the present-day continents may be composed of fragments of several different earlier continental masses.

Today's map of the world is, then, a record of a moment in time, a static view of the ever-moving continents. Although there is still much detailed work to be done on continental drift, there is enough information available to stimulate a little informed speculation. The area of the Pacific basin, for example, is shrinking, which suggests that perhaps, in the next 50 to 100 million years, Asia will close with North America and the Philippines will lie in the shadow of the Andes.

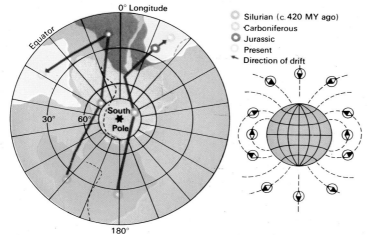

NORTH 30°

PACIFIC OCEAN

EQUATOR 0°

AUSTRALASIA

SOUTH 30°

DIA

Right: The major evidence for continental drift is provided by the magnetism found in ancient rocks. When molten rock crystallizes, magnetized iron grains settle in a direction parallel to the earth's magnetic field (far right). Assuming that the field has always been roughly parallel to the earth's axis, the inclination of the grains will indicate the latitude at which the rock was originally formed. Tracing the original latitudes of rock samples from Africa and South America (right) dramatically reveals the extent of drift. The coloured areas indicate the relative positions of the two continents at different periods.

WANDERING LANDS AND THE EARTH'S MAGNETISM

0° Longitude

Equator

30°   60°

South Pole

180°

○ Silurian (c. 420 MY ago)
○ Carboniferous
◉ Jurassic
● Present
↗ Direction of drift

The Spreading Sea Floor

The theory of continental drift, as put forward by Alfred Wegener more than 60 years ago, suggested that the continents had once been joined as parts of a large land mass and then slowly drifted apart. The evidence for this imaginative idea was impressive but the theory gained little acceptance among scientists. This was primarily because it was hard to envisage a driving mechanism powerful enough to force apart and then to propel the apparently static continents over many thousands of kilometres.

It was not until the early 1960s that substantial evidence was collated to establish a theory explaining not only continental drift, but also the world-wide distribution of volcanic and earthquake activity. This evidence was not found in the continents themselves, however, but in the other two-thirds of the earth's surface—the oceans.

When scientists examined the ocean floor, they found its geology to be profoundly different from that of the continents. Along many coasts the sea is shallow, often less than 200 m (110 fathoms) deep, and relatively flat-bottomed. This is the *continental shelf* and is part of the continent. Further out to sea, the shelf gives way to the *continental slope* which drops steeply to the ocean bottom 5 or 6 km (some 3.5 miles) down. The slope is also made of continental rocks and on it and at its base there may be piles of debris that have slipped down from the shelf.

The layer of sediment covering the deep ocean floor is thin and nowhere more than 200 million years old. This is young in comparison to continental rocks which may be over 3,000 million years old. Below the sedimentary material is solid, dark, dense rock of volcanic origin, going down some 7 km (4 miles) to the surface of the mantle. This underlying rock forming the oceanic crust is known as *sime* because it is rich in silicon and magnesium. The land masses are known as *sial*—the rock is dominated by silicon and aluminium. The dense sima meets the lighter sial at the foot of the continental slopes and is believed to pass beneath them.

Mountains under the sea

Another important discovery was that the ocean floor is not flat. A great mountain chain or *oceanic ridge* with peaks 4,500 m (15,000 ft) high lies under the waves. One of the first sections to be investigated was the mid-Atlantic ridge. This stretches from Iceland to Tristan da Cunha in the South Atlantic, rounding the Cape of Good Hope then linking up with the rest of the submarine mountain system—80,000 km (50,000 miles) long. This ridge, like many of the others, has a central rift valley some 50 km (30 miles) wide and 2 km (1.2 miles) deep.

In contrast to ridges, which stretch upwards and sometimes break the surface to form volcanic islands, are *trenches*. These run along the edge of continents or close

Right: The cross-section of the earth's interior from the Pacific to Africa reveals great activity above and below the earth's crust. The Atlantic sea floor is expanding but the Pacific is shrinking. New oceanic crust is continually formed at the mid-ocean ridges, carried aside by the spreading *plates* and destroyed in the subduction zones. The South American plate consists of both continental and oceanic crust embedded in the *lithosphere*, a rigid shell of rock which 'floats' on the molten *asthenosphere*. It is drifting west and riding over the denser Pacific plate, which descends and remelts, creating volcanic and earthquake activity.

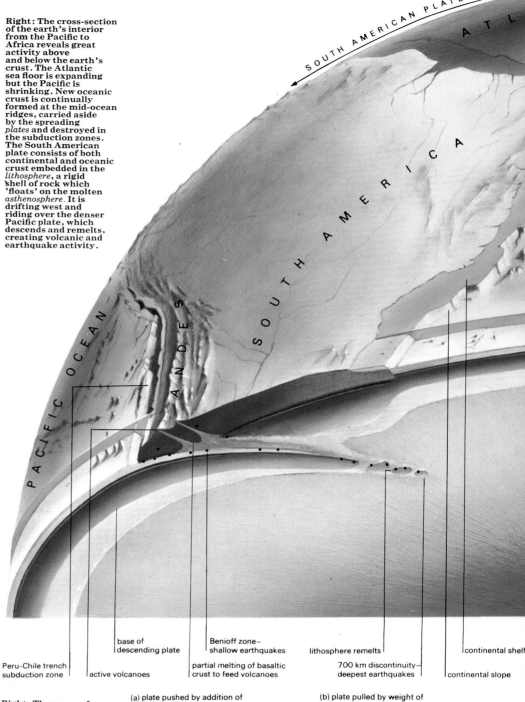

SOUTH AMERICAN PLATE MOVING

ATL

PACIFIC OCEAN

ANDES

SOUTH AMERICA

Peru-Chile trench subduction zone

active volcanoes

base of descending plate

Benioff zone— shallow earthquakes

partial melting of basaltic crust to feed volcanoes

lithosphere remelts

700 km discontinuity— deepest earthquakes

continental shelf

continental slope

Right: The cause of *plate tectonics* is unresolved. Four of the possible driving mechanisms are shown. The upwelling mantle may act as a wedge—pushing the plates apart as new material is added at the ridges (a). The raised ridges may provide a gradient down which plates slide under force of gravity. This may be coupled with sinking of cool, heavy ocean crust in subduction zones (b) due to the weight of very dense minerals formed as rocks pass under the overriding plate. Convection currents in the mantle may cause plate motion by (c) exercising a drag on the 'floating' plates. Alternatively, plate movements may be the outermost signs of powerful convection cycles (d), perhaps 700 km deep, of which the rigid *lithosphere* forms the cooled, brittle, upper boundary.

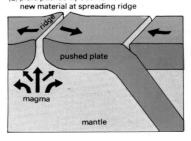

(a) plate pushed by addition of new material at spreading ridge

ridge

pushed plate

magma

mantle

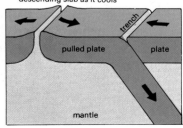

(b) plate pulled by weight of descending slab as it cools

trench

pulled plate

plate

mantle

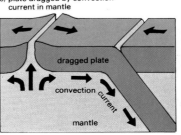

(c) plate dragged by convection current in mantle

dragged plate

convection current

mantle

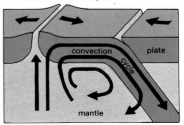

(d) plate is cooled, upper boundary of mantle convection cycle

convection cycle

plate

mantle

14

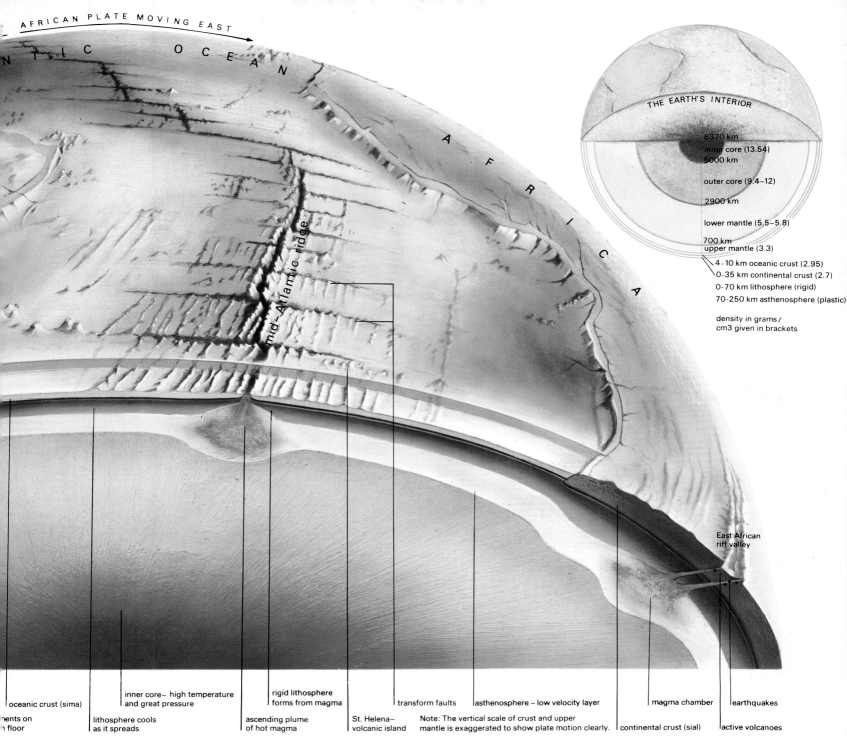

NTIC OCEAN

AFRICA

mid–Atlantic ridge

THE EARTH'S INTERIOR

6370 km
inner core (13.54)
5000 km

outer core (9.4–12)

2900 km

lower mantle (5.5–5.8)

700 km
upper mantle (3.3)

4 - 10 km oceanic crust (2.95)
0 - 35 km continental crust (2.7)
0 - 70 km lithosphere (rigid)
70 - 250 km asthenosphere (plastic)

density in grams /
cm3 given in brackets

East African
rift valley

oceanic crust (sima)   inner core– high temperature and great pressure   rigid lithosphere forms from magma   transform faults   asthenosphere – low velocity layer   magma chamber   earthquakes

nents on n floor   lithosphere cools as it spreads   ascending plume of hot magma   St. Helena– volcanic island   Note: The vertical scale of crust and upper mantle is exaggerated to show plate motion clearly.   continental crust (sial)   active volcanoes

to chains of islands such as Japan and are the deepest parts of the earth's surface. The deepest point, 11 km (6.8 miles) down, is in the Marianas Trench in the Pacific.

There is another major difference between ridges and trenches. The *heat flow*, the rate at which heat is lost from the inner zones of the earth to the atmosphere, is extremely high at the ridges. But as one moves away from them, the heat flow decreases and becomes exceptionally low along the trenches. This, and the height of the ridges, is believed to be caused by the expansion of heated mantle material pushing up from below the crust.

One characteristic common to both ocean ridges and trenches is volcanic activity. The continental side of trenches are chains of volcanic islands or mountains, and mid-oceanic islands tracing the path of a ridge above sea level, are invariably made of igneous rocks. Moreover, these volcanic belts contain the epicentres of nearly all earthquakes.

All this data was pulled together by an American geologist, Harry Hess. In 1960 he put forward an idea that became known as *sea floor spreading*. Because all the sediments on the ocean floor are young, he argued, the ocean floor itself could not be very old. Either the earth must have expanded enormously—by about five times in the last 200 million years—or new oceanic crust must be both created and destroyed continuously.

Undersea 'conveyor belts'

Expansion at anything like that rate is considered highly unlikely. Hess therefore proposed that new oceanic crust was created at the ridges, carried sideways as though on a conveyor belt, and then taken down into the mantle along the deep sea trenches. He suggested that the conveyor belt could be driven by *convection currents*, movements caused by heat differences, in the mantle.

Hot materials, less dense than cold, tend to rise and create an upward plume of heat. Near the surface, the warm materials spread sideways and cool steadily, until an opposing current is met. Both then turn down to form a descending cold plume. This area of downward movement along the trenches is called a *subduction zone*.

The growth of the Atlantic Ocean, for example, can be pictured as follows. About 150 million years ago, a rising plume of heat generated vulcanism along the line that was to become the mid-Atlantic ridge. (Volcanic rocks of appropriate age are found in places along the present margin of the Atlantic). New oceanic crust was created steadily and the new ocean opened and widened. The continents, firmly embedded in the oceanic crust, were carried sideways away from the ridge and away from one another.

In the 1960s new evidence became available which supported Hess's idea. During the Second World War, instruments called *magnetometers* were developed to detect submarines by the magnetic disturbance they caused. Since the war, scientists have

NASA

John S. Shelton

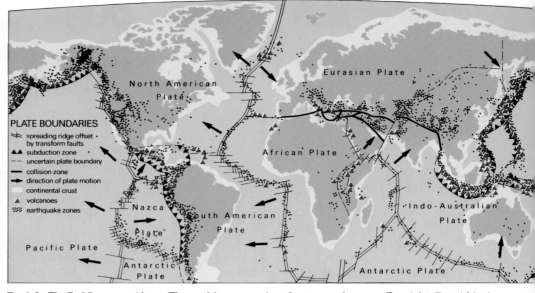

PLATE BOUNDARIES
- ⚡ spreading ridge offset by transform faults
- ▲▲ subduction zone
- --- uncertain plate boundary
- ▬ collision zone
- ← direction of plate motion
- ☐ continental crust
- ▲ volcanoes
- ⠿ earthquake zones

North American Plate

Eurasian Plate

African Plate

Nazca Plate

South American Plate

Pacific Plate

Indo-Australian Plate

Antarctic Plate

Antarctic Plate

Top left: The Red Sea is a new ocean in the making. Africa (left) is being slowly forced apart from Arabia.

Left: California's San Andreas Fault is the earthquake-prone margin between two plates. A stream is being carried north (to the right) by the Pacific plate (top).

Above: The earth's outer shell consists of a mosaic of rigid plates, seven of which cover considerable areas. Plate boundaries are clearly indicated by interconnecting belts of major earthquake, volcanic and mountain-building activity, whose distribution is explained by plate tectonics. They occur

along four types of plate margins. Plate material is created at *spreading ridges*. In *subduction zones* one plate is destroyed beneath another. Plates slide freely along *transform faults,* but push up high mountains along *collision zones.* Plate tectonics also confirms the theory of continental drift.

Top right: East Africa's Rift Valley, a volcanic area, may be the point of a future break-up in the African plate.

Right: Iceland is steadily growing larger. It is formed by the spreading mid-Atlantic ridge. The island has a jagged rift valley, and is an area of volcanic activity.

MAGNETIC PATTERNS ON THE OCEAN FLOOR

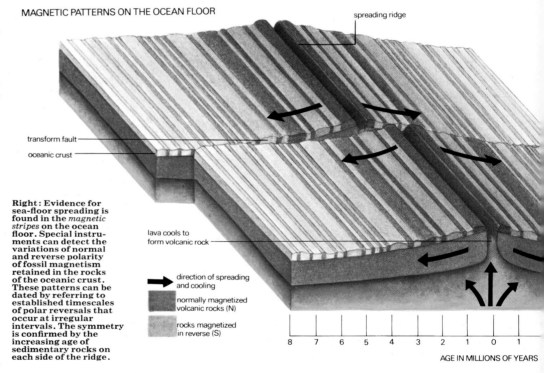

spreading ridge

transform fault

oceanic crust

lava cools to form volcanic rock

→ direction of spreading and cooling

▨ normally magnetized volcanic rocks (N)

▤ rocks magnetized in reverse (S)

8 7 6 5 4 3 2 1 0 1

AGE IN MILLIONS OF YEARS

Right: Evidence for sea-floor spreading is found in the *magnetic stripes* on the ocean floor. Special instruments can detect the variations of normal and reverse polarity of fossil magnetism retained in the rocks of the oceanic crust. These patterns can be dated by referring to established timescales of polar reversals that occur at irregular intervals. The symmetry is confirmed by the increasing age of sedimentary rocks on each side of the ridge.

continued to use these instruments to measure variations in the strength of the earth's magnetic field. Over large areas of the ocean the magnetic intensity was found to vary in narrow bands parallel to the ridges.

Cambridge geophysicists Frederick Vine and Drummond Matthews showed that this pattern of *magnetic stripes* could be due to the rocks of the ocean floor. As lava solidifies, it is magnetized by the prevailing magnetic field. The pattern of bands could therefore be explained if the earth's present north magnetic pole had from time to time switched to the south. During such a *magnetic reversal* the volcanic rocks forming at the ocean ridges would have been magnetized in the reverse sense from those erupted today.

When Vine and Matthews put forward their idea, magnetic reversal was still just a theory. Soon after, however, examination of suitable volcanic rocks showed that a series of reversals had indeed occurred over the last 5 million years. So, using the 'stripes' it is now possible to estimate the age of sea-floor rocks and see how they become progressively older away from the ridges.

These successive ages of the sea floor have been double-checked by dating the sediments resting on the igneous rocks. Knowing how old an ocean is means that its growth rate can be calculated. The North Atlantic, for instance, is spreading at about 2 cm (0.75 in) a year, while the east Pacific ridge is producing 10 cm (4 in) of new crust annually. The rate of sea floor spreading is remarkable. It means that North America is moving west the length of a man's body in a lifetime.

Earthquakes at plate margins

Also in the 1960s, a world-wide network of sensitive seismographs was set up to detect minute earthquakes and to differentiate between them and nuclear explosions. From this it was possible to map the points where earthquakes begin. It was found that along the ocean ridges earthquakes are almost all less than 100 km (62 miles) deep.

The deeper, stronger quakes are associated with the subduction zones. They all occur in a layer sloping at about 45°, the *Benioff zone,* and continuing down from the trenches to a depth of about 700 km (435 miles). There are a few shallow earthquakes situated at a maximum depth of 80 km (50 miles), probably caused by the rocks bending and cracking as they enter the subduction zone. Most of the quakes, however, happen much further down— between 300 and 700 km—and are probably the result of physical and chemical changes in the descending ocean crust.

In addition to ridges and trenches, another group of earthquakes is related to *transform faults,* great fractures that cut through the ocean ridges. These faults may extend for hundreds of kilometres across the ocean floor and, in some cases,

go into the continents like the San Andreas fault in California. The fractures divide the ridge systems into segments. This raises some problems for the idea of sea floor spreading, for how can the conveyor belt operate differently in adjoining parts of the ocean floor?

An even greater problem is presented by continents such as Africa and Antarctica. These are almost surrounded by ocean ridge systems without the corresponding subduction zones. This means that crustal growth must take place by movement of the ridge system away from the continents. Attempts to answer difficulties such as these have caused sea floor spreading to be developed into the more comprehensive theory of plate tectonics.

The earth's crust is divided into stable areas bounded by ocean ridges, subduc-

Mats Wibe Lund

Ardea

Scripps Institute of Oceanography

Below: The floating rig *Glomar Challenger* **operates for the US Deep Sea Drilling Project. Rated as one of the most successful scientific expeditions ever, the Project has gathered geological evidence at previously unreachable depths on the ocean floor.**

Right: Two protozoa, *radioiaria* **(top) and** *foraminifera* **(below), provide clues to the age of the sea floor. By dating the skeletons of these microscopic organisms, which sink to form sediments, Challenger proved that the oldest sea floor is recent in geological terms—less than 200 million years old.**

Oxford Scientific Films

4   5   6   7   8

tion zones and transform faults. Crust is created at the ridges, destroyed in subduction zones and moved passively along the transform faults. These stable areas are now called *plates,* and *plate tectonics* is the theory and study of their formation, movement, interaction and destruction, and of their relationship to the major geological features of the earth.

The plates are considered to be rigid internally but able to move with respect to one another. On the surface, they consist either entirely of oceanic crust or of oceanic crust in which the continents are embedded. The African plate, for example, includes continental Africa and parts of the Atlantic and Indian oceans.

These large, solid plates must be thicker than the depth of the oceanic crust. It is now believed that the plates are divisions

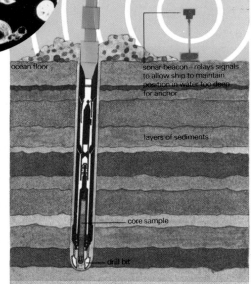

Glomar Challenger

sonar signal

drill string

ocean floor

sonar beacon - relays signals to allow ship to maintain position in water too deep for anchor

layers of sediments

core sample

drill bit

Left: Once on station, *Glomar Challenger* can drill without anchor. A sonar beacon is lowered and the ship uses four sideways thrusters to maintain position. From her 43 m tall derrick, the rig can lower as much as 6.7 km of pipe. Holes have been drilled more than 1.3 km deep into the ocean bottom.

Above: A scientist in a shipboard laboratory analyzes core samples. The fossil sequences and the stratas of sedimentary rocks tell the story of evolution and ancient climates in the oceans. The age and composition of the igneous rocks below the sediments confirm that oceanic crust is formed at spreading ridges.

of an outer, rigid shell of solidified rock, called the *lithosphere,* of which the crust forms the uppermost part. It is some 70 km (43 miles) thick under the oceans and perhaps 150 km (93 miles) thick under continents.

Floating continents in a sea of rock
Underlying the lithosphere is the *asthenosphere.* This is a world-wide 'plastic' layer through which seismic waves pass at low velocity and in which the rocks are partially molten or close to melting point. Its 'plasticity' bends to the shape of the lithosphere and allows the plates to glide relatively freely over the earth's surface. Continental drift is the result of plate movement.

The 'plastic' behaviour of the asthenosphere also explains the slow vertical adjustments which occur in the earth's crust. The continental crust is lighter than the rocks beneath it. Its average density is 2.7 grams/cm³ against 2.95 for the oceanic crust and 3.3 for the upper mantle. The lighter continents are in effect floating in a 'sea' of denser, but plastic, rock. The thickness of the continental crust is extremely variable.

This balancing act between 'floating' continents and underlying rock is termed *isostacy.* Isostatic adjustment is relatively rapid. About 10,000 years ago, for example, Scandinavia was covered by thick ice. The extra weight caused the crust in north-west Europe to sink, but now that the ice has melted, the land has risen some 200 m (650 feet) and is still rising.

Gradually the rates and directions of plate movement are being worked out, but its cause is still a mystery. Whatever its driving force, the theory of plate tectonics explains many aspects of earth history. Most changes occur at the plate boundaries, especially in the subduction zones where volcanoes and earthquakes are characteristic features. The moving plate theory is also important because it gives an idea of what will happen in the future. Knowing more about earthquakes, for instance, means that they can be predicted and, perhaps, controlled.

Mountain Building

There are two great chains of mountains on earth. One includes the South American Andes, the Rocky Mountains and other ranges encircling the Pacific; the other runs eastwards from the Alps of Southern Europe right across to the Himalayas and beyond. This system of 'linear' mountain belts appears to be unique to the planet earth.

Extending across the planet's surface for hundreds and even thousands of kilometres in continuous tracts, these mountains rise in places to peaks many kilometres above sea level. Their height means that most are snow covered. Frost-shattered fragments may break away to form jagged peaks surrounded by slopes covered in rock debris. Fast flowing streams cut gullies and gorges which are gradually widened and deepened, and may be cut still more savagely by glaciers flowing down from snow fields near the summit. Over millions of years such agents of erosion give mountains their characteristic features. Yet how did they originally form, and what forces were at work to create them?

Movements in the earth's crust

From the patterns revealed by volcanic and earthquake activity it has become clear that the earth's great mountain chains lie over unstable areas of the planet's crust. Indeed these mountains are not merely surface features, but are expressions of fundamental structures in the earth's crust. And it is this that has led scientists to regard mountain-building (known as *orogeny*) as part of an activity beginning beneath the earth's surface.

The earth can create mountains in a number of different ways, yet the great linear belts are an example of by far the most important mechanism, one which has been at work since early in the earth's history. These vast mountain chains of folded rock originate where the earth's crustal 'plates' converge, forcing layers of rock into great arcs which may rise far above sea level.

Investigation of the rocks of an 'oro-genic' mountain belt like the Himalayas shows that over millions of years they have undoubtedly suffered severe distortion and displacement from their original position. The layers of sediment, deposited in the sea long ago and hardened to form sedimentary rocks, contain fossilized remains of marine animals. When these fossils are found in rock strata of mountain folds thousands of metres above sea level it is clear that astonishing forces have pushed the layers upwards. The flat and continuous layers originally formed have been shaped into huge folds, tilted into vertical layers, or broken and stacked in a series of slabs. Such was the force of compression when the Indian continental plate met the vast plate of Asia that the Himalayas were formed.

The effect of this convergence of plates does vary from place to place. For example, it is particularly where the leading edges of both plates consist of 'continental' crustal material—which is less dense than crust of 'oceanic' type—that the

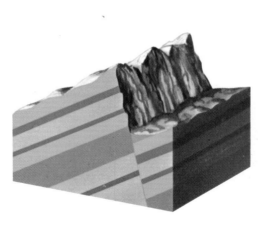

Left: Some of the world's most spectacular peaks are those formed by volcanic action. The classical shape of a volcanic cone is produced by the steady eruption of ash, pyroclasts and sticky lava from a central vent. Most volcanoes are located on the margins of the continental plates at mid-ocean ridges and deep sea trenches.

Right: The snow-capped peak of Mount Osorno reaches 2,660 metres into the South American skyline. A perfect example of a volcanic cone, Osorno is part of the Andes mountain range, formed when the Pacific plate was thrust under the South American plate.

Left: Most mountain ranges are the product of continual pushing and compression of the earth's surface. Sideways pressure on layers of sedimentary rock can produce fold mountains of a simple, open shape, as in parts of the Jura range in France and Switzerland. In more complex belts like the Alps and Himalayas, distorted folds—overturned and recumbent—are more common.

Right: The Himalayan range contains the highest peaks in the world. They are formed by the compression and uplift of a land area between the colliding mass of Asia and the subcontinent of India.

Left: Under strong compression blocks of surface rocks may fracture rather than bend, producing a fault rather than a fold. Normal faulting produces a mountain with a steep fault face raised above a plain and a gentle dip slope on the other side.

Right: The Sierra Nevadas are a good example of 'tilt block' mountains, formed by the uplift of a tilted fault block. This view shows the steep eastern face—up to 3,000 metres high—rising above the floor of the Great Basin of eastern California and western Nevada. The Sierra slope coincides with a major fault area, which includes the San Andreas fault.

Left: Some mountains are geological 'remnants' rather than 'constructions'. A mass of hard igneous rock such as granite intrudes into pre-existing rock, pushing up into the layers. Later, erosion of the softer surrounding rock leaves the igneous mass exposed as a dome or block-shaped mountain.

Right: Mighty Half Dome in the Yosemite Valley of California is a spectacular example of an intrusive mountain. Its tough granite face has resisted erosion better than the rock which once enclosed it. The sheer north-west face—now a mountaineer's delight—was carved by glaciation.

Left: Mount Ararat in eastern Turkey is a volcanic cone, 5,000 metres high. It lies in a 'collision zone' where volcanic and earthquake activity are caused by collision between the African and Eurasian plates. According to Biblical legend, Noah's Ark came to rest on Mount Ararat after the great flood.

Below: The sunlit slopes of Mount Ngauruhoe in New Zealand's Tongariro National Park. The mountain is a recently active volcano, the cone surmounted by an explosion crater which is still giving off gases. Mount Ngauruhoe lies on the fringe of the great 'linear' mountain belt that encircles the Pacific.

Below: The Elborz mountains near Teheran were formed by local tilting and faulting in an area of compression. They show a regular pattern of folding and deformation.

Below right: Diagram showing the features of a simple fold, created by horizontal pressure.

Right: Twisted layers of rock are clearly evident beneath the snow on a ridge along the western cwm of Everest, between Lhotze and Nuptse, at about 7,500 metres. These twisted strata indicate the kind of localized folding which produces minor anticline and syncline features in an area of compression.

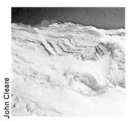

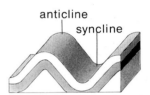

anticline

syncline

Above: The uplifted fault scarp of the tilt block of the Teton range forms a majestic panorama for visitors to the Grand Teton National Park in Wyoming, USA. Weathering processes have continually attacked the uplifted block, producing the present topography of sharp, angular peaks.

Left: A view of the Yosemite Valley from 3,000 metres up. Glacial action has smoothed a rounded valley in the granite rock, about 11 km long. The natural features of the area—sculptured granite cliffs and majestic waterfalls— are typical of heavy glaciation.

Right: The massive mountain dome overlooking Narssaq Harbour in Greenland. The slightly irregular shape is due to glaciation and frost action—exposure to extremes of temperature results in the fracturing of the rock which leaves jagged outlines and slopes which may be covered in a mass of rock debris.

flat lying strata   symmetrical   asymmetrical   overturned   isoclinal series   recumbent

  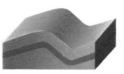 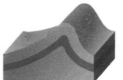  

Left: An example of the early stages of folding of rudimentary strata, producing a simple anticline. This arch-like fold of limestone is found at Chepstow in Gloucestershire.

Below left: The more advanced stages of folding in which many minor anticlines and synclines occur within a larger complex anticline. This example is on Anglesey, an island off the north-west coast of Wales.

Right: The Matterhorn peak in the Swiss Alps, 4,500 metres high, is one of the world's most spectacular mountains. The sharp peak is the product of extreme weathering—frost-shattering caused by icy temperatures.

forces of compression and uplift lead to formation of mountain belts. Where one of the plates consists of 'oceanic' crustal material, this may be overridden by the more buoyant continental plate, creating such features as oceanic trenches and volcanic island arcs. The Andes, the North American Cordilleras and the island arcs of Japan, the Philippines and Indonesia are products of the over-riding of the Pacific floor by the American and Asian continental plates.

The Geosyncline
Large parts of the world's orogenic mountain belts are carved from rocks which originated below the sea. Over periods of at least 100,000,000 years, marine sediments accumulated to thicknesses of ten or more kilometres on the sites of the belts. Most of these show features which indicate their accumulation in shallow seas and it is assumed that in the distant past, throughout the period of deposition, the sea-floor gradually subsided to make room for them. Such a well-defined region of long-continued subsidence of the earth's crust is called a *geosyncline*. For example, where the Appalachian Mountains (an 'orogenic' belt of mountains formed some 400 million years ago) now stand, a thick pile of sediment once lay beneath the sea. And this led two American geologists, Hall and Dana, to infer a connection between the development of a geosyncline and the subsequent operation of mountain-building forces.

The accumulation of great thicknesses of sedimentary and volcanic rocks in many such geosynclinal troughs has, however, been punctuated by phases of

crustal instability and volcanic activity. In these periods portions of the trough filling were raised above sea level and subjected to erosion. The successive layers visible today as mountain belts may therefore have gaps which reflect erosion at several different periods. Lower layers, for example, may show folds developed before the accumulation of the most recent deposits.

In many belts, the continued deposition of sediment ended with the collision of two continental plates. As a consequence, the 'geosynclinal' sea was eliminated as the layers folded upward to form the mountain belt. This mountain-building stage at the plate margin is marked by severe distortion of the deposits. Other changes are associated with the great heat generated in the active zone. For example, where rocks undergo slow deformation, and especially where they are weakened by high temperatures, they yield like plastic to give gigantic folds. Where forces uplift as well as compress the layers, sedimentary rock strata may break away and cascade down to pile up at lower levels in flat-lying or *recumbent* folds.

On the other hand, where deformation is rapid and the rocks cold or strong, fracturing of the layers is common. As a result folds may be severed from their roots and piled up again, together with slabs wrenched from the underlying basement. By all these means, the orderly layers of sedimentary rocks and lavas laid down one by one on the geosynclinal floor may be disturbed, reversed or disrupted. In the Alps, for instance, the characteristic structures are recumbent folds or thrust-slices piled one above the

Above: A view of the last 900 metres of the south-west face of Everest. Man's greatest mountaineering challenge, the peak was first conquered by Sir Edmund Hilary in 1953.

Below: The mechanism that is thought to have formed the Appalachian Mountains is illustrated by these six stages. (1) Some 600 million years ago the North American and African continents were parted by a spreading rift. (2) The Atlantic ocean opens up and sediments are laid down on the continental margins, their weight causing subsidence of the sea bed and the formation of *geosynclines.* (3) The ocean begins to close and a trench is formed adjacent to the North American continent as the lithosphere is re-absorbed into the earth's hot mantle. This underthrusting compresses

the North American geosyncline into folds, so creating the ancient Appalachians. An upthrust of magma and volcanic activity is triggered, so creating an intrusion of hard granite and surface volcanic mountains. (4) The Atlantic is now fully closed, so compressing the geosynclines of both continents and leaving only a vertical fault line. The two continents were joined in this way between 350 and 225 million years ago. (5) About 180 million years ago the Atlantic ocean began to open again along the old fault line, new oceanic crust material being formed as the continents drifted apart. (6) Today the rate of sea-floor spreading is some three centimetres per year, and new geosynclines are thought to be forming at the margins of the continents.

1 North America   Africa   2 continental shelf   shelf sediments   3   granite

continental slope   deep sea sediments   trench

rift   rift

lithosphere plate

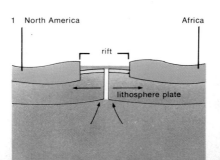 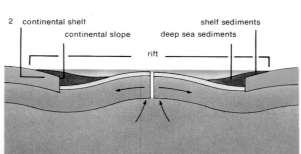 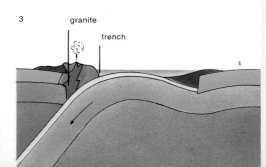

unfaulted blocks   normal   reverse   strike-slip   oblique-slip   hinge

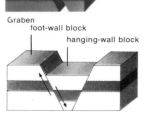

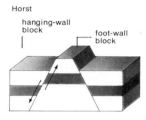

Left: A faulted anticline of shales and sandstones near Saundersfoot in Pembrokeshire. The shale core has been eroded, leaving a cave.

Below: Close-up of a section of rock from Trevaunance Cove, in Cornwall, showing small faults in layers of grit and shale.

Right: A rift valley, or *graben,* **is formed when the centre of an anticline slips down along fault lines.**

Below right: A block mountain, or *horst,* **is produced by a reverse movement—the middle block is forced up along fault lines. Erosion tends to round the rock surfaces.**

Left: The Grampian mountains in Scotland, an ancient, heavily-eroded mountain area. But crustal movements are still taking place— as erosion lessens a mountain's mass, it triggers movements to maintain a balance between the mountain's height and the depth of its 'roots' which lie in the molten mantle.

Graben
foot-wall block
hanging-wall block

Horst
hanging-wall block
foot-wall block

other.

Intense heat in the mountain-building belt results in two things: firstly, modifications, or the *metamorphism*, of the deformed rocks themselves; secondly, the rise of magma which is generated by partial melting of rocks at great depths. Chemical reactions during metamorphism lead to new minerals such as micas, garnet and hornblende. Different degrees of metamorphism also produce different rock types. For example, low intensities may produce slates, while higher intensities produce schists and gneisses whose parallel crystalline structure is related to the direction of the deforming forces.

The rise of granite is the dominant form of igneous activity during the mountain-building stage. The granite magma is derived largely from melting of rock near the base of the continental crust. Intrusive masses of up to several hundred kilometres in length occupy much of the interior of the Andes and the western Cordilleras of North America. Where one crustal plate over-rides another in a collision zone, magma may rise to the surface to build volcanic island arcs or volcanic mountain belts.

Mountain roots
The crumpling and disruption of rocks in a mountain-building belt do not only lead to a shortening of the belt, but also, in many instances, to a thickening of the crustal layer forming the belt. Like an iceberg in water, the mountain belt rises to a height above sea level which is balanced by a 'root' projecting deep into the denser material of the earth's mantle. This adjustment is the final stage in the mountain-building cycle, and is known as

the *isostatic* stage.

Mountain massifs may be the product of forces other than the collision of crustal plates. Blocks of the earth's crust for example, may rise vertically along deep faults in response to abnormal temperatures at great depth. At first this kind of block-uplift tends to give level-topped plateaux. But the effects of erosion on the plateaux, and especially at the boundary faults, may transform them into spectacular landscapes. The Colorado Plateau in the US and the Drakensberg Mountains of South Africa, are both the result of such forces at work.

Volcanic mountains, on the other hand, are built up by the extrusion of lava and ash from volcanic vents or fissures. The symmetry of the volcano depends on the style of volcanic activity. For example, eruptions from a single centre give conical mountains; eruptions through cracks or fissures in the earth's surface result in irregular ridges or lines of cones. Yet volcanic activity is so commonly associated with deep fracturing that the resulting mountains may reflect several processes. In the African Rift Valley, for instance, central volcanic cones such as Mounts Kenya, Elgon and Kilimanjaro rise in a highland plateaux which is the result of the uplift of a block along deep fault lines.

Erosion over millions of years
The emergence of all new mountain massifs, whatever their origin, is accompanied by intense erosion. Millions of years pass before a new mountain range emerges and long before it has ceased to rise the rock is subject to heavy erosion. The Brahmaputra and Indus rivers, for

example, which cross the Himalayas from sources in the Tibetan plateau, were able to deepen their valleys at the same time as the mountains rose, and so maintained their southward course to the sea. Continued denudation by the forces of erosion not only lowers the general level but also ultimately flattens out the topographical irregularities of the mountains. The end-product may be a *peneplain* of low relief and broad contours which exposes rocks and structures originally formed many kilometres below the surface.

The removal of rock-material as a result of erosion, however, also triggers off new crustal movements. This is because the isostatic balance is upset; the equilibrium is restored by a further rise of the eroded regions, which in turn stimulates further erosion. Many mountain terrains have been 'rejuvenated' more than once by this and other mechanisms. The Grampian Highlands of Scotland, for example, are the product of a mountain building belt 400 million years old which was rejuvenated comparatively recently. Successive cycles of erosion have revealed the roots of the old belt, made of deformed metamorphic rocks.

Indeed the forces which create and destroy mountains are at work all the time. Although uplift may occur at the rate of a metre or more in 100 years, erosion begins very rapidly, only slowing down as the elevation of the land diminishes. No highland area on the earth's surface can be regarded as 'stable'. All will change in some degree within a matter of a few hundred years. Within a hundred million years, the earth's surface will again be transformed.

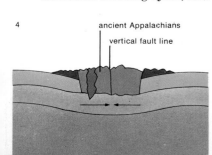

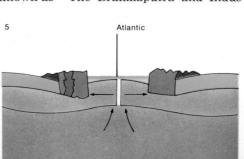

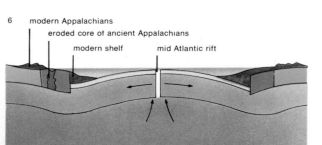

4   ancient Appalachians
vertical fault line

5   Atlantic

6   modern Appalachians
eroded core of ancient Appalachians
modern shelf   mid Atlantic rift

Minerals

Minerals are the building bricks of rocks. They are the basis of every rock except those of organic origin, like coal and chalk. A mineral is defined as any solid substance with a definite chemical composition occuring naturally in the earth, but which is not derived from plants or animals. By popular definition, anything that is mined is called a mineral, but the fossil fuels—coal, natural oil and gas—are excluded from the geological definition as they are formed from the remains of plant and animal life. One usual exception to the rule that a mineral must be solid is quicksilver, which is mercury in its native, liquid state.

Just as rocks are made up of combinations of minerals, the minerals themselves are composed of different fusions of chemical elements. Some minerals, however, such as gold or naturally-occurring copper and sulphur, contain only one element. The most common elements found in minerals, in descending order of occurrence, are oxygen, silicon, aluminium, iron, magnesium, calcium, potassium, and sodium. These are only eight of the 90 naturally-occurring elements, but they make up nearly 99 per cent by weight of the earth's crust. Oxygen and silicon alone account for nearly three quarters of the crust's constituents.

Secrets of atomic structure
The smallest particle of an element is a single atom. Examination of most minerals reveals that the atoms of the constituent elements have arranged themselves into a distinct and regular three-dimensional framework. These frameworks, known as *crystals* are geometric forms with their flat faces arranged symmetrically. Most minerals have this ordered atomic structure and are termed *crystalline*.

Under certain conditions that allow a crystalline mineral to grow without interference, it may form regular-shaped crystals. Silica, for example, may crystallize into perfect trigonal crystals of quartz. But if the growing crystals interfere with each other, then they may be distorted into mis-shapen grains of quartz which do not display regular crystal faces. Alternatively silica may develop into chalcedony, a *cryptocrystalline* mineral in which clusters of crystals are invisible except under the most powerful magnification. Finally, silica may take the form of opal, an *amorphous* or non-crystalline mineral, in which there is no regular arrangement of atoms. Each of these different manifestations of silica has a different atomic structure—directly affecting the crystal structure and thus the shape of each mineral.

How minerals are classified
Crystalline structure is an important clue in distinguishing one mineral from another. There are seven basic shapes of structural unity, and this gives rise to seven categories or *crystal systems*. Each mineral crystallizes in a particular system and can be identified accordingly. For example, a diamond belongs to the cubic system, whereas a ruby has a hexagonal crystal system.

Minerals display a dazzling variety of

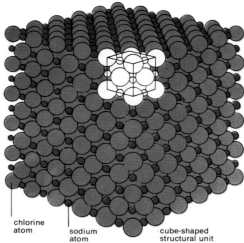

chlorine atom

sodium atom

cube-shaped structural unit

Above: Common table salt (sodium chloride) consists of finely ground crystals of a mineral called halite. When a crystal is magnified 100,000,000 times, its atomic structure is revealed. The large green circles represent chlorine atoms; the smaller red ones are sodium atoms. A 'detail' from the atomic structure model (right) outlines the molecular building block, or structural unit of the crystal. In this case it is the shape of a perfect cube.

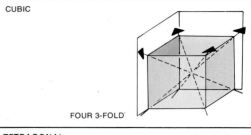

Below: A scanning electron micrograph of a common salt crystal, magnified 800 times. Even in small quantities the cubic crystal structure is recognizable.

Alan Windle

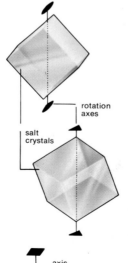

rotation axes

salt crystals

axis

crystal

An important clue in identifying one mineral from another is symmetry—a property which allows a crystal to be spun on an axis and to appear identical twice or more before it has rotated one full turn. The number of axes of symmetry in a crystal are then counted. The cube of a common salt crystal, for example, reveals three axes of symmetry.

Top left: Rotated on an axis taken through the centres of diagonally opposite edges, the cube appears identical twice in a complete rotation of 360°. This is termed a two-fold axis of symmetry. There are six such axes on a cube.

Centre left: On an axis taken through the opposite corners, the cube looks the same three times in a complete rotation, and reveals four three-fold axes.

Left: In the same way there are three four-fold axes of symmetry emerging through the centres of the faces of a cube. Minerals can be categorized into seven distinct systems determined by their crystal symmetry.

CUBIC

FOUR 3-FOLD

TETRAGONAL
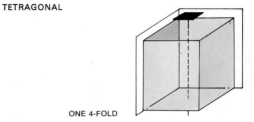
ONE 4-FOLD

ORTHORHOMBIC
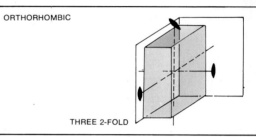
THREE 2-FOLD

MONOCLINIC
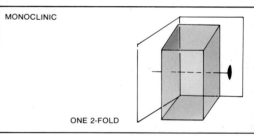
ONE 2-FOLD

TRICLINIC
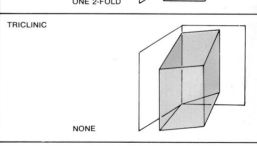
NONE

HEXAGONAL
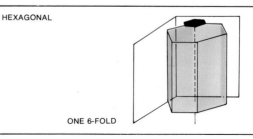
ONE 6-FOLD

TRIGONAL
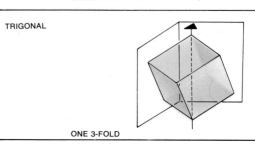
ONE 3-FOLD

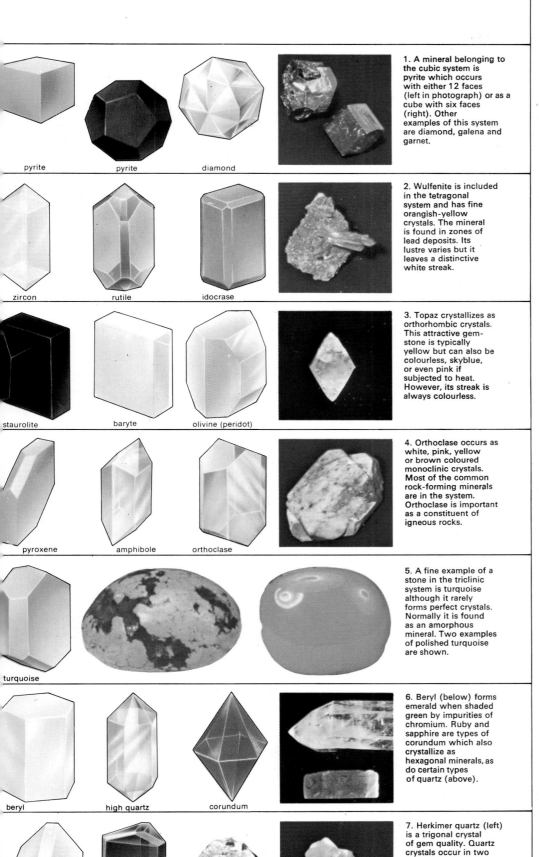

1. A mineral belonging to the cubic system is pyrite which occurs with either 12 faces (left in photograph) or as a cube with six faces (right). Other examples of this system are diamond, galena and garnet.

pyrite — pyrite — diamond

2. Wulfenite is included in the tetragonal system and has fine orangish-yellow crystals. The mineral is found in zones of lead deposits. Its lustre varies but it leaves a distinctive white streak.

zircon — rutile — idocrase

3. Topaz crystallizes as orthorhombic crystals. This attractive gem-stone is typically yellow but can also be colourless, skyblue, or even pink if subjected to heat. However, its streak is always colourless.

staurolite — baryte — olivine (peridot)

4. Orthoclase occurs as white, pink, yellow or brown coloured monoclinic crystals. Most of the common rock-forming minerals are in the system. Orthoclase is important as a constituent of igneous rocks.

pyroxene — amphibole — orthoclase

5. A fine example of a stone in the triclinic system is turquoise although it rarely forms perfect crystals. Normally it is found as an amorphous mineral. Two examples of polished turquoise are shown.

turquoise

6. Beryl (below) forms emerald when shaded green by impurities of chromium. Ruby and sapphire are types of corundum which also crystallize as hexagonal minerals, as do certain types of quartz (above).

beryl — high quartz — corundum

7. Herkimer quartz (left) is a trigonal crystal of gem quality. Quartz crystals occur in two systems and some authorities consider the hexagonal and trigonal systems as one. Dolomite (right) also occurs in two systems.

calcite — tourmaline

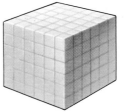

The symmetry of the structural unit controls the symmetry of the crystal structure. Since the structure governs the crystal shape, the symmetry of the whole crystal is an exact indication of the shape of the structural unit. The cubic structural units of the mineral pyrite can build two crystal shapes. In both cases the symmetry requirements —four 3-fold axes— are satisfied.

Above and below left: Cube-shaped iron pyrite (iron sulphide).

Above and below right: An eight-sided pyrite crystal, galena (lead sulphide).

Paul Brierley

colour, which is determined both by their structure and by the presence of impurities. But colour is not always a reliable clue to identity. Many minerals are commonly white or colourless and others, such as quartz or calcite, may occur in a whole range of colours.

The most reliable colour indicator is obtained by scraping the mineral against unglazed porcelain. This leaves a finely powdered trail, the colour of which is the mineral's *streak*. In this way, for example, crystals of haematite, which have a red streak, can be distinguished from those of magnetite which leave a black streak—although the crystals appear as the same colour.

The way in which a specimen affects light is another important clue to its identity. Minerals reflect light in different ways; this characteristic, known as *lustre*, ranges from the dull quality of clay to the adamantine lustre of diamond.

Hardness and *specific gravity* are two other reliable diagnostic properties. Hardness is actually rated in terms of the resistance of a mineral to scratching, arranged in ascending order from talc, which is easily crushed by a finger-nail, to diamond, the hardest mineral known to man. The hardness of a mineral is measured in terms of Mohs' Scale—an arbitrary scale with very irregular intervals, devised in 1822 by Mohs, an Austrian mineralogist.

The specific gravity of a mineral is the ratio between its weight and the weight of an equal volume of water. Taking the specific gravity of water as 1.0, the great majority of minerals have a specific gravity ranging between 2.2 and 3.2. Only those minerals which are as light as graphite (1.9) or as heavy as gold (15.0 to 20.0 according to purity) can be distinguished by their specific gravity when held in the hand.

The world's great mineral deposits
The geological processes in which minerals are formed determines both the distribution and the type of mineral deposits. *Magmatic* minerals are those

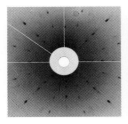

Above: The action of a crystal on X-rays is an important means of mineral identification. This X-ray diffraction photograph of common salt shows how the atoms deflect and reflect X-rays; the 4-fold rotation symmetry shown by the pattern of spots indicates that the atoms are packed in a cubic arrangement.

Paul Brierley

Paul Brierley

Left: A glowing piece of fluorite demonstrates the property of fluorescence. This refers to the way particular specimens of certain minerals emit visible light while bombarded with invisible radiation such as ultra-violet or X-rays. Fluorite, calcite and diamond all have this property.

Right: The vast salt deposits in the Danakil region of Ethiopia. This is an area where hot springs bring up minerals in solution —solid deposits are left behind when the solution evaporates.

Below: The 'Big Hole' at Kimberley in South Africa—one of the world's richest diamond mines.

George Gerster/John Hillelson

fracture   cleavage

Left: The atoms of the mineral mica are strongly bonded in layers, but between the layers the bonds are very weak. The crystal will thus split smoothly between the layers— this is known as its cleavage tendency. Where the bonding is strong, across the horizontal layers, it fractures irregularly.

Paul Brierley

Left: A spectacular formation of magnetite, a common example of a magnetic mineral—one which is strongly attracted by an iron magnet. Magnetite also has the property of exerting and retaining its own magnetic field; in the form of 'lodestone' it was used by the ancients as a compass.

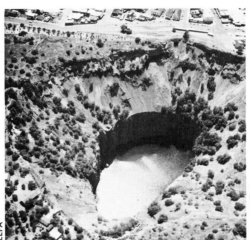

ZEFA

Right: A number of diamond stones can be polished simultaneously using modern methods. The extreme hardness of diamonds gives them an important industrial role, in glass-cutting tools, rock-drilling and cutting equipment.

Below: Flint hand axes, some 250,000 years old, were one of man's first uses of minerals.

De Beers

Michael Holford

which crystallize from molten magma as it cools to form igneous rock. The first minerals to crystallize in the cooling period—silicates with a high proportion of iron and magnesium—are free to grow without interference and form well-shaped crystals. For example, the important mineral chromite, used for toughening steel, was concentrated in enormous quantities in the huge Bushveld igneous complex of South Africa by this process.

As magma cools further, more minerals are formed until only a little 'residual liquid' is left between grains of rock. This liquid may be rich in volatile components and in elements that form valuable minerals, and may either be trapped in cavities known as *geodes, drusies* or *vugs* in which beautifully shaped crystals grow in towards the centre, or be violently squeezed out by pressure from solidifying minerals into cracks and fissures in surrounding rock. There it solidifies to form *hydrothermal veins* in which mis-shapen crystals of quartz grow, along with a wide variety of other minerals. These are commonly-mined deposits, as they often form at shallow depths.

Mineral deposits may also be of *sedimentary* or *metamorphic* origin. Deep down in the earth's crust, or near hot magma, metamorphic minerals are formed from pre-existing minerals in solid rock by intense heat and pressure. Most sedimentary rocks are the product of minerals weathered by wind, water and chemical action from igneous and metamorphic rocks and are consolidated in layers, such as shale and calcite-rich limestone. Other minerals, such as rock salts and gypsum, are *evaporites,* caused by evaporation in shallow seas or lakes.

1. As magma cools and forms igneous rock, minerals also form. Fine crystallized minerals, such as quartz, amethyst, galena and tourmaline, as well as feldspar and pyrite, occur in rock cavities called drusies, vugs and goedes. Diamonds from the Kimberley mine come from Kimberlite, an igneous rock.

2. River alluvial deposits have sometimes provided prospectors with easy pickings. Precious stones and metals may accumulate in places from the weathering and erosion of different types of rocks. Panning and dredging are used to sort out the potentially rich deposits from other sediments.

3. Limestone altered by heat-metamorphism and igneous gases is an important source of commercially valuable ores like copper, gold, 'fools gold' (pyrite), iron, lead and zinc.
4. Where heat has metamorphosed shale, minerals found include garnet, chiastolite, biotite and cordierite.

5. Hydrothermal veins are heavily mined for their rich supplies of gold and silver, as well as the silver- and lead-bearing galena, gems such as opals, emeralds and tourmaline, and sulphide minerals like pyrite and chalcopyrite. Secondary minerals like copper-bearing azurite and malachite occur.

HOW AND WHERE MINERALS OCCUR

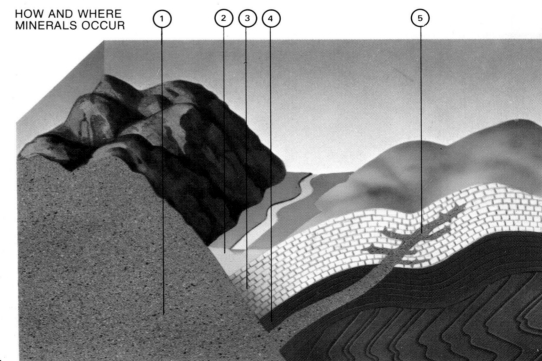

Right: A variety of agate known as **Mexican Lace**, typical of the fantastic and colourful structures which make agate popular as an ornamental stone. Agate is in fact a variety of chalcedony, a mixture of quartz and opal.

Left: Panning gravel for diamonds in Borneo, a prospecting method still used today.

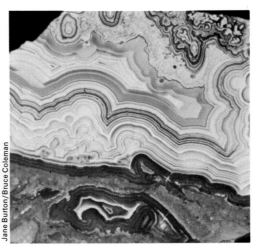

Left: An asbestos suit in action in an industrial test. As well as withstanding heat, asbestos has a high electrical resistance and is immune to chemical action. Chrysotile (above) is one of a number of minerals which occur as long fibrous crystals which can be spun to form asbestos.

Above: A crystal of diamond, as it occurs in Kimberlite, the igneous rock which forms the famous South African 'diamond pipes'.

Left: The breathtaking Kohinoor diamond, originally found in India. It was cut in 1852 and is now part of the British crown jewels. This is one of the world's largest diamonds.

MOHS SCALE OF MINERAL HARDNESS

HARDNESS	MINERAL	TEST
1	talc	can be scratched by fingernail
2	gypsum	
3	calcite	
4	fluorite	can be scratched with steel point
5	apatite	
6	orthoclase	
7	quartz	will scratch glass easily
8	topaz	
9	corundum	
10	diamond	will scratch any other material

6. Beach sand and gravel retain deposits eroded from rocks and sorted by the continual action of waves. For example, chalcedony and calcite are eroded from limestone and sandstone, and pyrite and marcasite from shale. Some normally rare minerals like monazite may be concentrated here.

7. Ancient metamorphic rock, subject to great pressure and change, is the setting for garnet, asbestos, talc, serpentine, turquoise and some emeralds.

8. Sedimentary strata contain large deposits. Dolomite is an example of a constituent of many sedimentary rocks. Others are gypsum and halite.

Some rare minerals are very hard and have an unusually attractive colour and lustre. Those of greatest rarity, and therefore of greatest monetary value, are the precious gemstones, diamond, emerald, ruby and sapphire. Platinum, gold and silver, the precious metals, have also acquired great value because of their beauty, rarity and durability. These three metals together with copper and iron are the only metals to occur as *native*, or uncombined, elements in nature.

The precious minerals are both hard and, except for silver, chemically unreactive. When rocks bearing minerals of high specific gravity are exposed to weathering, the lighter material is gradually eroded away while the heavier, chemically stable minerals are concentrated in *placer* deposits.

Such deposits are called *residual* if they have remained at or near their original position, *eluvial* if they have been concentrated by rain-wash and gravity, and *alluvial* if they have been formed by streams. The famous deposits which sparked off the 1849 gold rush to California were alluvial placers. The discovery of diamond-bearing gravels caused a similar great rush to Lichtenburg in South West Africa in the 1920s.

Finding precious stones is still largely a matter of luck. Most occur in close association with particular types of rock, but suitable geological locations only rarely contain precious minerals and only exceptionally are these of gem quality. The most productive diamond mines are at Kimberley in South Africa, where the stones crystallized in an igneous rock called kimberlite. Other major producers are Angola and Zaire.

The weight of precious minerals is measured in *carats*, one carat weighing a mere 200 milligrams. Stones of gem quality are closely inspected for flaws and weaknesses, before being carefully cut and used in jewelry. The emerald, for example, owes its great value to the rarity of flawless crystals. This dark green variety of the mineral beryl occurs in highly metamorphosed shales called mica-schists. The finest emeralds come from near Bogota in Columbia, but other important deposits have been found in the Ural Mountains in the Soviet Union and in Austria, Norway and Australia.

The world's supply of fine rubies has come largely from the Mogok mines in Upper Burma, where they occur in metamorphosed limestone. The presence of minute quantities of chromium causes the red colour of ruby in the mineral corundum. Another gem variety of the colourless corundum is the sapphire, tinted blue by iron and titanium impurities. Fine sapphires are found in gravels in Sri Lanka, Thailand and Kashmir.

Technological progress in exploiting minerals has determined the growth of civilization. The Stone Age began when the first crude but handy tools were fashioned from flint. From the Copper Age—when man first discovered a method of isolating metal from its natural mineral state—through the successive Bronze, Iron and Atomic Ages, man's activities and well-being have been affected by his increasingly sophisticated use of earth materials. The industrial and technological revolution which has reshaped society in every continent relies massively on a continued supply and large-scale exploitation of the earth's mineral wealth.

Metal Ores

The search for metals dates back almost to the beginning of civilization. Ores are minerals from which metal can be extracted, yet the first metal to be recognized by man was undoubtedly gold—which occurs naturally in a metal state and needs no extraction. Unaffected by weathering and other chemical processes, gold occurs in veins in rocks or as flakes and nuggets in river gravels. Gold was prized by the ancients for its unrivalled colour and lustre and for the ease with which it could be worked into objects of beauty and value. The Egyptians believed that gold had divine significance and established a state industry to exploit the metal over 4,000 years ago.

The Middle East also saw the beginnings of *metallurgy*, the extraction of metals from their ores. Archaeologica[l] excavations in Iran and Afghanistan have revealed that around 5,000 BC copper was being extracted from its easily-smelted ore, the beautiful emerald-green mineral malachite. The Greeks and Romans controlled extensive mining industries and their empires owed much of their preeminence to their wealth in metals.

In response to the needs of the technological revolution came a more scientific understanding of the formation of ores and their distribution patterns. Geologists now realize that nearly all the metals used in industry are very scarce. Copper forms 0.007 per cent of the earth's crust, tin 0.004 per cent, lead 0.0016 per cent, uranium 0.0004 per cent, silver 0.00001 per cent and gold a mere 0.0000005 per cent.

Usable ore deposits are therefore extremely rare features because they require a concentration of metals to as much as a million times their average distribution. There are two main processes by which ore deposits are formed. They may be concentrated within rocks formed by cooling magma or deposited by surface processes of erosion.

When magma cools slowly, insulated by the thickness of surrounding rocks, the minerals crystallize out in a particular order. Some minerals separate out early and sink to the bottom of the magma to form *magmatic segregations* such as the enormous quantities of chromite found in southern Africa. The remaining liquid then becomes more concentrated in other ore minerals and contains large amounts of dissolved gases and water vapour. At a late stage of the cooling process, the liquid may squeeze into cracks and fissures in the igneous rock to form *pegmatite* deposits.

The crystallizing minerals of pegmatite may grow very large. In the Black Hills of South Dakota, USA, for instance, one crystal of the lithium-aluminium mineral spodumene measuring over 15 metres in length and weighing over 90 tonnes was taken out of the pegmatite mine. Many of the rarer and more exotic minerals are found in pegmatites, including monazite, an ore of the radioactive metal thorium.

The solutions remaining in the late stages of separation are under great pressure and are chemically highly reactive. As they stream into the surrounding rocks they may react with them and deposit the metals they hold in solution as *pneumatolytic* mineral deposits. Deposits

Paul Brierley

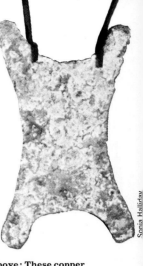

Sonia Halliday

Above: These copper ingots, probably used as a trading currency, came from the oldest known shipwreck, dated 1000 BC, off the coast of Turkey.

Below: Geophysical techniques are used in the search for ores. The operator in this crew using a portable ground system carries a coil. This measures the responses to signals from an electromagnetic source.

Above: A polished example of malachite. This beautiful emerald-green mineral is often a result of secondary enrichment. Metallic copper was extracted from this easily-smelted ore as long ago as 5000BC.

IGS

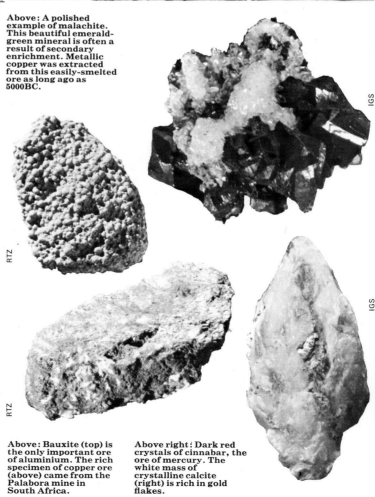

RTZ

RTZ

IGS

Above: Bauxite (top) is the only important ore of aluminium. The rich specimen of copper ore (above) came from the Palabora mine in South Africa.

Above right: Dark red crystals of cinnabar, the ore of mercury. The white mass of crystalline calcite (right) is rich in gold flakes.

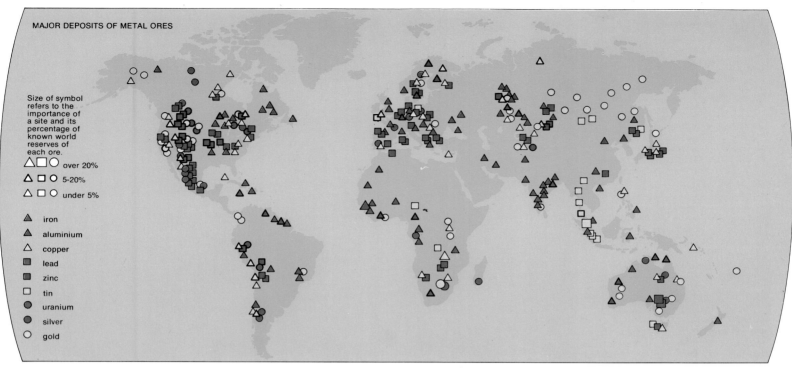

MAJOR DEPOSITS OF METAL ORES

Size of symbol refers to the importance of a site and its percentage of known world reserves of each ore.

△ □ ○ over 20%
△ □ ○ 5-20%
△ □ ○ under 5%

▲ iron
▲ aluminium
△ copper
■ lead
■ zinc
□ tin
● uranium
● silver
○ gold

Above: The world map indicates the known distribution of major metal ore deposits. There are several thousand minerals but only about a hundred are of economic value. Distribution and production of the most important metal ores are detailed (right).

Below: This spectacular photograph of the southern half of Rhodesia was taken at a height of 500 miles from an orbiting NASA satellite. The picture emphasizes certain bands of the light spectrum and reveals many large-scale geological features unrecognizable on the ground. The long green strip is the Great Dyke, a major source of chromite ore.

RTZ

Iron is the fourth most plentiful element in the earth's crust and rich ores are widely spread. This is fortunate for the world uses over 800 million tonnes annually. USSR, USA, Australia and Brazil produce the most.

Aluminium is the most abundant metal in the earth's crust, but production is only 15 million tonnes, mostly from USA, USSR, Japan, Canada and Norway.

Copper production is some 6.6 million tonnes a year. Two-thirds comes from Chile, Zambia, Zaire and Peru whose economies largely depend on copper.

Tin is mined in large quantities in only a few areas in Asia, Africa and Bolivia. Low output—under 200,000 tonnes— makes tin an expensive metal.

Lead and **Zinc** usually occur together. Lead production is some 4 million tonnes annually, mostly from USA, USSR, Canada and Australia. The 6 million tonnes of zinc come mainly from the same four countries.

Gold is associated with South Africa which produces two-thirds of the world total of less than 1,500 tonnes. Other major sources are USSR and Canada.

Silver is also valuable but less rare. Leading producers are Mexico and Peru followed by USSR, Canada and USA. Annual supply is under 1,000 tonnes.

Uranium ore of a high-grade is of limited supply. Estimated consumption is 30,000 tonnes a year. Rich deposits occur in Canada, Australia and Africa.

of the tin ore cassiterite in Cornwall in southwest England, once a major source of the metal, are of this type.

The final stage of the formation of ore deposits of magmatic origin involves the watery hot, liquid residues called *hydrothermal* solutions. Under the right conditions, these solutions can move great distances and, being chemically and physically so different from the rocks in their path, they react with them to deposit their load of ore minerals. In cavities and fissures, *lodes* and *veins* are formed, while in the minute spaces between the grains of rocks, *impregnations* result.

Hydrothermal deposits are classified according to their temperature of formation. The Morro Velho gold mine in Brazil, still worked after two centuries of mining, is an example of the highest temperature deposits which formed nearest to the magma source. This is known because some of the minerals accompanying the gold only form at high temperatures.

Many of the world's great copper ore deposits are considered to have formed at a more moderate temperature. The enormous copper deposits found in the geologically-young mountain chains of the Andes, for example, are typically

great masses of igneous rock peppered through with copper minerals. The world's largest copper mine is at Chuquicamata, some 3,000 metres up in the Andes. The richest mercury mine in the world is at Almaden in Spain. This is an example of the coolest hydrothermal deposits, usually formed at shallow depths.

The second major group of mineral deposits includes those formed by sedimentary processes. The action of rivers, seas and wind on rocks gradually wears them down and the heavier, ore minerals become concentrated together to produce deposits, such as the beach sand deposits along the eastern coastline of Australia, mined for titanium and zirionium.

Sedimentary deposits have also been formed by chemical or organic action. Many important iron ore deposits, such as the ironstones of the English Midlands and of Alsace-Lorraine in France, were formed by the action of acidic water on iron-bearing rocks.

More often, the chemical action of weathering produces new minerals. Under intense tropical weathering conditions, clays are broken down to leave their constituent aluminium minerals. The extensive layers of bauxite (aluminium oxide combined with water), like those

27

Left: Sinking a shaft at a diamond mine in Cape Province, South Africa. The deepest shafts extend over 3 km (2 miles) down into the earth at the Witwatersrand gold mines. Problems of water pumping, intense heat (rock temperatures increase 1°C for every 60 metres in depth) and high humidity have to be overcome before mining is possible.

Below: The gold mine at West Driefontein in South Africa is one of the world's largest. The tower on the right lies over the shaft. Winding gear hauls the skips of ore to the surface. The ore is then crushed at the plant in the centre and gold extracted. Waste is carried away by conveyor belt.

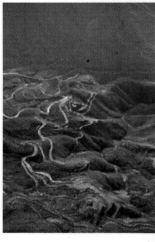

Above: The open-cast Toquepala copper mine in the Peruvian Andes. The open-cast method is suitable for mining large tonnages of low grade ore. First the barren rock or over-burden is removed and then each terrace or bench is mined back into the sides of the pit. After blasting, the ore is scooped up with mechanical shovels into waiting trucks. Ores with as little as 0.3% copper—once rejected as waste—can now be profitably mined.

Right: The residual deposits of gernierite on the Pacific island of New Caledonia form one of the world's most valuable reserves of nickel. It is mined by an open-cast method called strip-mining.

found in Jamaica which built up in this way, form residual deposits of virtually the only ore of aluminium.

Ore deposits, like other rocks, are also subject to chemical weathering at their surface outcrops. Water percolating through rocks often contains acid which attacks the ore and forms a metal-bearing solution. *Secondary enrichment* is the term applied to ore deposits carried downward in solution and later solidified in rich concentrations.

Exploration for the world's deposits

Many of the world's major ore fields have been discovered by chance. The great nickel deposits of Sudbury, Ontario, were found accidentally in the 1880s by workmen on the Canadian Pacific railway. Before the development of modern ex-

ploration techniques, minerals were located by prospecting. This involved searching directly for ore deposits on the surface, as in gold-panning, or indirectly by looking for the tell-tale signs of buried ore deposits. These signs include the *gossans* or 'iron hats' of rusty, spongy rock which sometimes cap sulphide ore deposits, or the staining of rocks by traces of the brightly coloured minerals of some metals.

Modern exploration involves searching an area in a much more elaborate way. Mining companies spend millions of pounds every year on exploration, with only very small chances of success. It has been estimated that perhaps one in a thousand prospects examined ever leads to a major ore discovery and an eventually productive mine.

Exploration usually follows a set sequence. First, a large area is selected because the right rock types and structure exist for a particular type of ore deposit. For example, rock fractures such as joints or faults may provide channels of easy access for metal-bearing hydrothermal solutions. At each stage in his exploration the geologist will build up knowledge of the type and distribution of rocks in the area by making geological maps. Here, he may be aided by aerial photographs. By careful interpretation, an enormous amount of information can be gained about the rocks and structure of the area which would otherwise take a great deal of time and work on the ground to obtain. A development of this technique on an even greater scale is the use of satellite photographs.

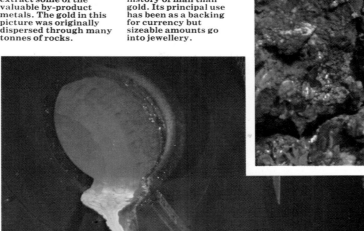

Below: Molten gold poured from the furnace cascades into a set of moulds. After cooling, these ingots contain almost 99% pure gold but they are then even further refined to extract some of the valuable by-product metals. The gold in this picture was originally dispersed through many tonnes of rocks.

Gold generally occurs as the native metal, often mixed with silver and other precious minerals. Probably no metal has had more influence on the economics, politics and history of man than gold. Its principal use has been as a backing for currency but sizeable amounts go into jewellery.

Above: Most of the world's tin is mined from alluvial deposits of cassiterite (tin oxide) in South-East Asia. This dredger operating in Malaysia slowly works up and down a shallow lake. It is fitted with a large bucket-wheel which scoops up the tin-bearing gravels from the bottom. Malaysia is the world's largest tin producer.

Above: This specimen of meteoric iron was found at Krasnoyarsk in Siberia. Meteorites are material from outer space which have broken through the earth's atmosphere to fall on the earth's surface. They provide important clues to geologists of material and metals that exist on other planets.

Right: The tough shell of an Apollo spacecraft and the complex equipment carried are made of a variety of metals. Aluminium alloys for the hull are toughened with small amounts of other metals to enable it to withstand great heat. Tiny quantities of gold are used in some electronic components.

Right: Copper is an excellent conductor of electricity and some 60% of all copper extracted goes to the electrical industry. Several kilometres of copper wire were used in this modern telephone exchange system. Copper is also an essential ingredient of the alloys brass and bronze.

Direct geological observations are supplemented by the techniques of geochemistry and geophysics. Geochemistry utilizes the fact that traces of the metals in minerals can work their way to the surface, carried there by the water which circulates through the rocks. These metals then become dispersed in the soils carried into the sediment of streams and rivers or are even taken up by trees and plants. Geophysics depends on the fact that the physical properties of concentrations of ore minerals are measurably different from those of surrounding rocks. Instruments have been developed to detect the minutely different electrical, magnetic and gravitational response of ore bodies.

Both geochemistry and geophysics can only give a hint of what lies beneath the surface. Many features other than ore deposits can give rise to false indications and the real test of whether an ore deposit exists is to probe beneath the surface. The most widely used technique is *diamond drilling*. The cutting action of the rotating diamond-tipped drill bit produces a cylindrical *core* of rock. This is hauled up at intervals and examined.

Drilling can provide the first direct evidence of ore minerals. Using a grid pattern of drill holes over an area containing a deep-seated deposit, it is possible to get an estimate of a deposit's shape, size and grade of the ore even before the first tunnel is driven into the deposit.

Detailed exploration work provides enough information about the ore deposit for an entire modern mining operation to be planned and designed several years before mining actually starts. Advances in mining technology have meant that very low grade ores can be worked economically, provided the tonnages mined are sufficiently large. The bulk of the major, large-tonnage, new mines brought into production are enormous quarrying operations called *open cast*.

For ores deposited in veins or narrow layers, as well as for those lying too deep or at too steep an angle, underground mining methods have to be used. Shafts are sunk and horizontal tunnels driven at different levels into the ore deposit. The deposit is then explored from subsidiary tunnels. Alluvial deposits which are not amenable to either underground or open cast mining are extracted by dredging. For example, large dredgers scoop up tin-bearing gravels in lakes in Malaysia.

Coal

Coal is a unique deposit. No other rock (for coal is as much a rock in the geological sense as sandstone, limestone or granite) has played such an important role in the development of major industrial countries. Without coal, many modern technologies would be impossible, or prohibitively expensive. For example, coal is not only a fuel, but also—in the form of coke—an essential ingredient of steel. In addition, through making coke, many useful chemical by-products are generated.

The formation of coal

Coal is formed from the compacted and deeply buried remains of trees and plants which grew in forests millions of years ago. It is usually found in layers, or seams, each covering a large area, often hundreds of square kilometres, and ranging from one or two centimetres to several metres thick.

The oldest coal occurs in rocks of the Upper Devonian period, some 360 million years old, and is found subsequently in rocks of all ages up to the Tertiary period, which began 70 million years ago. However, most coals of economic importance were formed in the latter part of the Carboniferous period (the name means coal-bearing) some 265-290 million years ago. In this period conditions were just right for the prolific growth of forests, whose later burial led to the formation of the coalfields of North America, Europe and USSR. The climate was tropical and the trees grew in extensive swamps similar to the present-day jungles in such places as the Amazon basin and the Irrawaddy Delta of Burma.

Under these conditions, growth is very rapid. Dead trees and plant debris falling into the swamps quickly become waterlogged, and accumulate on the bottom. The stagnant swamp waters contain little oxygen, inhibiting the action of bacteria which would normally cause the vegetation to decay. Instead, the leaves and other soft parts gradually turn into a dark, jelly-like *humus*. This impregnates the harder, more woody plant debris until the end result is a layer of peat. (In present day swamps, peat layers 10 m (30 ft) thick have been found.) This is the first stage in the development of true coal. During peat formation, the weight of the upper layers compacts the lower layers, squeezing out some of the water. Chemical reactions accompany this compaction and result in the gradual enrichment of the peat with carbon. At the same time *methane*, or marsh-gas, is released.

To turn peat into coal, it must be buried and compacted still further beneath a thick pile of sediments. The consequent increase in pressure and slight rise in temperature results in progressive chemical changes. Water, methane, and other gases (known as *volatiles*) are further driven off and increasing carbon enrichment occurs until, ultimately, coal is formed. Such a decrease of volume takes place that a layer of peat more than 10-15 metres thick will produce only 1 metre of coal.

In Upper Carboniferous times, when coal formation was at its peak, the earth was in a general state of unrest. Fluctuating periods of earth movement caused

IGS

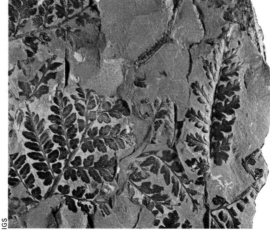

IGS

Above: Reconstruction of a typical coal-forming forest in the Carboniferous period reveals the luxuriant vegetation. Giant club-mosses, 'horsetails' and a dense undergrowth of smaller fern and creeper-like plants flourished in swampy terrain similar to the tropical jungles found in the Amazon basin.

Below: The types of plants which grew in coal-forming forests are known because of fossilized remains commonly found in the rocks near coal seams. These well-preserved fossil ferns came from a coal measure in Yorkshire. Dead ferns and trees accumulated in the swamp to form peat and, later, coal.

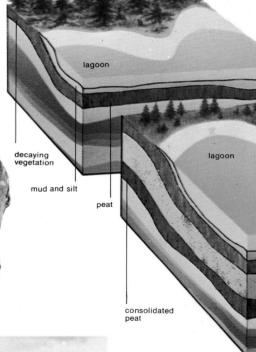

forest

lagoon

decaying vegetation

mud and silt

peat

lagoon

consolidated peat

Picturepoint

Left: Peat forms also in temperate climates. In this hilly area of Scotland, with poor drainage, thick peat deposits have formed from fallen trees, heather and mosses. After digging and stacking to dry, the peat is used by local people as fuel but it gives off little heat and much smoke.

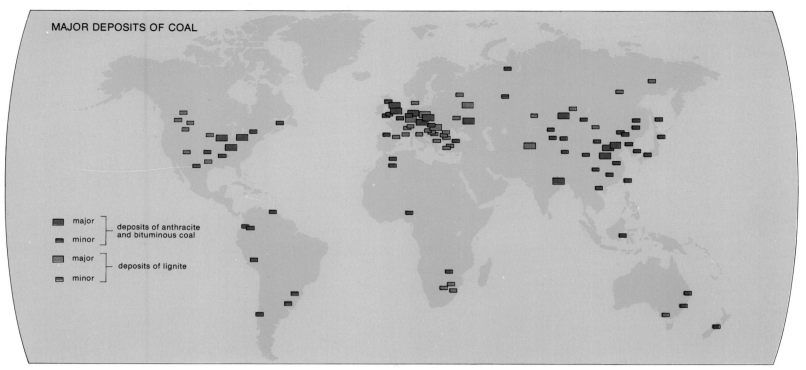

MAJOR DEPOSITS OF COAL

■	major	deposits of anthracite and bituminous coal
■	minor	
▭	major	deposits of lignite
▭	minor	

Below: Three stages in the formation of coal seams are shown. Dead vegetation falls into the swamp to form peat. After subsidence, water floods the forest and deposits a sedimentary layer of mud and silt which buries the peat to form coal eventually. As the water recedes, new forests grow and a new cycle begins.

Above: Coal deposits are widely distributed throughout the world and will offer a continuing supply of fuel to an energy-hungry world for many centuries. It is estimated that remaining resources are some 2.9 million million tonnes. Annual production is 3,000 million tonnes.

Right: The three main types of humic coal are classed by their degree of alteration. Lignite (right) is a soft coal, dark brown in colour, with a woody texture. Coals are broadly made up of carbon, hydrogen and oxygen. With high rank coals, carbon content increases. Lignite is typically 70% carbon.

LIGNITE

BITUMINOUS

Left: Bituminous coal is the type most commonly used in the home. It is black and brittle with alternating bands of shiny vitrain and dull durain layers. Anthracite (below) is the highest rank coal produced by the greatest degree of alteration. It is very hard and has a 96% carbon content.

ANTHRACITE

gradual subsidence of the coal-forming forests, with occasional periods of rapid subsidence in which the sea frequently flooded the forests and accumulating peat beds.

The forests occupied vast areas of swampland through which rivers and streams flowed. When they reached the sea, the rivers formed extensive deltas which were also colonized by forests. As rapid subsidence took place, the plants became submerged, and thick mud was deposited on top of the forests, burying and compacting the peat. When rapid subsidence ceased, the sea level remained much the same, but the waters became shallower as rivers carried down more sediments.

Eventually, so much sediment accumulated that sand-banks and mud flats appeared above water level. These were quickly colonized by plants and soon became new swampy forests. Peat formation started again, continuing until another rapid subsidence flooded the area, starting the whole cycle over again. Such a sequence of events is known as *cyclic sedimentation*.

Types of coal

Coals which have formed in seams by the process outlined above are known as *humic* coals and may be classed by the degree of alteration which the original peat has undergone. This is known as their *rank*. A whole range of coals can occur, but the main types are *lignite*, *bituminous coal*, and *anthracite*.

Lignite is a softish coal which is dark brown in colour. Nearest to peat in composition, it gives off a lot of smoke when burnt, without a great deal of heat. There are extensive deposits in central Europe and North America. Bituminous coal, on the other hand, is the type with which most people are familiar. It is black and brittle, with a tendency to fracture along one or two vertical planes, forming straight-sided blocks of coal.

Bituminous coals usually have horizontal bands of alternating shiny and dull layers. These represent different types of 31

FORMATION OF COAL

new forest

sedimentary layer

fresh layer of peat

lagoon

consolidated peat

lignite coal

J. Pfaff/Zefa

Left: Open-cast mining for low quality brown coal up to a depth of 50 metres near Cologne in Germany. This method is applied to shallow seams and vast excavating machines are used to mine a deep pit.

Right: For deeper deposits, underground mining is required. Miners working at the coal face are hampered by dirty and dangerous conditions. Modern mining techniques involve increasing use of mechanization.

Below: A plan of a typical coal mine shows the tremendous amount of careful planning and costly machinery needed to extract coal from deep coal seams.

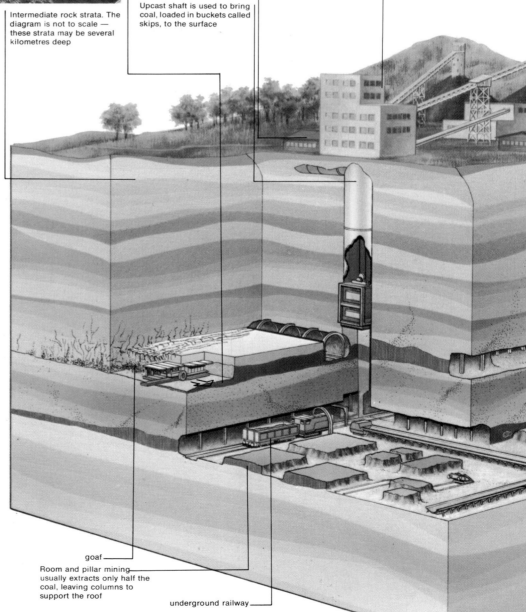

A cutaway section through the unmined coal shows the machinery used in longwall mining at work. The arrow shows the direction of mining into the coal face

Fan-house, with powerful fan to extract the foul air

The top of the upcast shaft is housed in a sealed building, to ensure that the fan operates efficiently in removing used air from the whole underground area

Intermediate rock strata. The diagram is not to scale — these strata may be several kilometres deep

Upcast shaft is used to bring coal, loaded in buckets called skips, to the surface

goaf

Room and pillar mining usually extracts only half the coal, leaving columns to support the roof

underground railway

original plant debris. The hard shiny, almost glassy, layers are known as *vitrain*. Microscopic examination shows that they consist of highly compressed bark and woody material. The dull layers are called *durain* and are formed mainly of the smaller and more resistant plant debris, such as spore-cases. Neither durain nor vitrain soil the fingers when touched. It is the presence of *fusain* that makes coal dirty to handle. Fusain is a soft and friable substance resembling charcoal, and was most probably formed from dead branches and trunks exposed to the air.

Anthracite is the highest rank of coal. Durain and vitrain bands are both present, but rarely fusain, and so anthracite is clean to handle. It burns with a very hot flame with hardly any smoke.

By contrast with the humic coals, the *sapropelic* coals are a group which do not appear to have formed from extensive tropical forest peat. There are two main types: *cannel coal* (the name is probably a corruption of 'candle' since it burns with a bright, smokey flame) is unbanded and breaks like glass. It is thought to have originated from the accumulation of fine floating plant material, such as spores. The remains of algae often form some of the constituents. *Boghead* coals, on the other hand, are dark brown or black, and resemble tough leather. They consist mainly of the remains of algae, which probably lived in large, well-oxygenated lakes.

The process of repeated seam formation leads to a great thickness of coal-bearing sediments being built up. These are given the general term *coal measures* and may reach a thickness of at least 1500 m, containing 20-30 main coal seams between one and three metres thick and many additional, much thinner ones. Their original horizontal layers, however, have often been disturbed by folding, tilting and faulting as a result of earth movements during the hundreds of millions of years in which they formed. Where coal-measures outcrop at the surface, an exposed coalfield is found but, over many

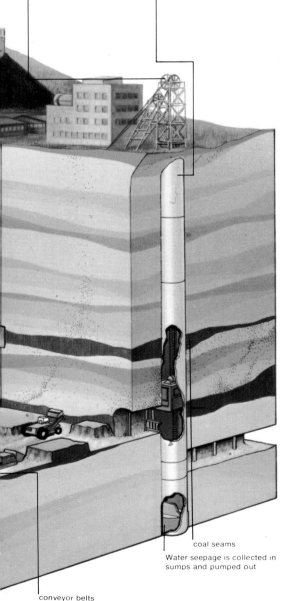

Left: American coal mining is carried out on a large scale. Here an automatic loader is picking up the coal cut from the seam face and loading it on to a transporter. This is driven through the underground tunnels to a central conveyor belt.

Below left: Two types of drilling bit are commonly used in coal exploration. An open-hole bit simply bores a hole through the rock. A coring bit is hollow with numerous industrial diamonds set in the rim. It retains a core of rock which is analysed for traces of coal seams. Often the borehole drilling rig is small enough to be mounted on a truck and moved from site to site.

Right: The Industrial Revolution began in Britain when the steam engine, fuelled by coal, replaced the water-driven wheel. This quiet valley town in Wales, now centred around the winding gear of a coal mine, grew rapidly in the 19th century as its rich seams were exploited.

The headgear of the downcast shaft is made of an open lattice of steel girders, so that fresh air can enter to ventilate the mine

Downcast shaft is fitted with a cage, used to convey man and equipment into and out of the mine

coal seams

Water seepage is collected in sumps and pumped out

conveyor belts

areas, erosion has removed all trace of the coal. In other regions, younger rocks cover the coal measures completely, resulting in a concealed coal field at depth.

The search for coal

In completely unknown country, a thorough geological survey normally reveals coal deposits of some importance. The geologist will often employ aerial photography to help him with surface mapping but to prove the existence of a concealed coalfield boreholes have to be sunk.

The cores which are taken from the boreholes are analysed to determine their physical and chemical properties. These will indicate whether it would be economic to mine. Open-hole boreholes can also provide useful information, using a remarkable new technique called *electrical logging*. This involves lowering various instruments on a cable down the hole. These send back electrical impulses which vary according to the nature of the strata and the type of probe used. The results are recorded on graph-charts which build up an accurate picture of the borehole.

A comparatively new technique in coal field exploration is *seismic* surveying, although it has been used for many years in the search for oil. This kind of survey is carried out by drilling a line of shallow holes three metres deep. A small quantity of explosive is loaded into each hole, and then fired in succession. This produces a series of miniature earthquakes whose shock waves pass down into the ground. The different layers of rock reflect the waves back up again with different intensities, and these are picked up on the surface by special microphones, called *geophones*. The resulting picture built up shows different types of strata and, more importantly, the *structures*—for example, the folding or faulting of the layers.

Mining methods

Coal is extracted by either open-cast workings at the surface, or by deep mines underground. The average depth of open-cast mines in Britain is 33 metres (110 ft),

although a working depth of 213 metres (700 ft) is planned at a Scottish site. To reach the coal seams, all the overlying soil and rocks, or overburden, must first be removed by large draglines and excavators. Later the overburden is replaced.

The main method of mining, however, is by fully mechanized *longwall* extraction. Two parallel tunnels or roadways, usually about 200 m apart, are driven into the coal seam. These are connected at right angles by a third tunnel, the height of the seam, which forms the coal face. Successive strips of coal are cut from the face, advancing it forward. Simultaneously the two roadways at each end are lengthened, to keep pace with the coal face.

The coal is cut by an electrically operated machine, mounted on a special armoured steel conveyor running along the length of the face. It pulls itself along the conveyor track by a chain and sprocket arrangement, cutting a strip of coal from the face, which falls onto the conveyor to be taken to one end of the face. There, it is loaded onto a belt conveyor which transports it to the mine shafts, where it is lifted to the surface.

Longwall *retreat* mining differs from advance mining in that the two parallel roadways are initially driven right to the furthest extent of the coal panel. The coal face is formed at the far end and retreats back towards the mine shafts. By 'blocking out' the panel in this way, any geological hazard like a fault can be assessed before the face starts production.

The world's remaining coal resources are estimated at 2,900,000,000,000 tonnes, of which only some 12 per cent can be economically worked by present day mining methods. Techniques such as *in-seam gasification* (which obtains energy by igniting the coal in its seam), however, may enable some of the energy of the remaining 88 per cent to be tapped. But in the meantime, much research is being carried out into methods of using coal more wisely and efficiently. The world is using coal many hundreds of thousands of times faster than it took to form—and the supply is not inexhaustible.

Petroleum

Petroleum, defined broadly to include crude oil, inflammable natural gas and the semi-solid black substance known as asphalt or bitumen, has been exploited on a small scale for centuries. Bitumen, for example, was used more than 5,000 years ago in waterproofing ships and as a mortar for bricks. But these early uses relied on natural escapes or *seepages* of oil and gas to the earth's surface and on hand-dug shafts near such places. Oil had also been recovered from the surface of some rivers, again provided by seepages, and small amounts had been found to contaminate wells drilled for water.

In Pennsylvania, on 27 August 1859, a retired railway guard named Edwin L. Drake sank a steam-powered drill into the ground, to produce petroleum commercially for the first time. Drake struck oil at a depth of only 21 metres (69 feet). Today, however, advanced technology enables oil and gas to be produced from depths well in excess of 6,000 m (20,000 ft), and the deepest well drilled to date in search of oil is 9,583 m (31,441 ft). Oil and gas fields have been developed in more than 60 countries, as well as offshore in many parts of the world, with wells in some cases more than 275 km (170 miles) from land and in depths of water of over 140 m (450 ft).

The Origin of Petroleum

The origin of crude oil and natural gas is still a subject of investigation and debate. However, most geologists now believe that oil and gas formed from changes in the remains of a variety of animals and plant life. This organic matter is thought to have been deposited with inorganic minerals as sediments on the bottom of ancient seas and lakes, most commonly in shallow, calm tropical seas. The organic matter generally constituted only a small amount of the total sediment, which was buried deeper by successive deposits of sediment and turned into rock.

The organic remains, imprisoned in the mud and sand, then underwent considerable change. They were partially modified by the action of bacteria and, after biochemical changes ceased, the total organic complex was slowly acted upon by heat. As the sedimentary strata were buried progressively deeper in the earth's crust, they entered zones of greater pressure and higher temperature. This heating, never strong, caused changes in which *hydrocarbons*—compounds of carbon and hydrogen—and other petroleum components were formed directly or developed by further alteration of previously released compounds.

Many of these changes may have taken place over several millions of years and at temperatures not more than about 180°C. In the process, an entire range of products—including crude oil and natural gas—were released. In the early stages in particular, the products will have been influenced by the nature of the parental matter. For example, coaly type organic matter is prone to give methane gas, and not the decidedly heavier hydrocarbons characteristic of crude oils. Like coal, which is also derived from organic material, oil and natural gas are known as *fossil fuels*.

Picturepoint

Above: Excess petroleum gas is burnt off at a field in Abu Dhabi. Much of the natural gas which occurs with oil is burnt off at the point of production, because of the cost and difficulty of transporting it to areas of consumption great distances away.

Right: Edwin Drake drilled the first ever well in a specific search for oil at Titusville, Pennsylvania in 1859. The Pennsylvania Oil Company, founded in the same year, was the ancestor of the international oil companies of today. Drake was lucky—he picked a spot where oil lay just 21 metres below the surface.

Drake Museum

FAULT TRAP

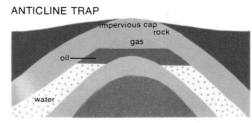

ANTICLINE TRAP

SALTDOME

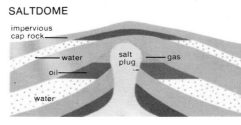

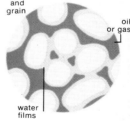

Above: Oil and gas are trapped between the pores of reservoir rock—the mineral grains are usually surrounded by a thin film of water.

Above right: Pools of iridescent colour created by natural seepage from a Venezuelan oil field. If petroleum leaks from underground, via a fault or crack, it floats on top of surface water.

Left: Three examples of the natural traps in which oil may be found. Oil is formed from microscopic marine organisms which died and sank to the bottom of water, becoming trapped beneath mud. Oil then rises until it reaches impervious rock.

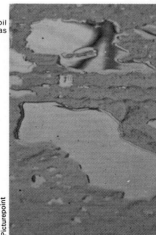

Picturepoint

THE WORLD'S SUPPLY OF OIL AND GAS

Middle East	Communist countries	Africa
56% / 38%	16% / 19%	9% / 9%

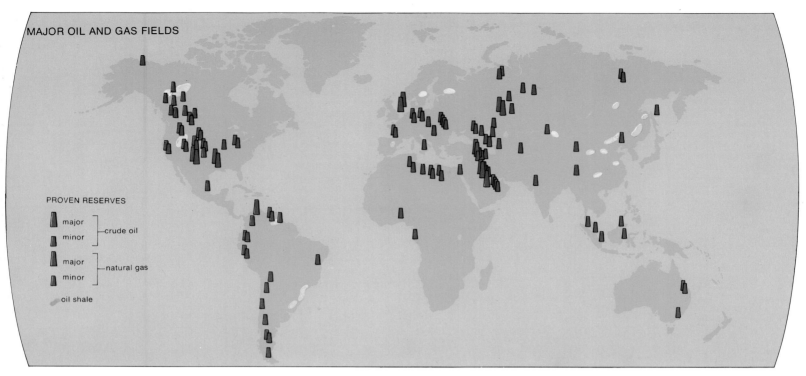

MAJOR OIL AND GAS FIELDS

PROVEN RESERVES

major ⎤
        ⎬ crude oil
minor ⎦

major ⎤
        ⎬ natural gas
minor ⎦

oil shale

Where petroleum is found

Organic matter is generally deposited in greatest abundance in fine-grained rocks such as clays. Because only a small proportion of it is split off to give hydrocarbons, its concentration in these, the *source rocks*, is very low. Quite early it was recognized that, in order for oil or gas to accumulate to form a *field* or pool, the hydrocarbons must have moved away from their point of origin and that certain rocks with significantly different physical characteristics to those of the source rocks must be present. This movement, or *migration*, is caused by the pressure from the weight of overlying sediments.

Water trapped in the source rock is squeezed out and carries the petroleum with it into porous *reservoir rocks*, where the openings between the mineral grains allow fluid to percolate towards the surface. As the fluid slowly migrates through the porous rocks, the less dense petroleum separates from the salt water, which then accumulates below the crude oil and natural gas or occupies parts, sometimes as much as 20 per cent, of the pores in which the oil and gas occur.

Crude oils range widely in their physical and chemical properties. The colours range from green and brown to black with rare examples of straw-coloured oils. When they reach the surface, some oils are more fluid than water, yet others may be as viscous as treacle. The principal elements in their composition are carbon and hydrogen, with appreciable amounts of sulphur, oxygen and nitrogen, and yet smaller amounts of metallic elements, among which nickel and vanadium are outstanding. Natural gas is largely composed of methane in most cases, but small amounts of ethane and propane are commonly present. In addition some gases contain significant amounts of nitrogen, carbon dioxide, hydrogen sulphide and, more rarely, helium.

The most common reservoir rocks are sandstones and various types of limestones. Especially in the latter, some storage space is provided by openings other than inter-grain or inter-crystal openings, some of which may be decidedly larger than the pores between the sand grains. These are openings inside fossils, or between irregular fossil fragments; spaces are also formed by the solution or replacement of minerals, and by open fractures. Fractures are especially important in the finer-pored rocks, not so much because of the 'storage space', but because they make the rock mass much more permeable.

Accumulations occur when the petroleum is trapped in the reservoir rock by an overlying layer of suitably shaped impervious rock. This is known as the *cap rock*. Shales, clays, salt, gypsum and anhydrite are the principal cap rocks. Any pores in these rocks are much smaller than those in reservoir rocks, and are occupied by water. There is little if any penetration of the oil or gas into the cap rock. Natural gas may collect above salt water without the presence of oil. Free gas may also occur in a *gas cap* overlying crude oil containing dissolved gas. This in turn rests on the main body of salt water. On the other hand, some accumulations of petroleum have no associated gas cap, but do have dissolved gas in the oil.

Various types of geological formation

Right: An exploratory drilling rig. Mud is pumped down the drill shaft to lubricate the drill bit. Drilling mud disappearing below ground is a sign of porous rock and this in turn means there is possibly oil present. The cutting bit of the drill is rotated by turning the whole length of the pipe.

Shell

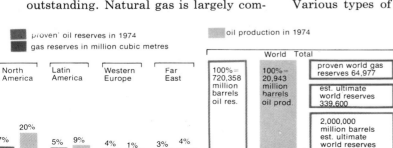

proven oil reserves in 1974
gas reserves in million cubic metres

oil production in 1974

North America	Latin America	Western Europe	Far East		World Total	
				100% = 720,358 million barrels oil res.	100% = 20,943 million barrels oil prod.	proven world gas reserves 64,977
						est. ultimate world reserves 339,600
20%						2,000,000 million barrels est. ultimate world reserves
7%	5% 9%	4% 1%	3% 4%			

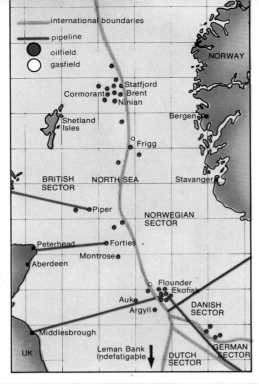

Right: The North Sea is among the most active fields for offshore oil exploitation. Worldwide, offshore fields offer a large potential of untapped oil and gas—they contribute only 17% of total world production but make up 21% of known world reserves. In the North Sea, oil reserves in the British sector alone may exceed 8,400 million barrels. Oil first came ashore in 1975 by tanker from the Argyll field. Since then, most oil has been pumped ashore via pipelines.

Below: The Forties rig—an anchored production rig standing on legs on the sea floor—is joined to the Scottish mainland by pipeline. The derrick, set high up on the rig platform above the waves, moves laterally so that the drill can be lowered to several positions down any one of the fixed drill pipes. These protect the drill which is driven through the *anticlinal cap rock* trapping the oil.

Right: A giant torch lights up a North Sea oil rig as excess gas is burnt off during production tests. Natural gas occurs both alone and with oil; its principal component is methane, an important raw material for the chemical industry.

Below right: The massive Esso refinery at Fawley on Southampton Water, is one of the largest in the world. Crude oil is refined into a vast number of primary products. Besides its use as a major fuel for all forms of air, sea and land transport, oil is also the raw material for a multitude of chemicals and synthetics. These are used in the manufacture of a range of products from agricultural feeds and fertilizers to perfume and plastics. Current research may lead to petroleum by-products providing a massive source of protein for a hungry world.

Shell

OIL PRODUCTION PLATFORM

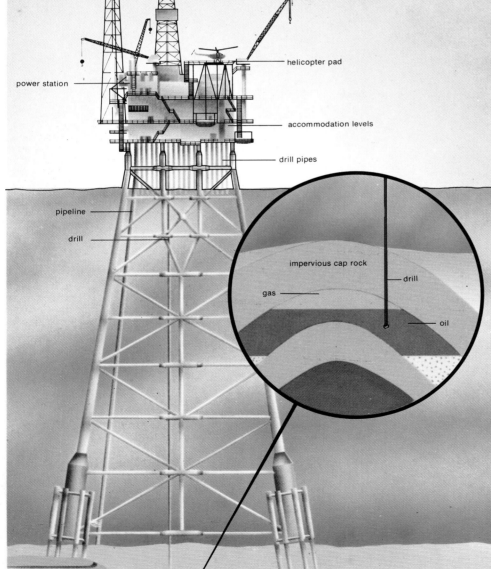

flare stack

drilling tower

helicopter pad

power station

accommodation levels

drill pipes

pipeline

drill

impervious cap rock

gas

drill

oil

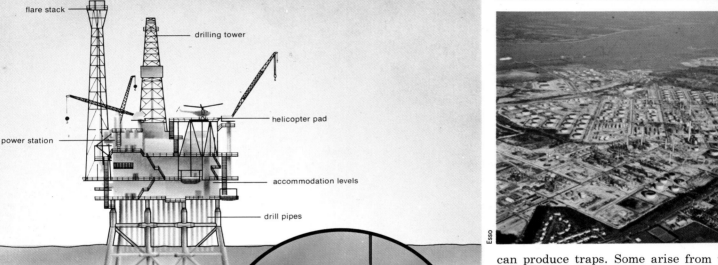

Esso

can produce traps. Some arise from the way the layers of sediment were at first deposited. Others are *structural traps*, formed by the folding or faulting of the earth as in *anticlinal* or *fault* traps, or by intrusions of different rocks, of which the *salt dome* is an example. Fields can also be dependent on more than one trapping feature. In the North Sea, for example, 'Leman Bank', a large gas field, is a broad, gentle, faulted anticline, while 'Indefatigable' has several pools on separate fault blocks. The 'Forties' field to the north, where estimated reserves of 1,800 million barrels have cost more than £750 million ($1,600 million) to put on production, is on a broad, low-relief anticline.

The quantity of oil and gas in commercial accumulations varies widely and always exceeds the recoverable amount (known as reserves) sometimes by as much as 20 times. Yet changes in the economic climate and technical advances may quickly alter the amount of designated reserves. Commercial viability simply requires that the exploration, development and operating costs of the field shall be amply covered by the income from the sale of the oil and gas. What constitutes a commercial oil field depends on many factors and these

Above: The giant oil tanker *Esso Scotia*, launched at Bremen in 1969, capable of carrying almost half a million tons of crude oil.

Below: Sheik Rashid of Dubai, one of the Arab rulers who have amassed great wealth from oil. Major producers like the Arabs have great economic influence.

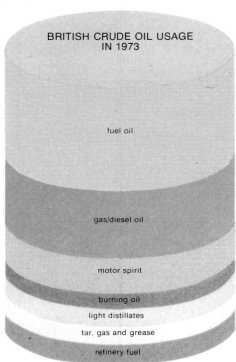

BRITISH CRUDE OIL USAGE IN 1973

fuel oil

gas/diesel oil

motor spirit

burning oil

light distillates

tar, gas and grease

refinery fuel

include the quality of the oil, the current price of oil and the depth of the reservoir.

Among the highest known reserves are the 66,500 million barrels of oil at the Ghawar field in Saudi Arabia and 65 million million cubic feet of gas under Slochteren in Holland. (One barrel of oil is about 0.16 cubic metres and contains 35 gallons. Gas reserves are in volumes calculated at atmospheric pressure and temperature.) Field areas vary from over 2,800 sq km (1,100 sq miles) to as little as 2.5 sq km (1 sq mile) for some pools. Individual well producing rates range from more than 20,000 barrels a day to less than 100 at the peak, and gas wells may flow at rates of tens of millions of cubic feet per day. There are, however, inevitable declines as the fields and wells are depleted.

There is no means of recognizing with certainty whether masses of oil or gas exist at depth before wells have been drilled. However, geologists can make reasonable predictions on the basis of rock forms which could constitute traps. In some areas, the surface rocks give clues to the different rock layers at depth. Surface mapping, often aided by the examination of aerial photographs, will often dictate accurately the positions of anticlines and faults at depth.

Where surface rocks are not a guide to the position of underground geological structures, or at underwater sites, geophysical techniques must be used to indicate the sites of structures at depth. One method uses readings of the intensity of the earth's gravitational pull. This may show where denser, and hence commonly older, rocks are nearer the surface than elsewhere. This indicates to geologists that violent earth movements have occurred in the past and could imply the existence of an anticline or point to a fault, both of which are capable of providing traps.

Seismic surveys are carried out as an alternative technique, or to confirm other indications. Pulses of energy, generated by explosives or other means, travel down from the earth's surface and, after reflection or refraction at boundaries between the rock layers, return to the surface and are detected by seismometers. Measurement of the travel times and the recognition of what are apparently the same boundaries from a series of observations allow the shapes of sub-surface boundaries to be plotted. In this way trapping forms can be recognized. Aeromagnetic surveys throw light on the broader features of sedimentary basins in which oil and gas accumulations are formed.

Drilling is an expensive operation, particularly in marine areas. Success is not assured even after extensive geological and geophysical surveys, because for various reasons traps can lack hydrocarbons, or contain quantities of hydrocarbons which are too small to justify commercial development.

The cuttings and other rock samples from a test drilling are carefully examined. These reveal the nature of the rocks penetrated and their fluid contents, and checks are kept on the returning mud for evidence of oil or gas. In addition, instruments are lowered into the hole from time to time to make electrical, radioactivity and other measurements. From these results, geologists can assess the type of rock, its porosity and the content of gas, oil or salt water. When hydrocarbons are recognized or thought to be present in exploratory wells, further special tests are made to check whether oil or gas can be produced at adequate rates. All of this is done before finally deciding to complete the well for production or to abandon it. Additional wells are normally needed to estimate the approximate size of the accumulation before embarking on full development, which includes the costly installation of pipe lines, storage and other major facilities.

To bring oil or gas to the surface, oil producers largely rely on the great pressure to which the petroleum at the bottom of a well is subjected. This pressure is reduced by opening surface valves or by other means, permitting fluids as a whole in the reservoir rock to expand, with gas coming out of solution in the oil, and the fluid itself being forced into and up the well.

Wells commonly produce oil unaided, for a time at least, but later many have to be helped in some manner, such as by pumping, in order to bring oil to the surface. Oil reaching the surface, as well as being accompanied by gas, is sometimes also associated with salt water, especially as the wells grow older. Gas, oil and water have to be separated before the saleable products are dispatched from the fields.

As the reserves of known accumulations of liquid hydrocarbons are used up, other sources become increasingly important. One such source—still so expensive that full exploitation lies in the future—are rocks impregnated with extremely viscous petroleum which will not flow into wells. These are referred to as *tar sands*, and include an enormous accumulation, known as the Athabasca Tar Sands of northern Canada. Special means, amongst which are excavation and washing, have to be employed in order to utilize these deposits. Such operations are commercially viable only rarely at present.

Another potential source may be the oil obtainable from *oil shales*. These are rocks rich in solid organic matter called kerogen, but not in free oil. However, by heating these shales at temperatures of several hundred degrees centigrade, the organic matter breaks down to yield considerable amounts of oil. This oil differs in various ways from crude oil, but may be refined by similar procedures although environmental problems arise from the disposal of large amounts of baked rock produced as waste. However, very extensive oil shale deposits exist, and they are potential sources of large volumes of oil, at a price.

Geological Time

The most accurate estimates available today indicate that the earth is about 4,500,000,000 years old. This figure presents a dramatic contrast with some estimates in the past. In 1644 John Lightfoot of Cambridge produced the unequivocal assertion that the moment of all creation was 9.00 am on September 17, 3928BC. Ten years later this was amended to 4004BC by Archbishop James Ussher of Ireland (1581-1656), who drew his date from a literal interpretation of the Book of Genesis. As late as 1900, his view of the creation was printed in the Authorized Version of the Bible by Cambridge University Press. This belief in a literal six-day creation and a 6,000 year-old earth was unquestioned by many Christians, until geologists began to produce conclusive evidence against it.

Leonardo da Vinci (1452-1515), the brilliant Italian artist and scientist, was perhaps one of the first to have an inkling of the modern concept of geological time. He recognized marine shells, found in the rocks of high inland mountains, as fossils —the remains of once-living organisms buried in the rocks by natural processes. He was convinced that the sea had covered the area at some time in a distant past. He rejected the interpretation of scholars who saw fossils as the Devil's work, put there to confuse mankind, or as evidence of the Biblical Flood, dated by theologians to 2348BC. Da Vinci sketched the rocks, showing their layered arrangement and the way in which they were buckled into folds.

Even so, it was not until 150 years later that Nicolas Steno (1638-87), a Dane living in Italy, rediscovered fossils and layering in rocks. Interpreting these features in the conventional manner, he attributed them to the Biblical Flood. But he did see that the layers stretched for great distances and that the upper beds of rock must have been deposited on the lower. This simple observation was to become the *Law of Superposition* and the basis of a geological time scale: more recent sedimentary rocks will always lie on top of the older rocks, unless later disturbed.

Steno's law of superposition was taken further by William Smith (1769-1839), a British engineer employed in canal construction. During his travels he collected fossils and noted that each form was restricted to certain beds. He found that the layers were always in the same order and contained the same sequence of fossils wherever they occurred.

After a quarter of a century of diligent observation, in 1815 Smith was able to publish a remarkable map of England and Wales. This showed the areas where each of his groups of beds came to the surface and their succession from oldest to youngest. Smith was unaware of the idea of organic evolution, which was put forward 44 years later by Charles Darwin, but he recognized that fossils were evidence of a constant process of change over a long period of time. By means of fossils, he proved that rocks in different places can be *correlated*, or shown to be of the same age, and that successions of

Heather Angel

Mary Evans

W. J. French

rocks can be arranged in a relative time sequence.

Hutton's 'Theory of the Earth'
The greatest step towards modern geological ideas, however, is justly attributed to a Scottish physician, James Hutton (1726-97). In 1788 he proposed a *Theory of the Earth* in which the formation of rock strata was only part of a process with 'no vestige of a beginning— no prospect of an end'. His great contribution lies in the recognition of the cyclical nature of geological change, with the implicit assumption that the earth must have had a very long history.

From his observations, Hutton reasoned that rocks were slowly weathered and eroded by the action of water and air and the debris transported to the sea to form new sedimentary beds. These beds in turn sank lower into the earth under the weight of successive deposition. In the depths they became crumpled and heating and compression produced new minerals and new structures. Along with this metamorphism, molten rock was forced into the strata which, upon solidification, gave rise to granites and related igneous rocks. Uplift of all this to make new land initiated a new cycle. According to Hutton the 'elements' that batter the land have always done so. 'The present,' he asserted 'is the key to the past.'

Hutton also described evidence of the relative age differences between rocks. On the island of Arran in Scotland, for example, he found sedimentary rocks folded by earth movements and metamorphosed, and then intersected from below by numerous thin granite veins. Here was evidence that not only did certain rocks

W. J. French

Top: At Loch Assynt in Scotland, the mountain structure has two unconformities. Quartzite on the surface rests on sandstone, deposited on older, folded gneiss.

Centre: Further evidence of relative age is found in conglomerates, which are formed of pebbles and boulders eroded from some pre-existing rocks.

Above: On this Yorkshire beach, marine erosion originally carved a cliff and shore platform out of chalk and clay. On the platform a beach deposit of chalk cobbles has been formed. Wind-blown sand coated this beach, and later deposits of glacial clay blanket the chalk, sand and old beach. Present marine erosion exposes the sequence.

Ronan

Right: Hutton, known as
the 'Father of Geology'
for his pioneering work.

Below right: The law of
superposition is assumed
to apply unless it can
be shown that the beds
have been inverted as a
result of earth
movements. In the event
of folding, the strata
can become overturned
so that some beds are
upside-down and older
beds rest on top of
younger beds. Geologists
are then faced with the
problem of deciding the
strata's original 'way-
up'. Unfolded beds,
occurring above an
unconformity with folded
beds, will be younger
than the altered beds.
Similarly, an igneous
vein will be younger
than the folded or
metamorphosed rock
into which it is intruded.

James Hutton based his
unconformity principle
on findings at Siccar
Point (above) and Arran
(right) in Scotland. The
print, from an early
geology book by Charles
Lyell, and photograph
both show strata of
slightly inclined red
sandstone resting on
vertical schist. Here was
proof to Hutton of a
long interval of time.
Hutton's work was not
widely known until
championed after his
death by a student, John
Playfair. Taken by
Hutton to Siccar Point,
Playfair later wrote: 'The
mind seemed to grow
giddy looking so far into
the abyss of time, and
while we listened . . . we
became sensible how
much farther reason
may sometimes go than
imagination can venture
to follow.'

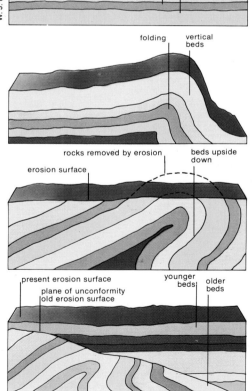

Mary Evans

W. J. French

originate below the earth's surface, but
also, as Hutton recorded, the granite must
be younger than the pieces of sedimentary
rock it engulfed.

Also on Arran, Hutton found the
junction, termed an *unconformity*, between layered rocks of two different ages.
An unconformity marks an interval in
which deposition temporarily ceased
and rocks already formed were eroded. On
Arran, the older strata formed in some
ancient sea had been buried deep in the
crust, folded and recrystallized before
being injected with quartz veins. Uplift
and erosion eventually brought them to
the surface where they formed the
floor, upon which pebbly and sandy layers
were deposited.

Hutton found additional evidence of
relative age in the pebbly layers themselves, for the pebbles must have been
made from some pre-existing rocks. The
total series of events leading to the
formation of a plane of unconformity
obviously may occupy a very long period
of time.

Layers of rock cannot themselves be
considered as time planes. Nor for that
matter can planes of unconformity. As the
sea migrates over a land mass it may
deposit similar material at each stage of
its advance. These materials will not be
of precisely the same age for they become
younger as the sea spreads progressively
over the land surface. Such deposits are
termed *diachronous*, and are of only
limited use in age correlation.

With these principles established, geologists began the task of building a chart
of the relative ages of different rocks and
areas of the earth. The law of superposition clearly had to be adjusted, how-

ever, where earth movement had occurred.
For rocks may be folded and the strata
then become inclined or vertical, or even
over-turned. In such cases, the older
rocks will rest upon the younger. It is
then necessary to find ways of determining
the original sequence of strata before the
relative ages become clear.

Fortunately for the geologist, there are
several types of evidence which point to
the *way-up* in which rocks formed. Formation of sediments is a complex process
involving deposition of fragments, chemical precipitation and the accumulation of
organic debris. There are usually intermittent pauses in accumulation or even
periods of erosion. One clue here is the
ripple marks left by wind, wave or current
action on the top of sediment. Traces of
animals having bored or burrowed into
the sediment while still in its soft state or
even after it has been consolidated, may
indicate what was then the surface. Any
of these aspects of sediment formation can
lead to preservation of evidence of
'way-up'.

The geologic column

Using the law of superposition, the
fossils found in the rocks and the evidence
of 'way-up', the sequence of layered rocks
may be described and world-wide correlations made. Placing the rocks in order
according to their relative ages makes it
possible to construct a scale or *geologic
column*. Until recently it was conventional
to recognize at the base a series of rocks
without fossils, the *Archeozoic*, and a
younger series with scanty evidence of
life known as the *Proterozoic*.

Resting on these old rocks are the
Phanerozoic rocks containing many fos-

1 CROSS BEDDING

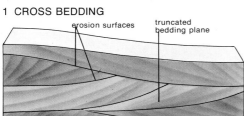

erosion surfaces — truncated bedding plane

2 GRADED BEDDING

pebbles and sand at base
silt and mud towards top

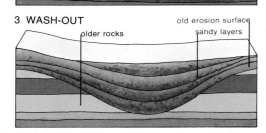

3 WASH-OUT

old erosion surface
older rocks
sandy layers

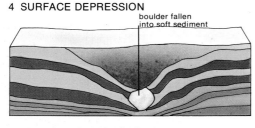

4 SURFACE DEPRESSION

boulder fallen into soft sediment

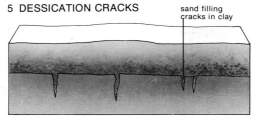

5 DESSICATION CRACKS

sand filling cracks in clay

Left: Geologists use a variety of clues to determine 'way-up'. (1) In cross bedding, thin layers are deposited obliquely to the main bedding surfaces. These layers are usually abruptly truncated at the top by succeeding beds. This feature is found in Zion National Park, USA (above left) (2) Graded bedding may be a clue, *where coarser deposits collect at the bottom. (3) Wash-outs occur where channels have been cut into older sediments, and then filled with sandy layers, leaving a record of the original 'way-up'. (4) Falling boulders form depressions in the upper surface of beds and (5) sand will fill surface cracks in drying clay.*

Above left: Horizontal strata are usually no problem to the geologist interested in their relative ages. Using the law of superposition, he can assume that the younger rocks are at the top. The layers shown of light limestone and dark shales represent a few million years, only a relatively short span in earth's history.

sils. So much detailed evidence is available from these beds that they have been divided into numerous rock *systems*, each formed in a specific geological *period*. The oldest belong to the *Cambrian* system, all older rocks are therefore collectively termed the *Pre-Cambrian*.

Most of the Phanerozoic systems and periods were worked out during the nineteenth century. The recognition of the systems took place in different regions and some of the names, such as Devonian, Permian and Jurassic, reflect these localities. Even today geologists continue to argue over the precise boundaries between the systems and the detailed correlations of rocks from one area to another. In the early days, definition was usually based on some strongly marked break in the rock sequence, such as an unconformity. However, where in one area there is an unconformity, in another area of the same age there may be successive strata undisturbed. Boundaries are therefore today based on detailed fossil lists and correlations.

Towards an appreciation of time
The work of Hutton and others allowed later geologists to grasp one concept of time—that of *sequence*, or the order of geological events. The other use of time is as a measure of *duration*—the length of time an event continues. At first there were few facts, but the evidence indicated that it had taken a very long time for the earth processes of erosion, deposition and uplift to occur.

Serious efforts to calculate the length of geologic time began in the late nineteenth century. The data gathered for the fossil record from the Phanerozoic led to

attempts to estimate the age of the rocks from the number of evolutionary stages shown by the fossils. In 1867, Sir Charles Lyell (1797-1875), a friend of evolutionist Charles Darwin, decided by this means that the *Tertiary* period was 80 times as long as the *Quaternary*. Guessing one million years for the Quaternary gave 80 million years for the Tertiary and put the age of the Phanerozoic as a whole at 240-million years. Later studies of fossil horses again indicated that the Tertiary was about 80 times as long as the Quaternary. These figures, based on so many dubious assumptions, have little value, but the recognition of the origin, development and extinction of so many fossil forms testifies to the immensity of geologic time in relation to historic time.

Hutton's dictum that 'the present is the key to the past' leads to other ways of estimating age. Some geologists thought that if they found the rate at which sediment accumulates today and the total thickness of sediment formed throughout Phanerozoic time, they would have a simple method of assessing age. Obtaining these figures, however, is fraught with difficulty. Rates of sedimentation vary tremendously from place to place and the maximum thickness of sediment in each period is difficult to assess.

Another calculation giving an indication of the magnitude of time was first made by an Irish geologist John Joly (1852-1933). He calculated the minimum age of the oceans to be 90 million years by measuring the total amount of salt in the seas and its rate of accumulation.

Kelvin and the age of the earth
One of the great physicists of the nine-

Zefa

W. J. French

C. R. Roberts

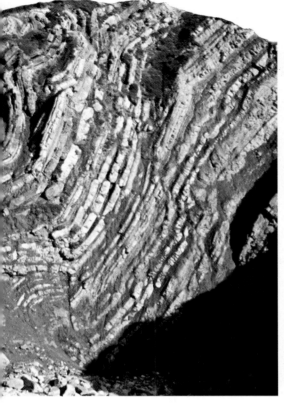

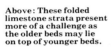

Above: These folded limestone strata present more of a challenge as the older beds may lie on top of younger beds.

Left: Trace fossils are valuable as a means of determining 'way-up'. Animal bores or burrows and trails indicate the position of the surface of sediment when the animals were active.

Jacana

Below left: The Petrified National Forest Park, USA, has a vivid example of strata to be found on a large scale in their original sequence of deposition. Here the beds of shales, marls and sandstones have been eroded over millions of years to reveal a wide range of bright colours, earning the area the name of Painted Desert.

Above: When strata occur vertically, as here in New Zealand, it is not immediately evident which rocks are older. Once 'way-up' has been discovered, age correlations can be made with rock systems throughout the world. These stratified rocks are of Jurassic age, a period of widespread deposition.

Bruce Coleman

teenth century, Lord Kelvin (1824-1907), sparked off a controversy by making three calculations, each indicating that the age of the earth was probably less than 100 million years and most likely about 30 million. Kelvin obtained his maximum age from studies of the rate of the earth's rotation and of the amount of heat given out by the sun.

For his more exact calculation, Kelvin assumed that if the earth began as a molten globe, the length of time required to cool to the present temperature could be obtained. Making the most reasonable assumption for the temperature at which crust would begin to form, the age of the earth was calculated to be about 30 million years. These results caused confusion and argument for a few years until another physical discovery proved them wrong.

Kelvin himself pointed out that the supposed cooling history of the earth depended on there being no other source for the generation of heat. The discovery in 1895 of radioactivity gave such a mechanism and quickly led to an explanation for the long period without notable change in the temperature of the crust. The decay of radioactive atoms involves the emission of radiation; the absorption of this radiation by the rocks liberates heat.

The discovery of this process of radioactive decay now also provides the method for measuring the age of rock beds by direct, rather than relative, means. Its discovery eventually resolved the long and bitter argument over geological history. The earth was shown to be not millions, but thousands of millions, of years old.

GEOLOGICAL TIME SCALE
showing the Geologic Column with explanations of the names used
(dates indicate numbers of million years ago)

C. R. Roberts

ERA	PERIOD of time SYSTEM of rocks	EPOCH of time SERIES of rocks
CAINOZOIC recent life	QUARTERNARY an addition to the old tripartite 18th Century classification	RECENT
		PLEISTOCENE most recent
	2	
	TERTIARY third from the 18th Century classification	PLIOCENE very recent
		MIOCENE moderately recent
	7	
	26	OLIGOCENE slightly recent
	38	EOCENE dawn of recent
	54	PALAEOCENE early dawn of the recent
	65	
MESOZOIC middle life	CRETACEOUS chalk	
	135	
	JURASSIC Jura mountains in Europe	
	193	
	TRIASSIC from the three-fold division of the period made at a locality in Germany	
	225	
PALAEOZOIC ancient life	PERMIAN from Permia province in Russia	
	280	
	CARBONI-FEROUS coal abundance	UPPER Pennsylvanian in USA
		LOWER Mississippian in USA
	345	
	DEVONIAN Devonshire, England	
	395	
	SILURIAN Silures, ancient British tribe	
	435	
	ORDOVICIAN Ordovices, ancient British tribe	
	500	
	CAMBRIAN Roman name for Wales	
	570	
PRE-CAMBRIAN	PROTEROZOIC	
	ARCHEAN	

(PHANEROZOIC obvious life — spanning Cainozoic, Mesozoic, Palaeozoic)

The Age of the Earth

The longstanding argument about the age of the earth was finally resolved by a breakthrough in a field of science quite separate from geology. In 1895, Henri Becquerel, a French physicist, realized that a mysterious form of energy was given out by certain substances independently of any external action. What Becquerel had discovered was the energy released by the spontaneous disintegration of the atoms of certain substances, the *radioactive elements*, into atoms of a different, stable element.

The process by which an unstable element spontaneously breaks up to form a second element is called *radioactive decay*. From the moment they exist, all radioactive elements are subject to decay from one form, or *isotope*, to isotopes of other, stable elements. The isotopes of an element differ in the number of particles in their atomic nucleii. They are therefore labelled according to this number. For example, uranium has two important radioactive isotopes—U^{235} and U^{238}. These *parent* atoms change slowly to the *daughter* lead (Pb) isotopes Pb^{207} and Pb^{206} respectively.

Just ten years after Becquerel's discovery of radioactivity, the pioneer English nuclear physicist Ernest Rutherford suggested that radioactive minerals such as uranium could be used to date rocks. Although the spontaneous decay of an individual atom is unpredictable, the overall rate of decay of the large number of atoms of uranium, as in all radioactive material, is constant and can be measured. Knowledge of this constant and of the ratios of parent to daughter isotopes provides geologists with a 'clock'.

The half-life

The intervals of time involved are enormous. It is more meaningful to express the rate of decay as the *half-life*, the time required for half the atoms in a specimen to have changed to the daughter isotope. Uranium-235, for example, has a half-life of 713 million years. This means that if there were 1,600 atoms of U^{235} in a specimen at the start, after one half-life there will be 800 atoms of U^{235} and 800 of Pb^{207}. After the next half-life of 713 million years, 400 atoms of U^{235} will remain and 1,200 atoms of Pb^{207} will have formed. The process of disintegration is effectively infinite, for as the radioactive material declines in abundance, its decline becomes progressively slower. The proportion of lead formed from decay indicates the length of time since decay began, and thus the age of the mineral.

Early results from this method were unreliable. Difficulties existed in measuring the proportions of the minute amounts of the isotopes. The development in the 1950s of the *mass spectrometer*, a machine capable of isolating different isotopes, meant a vast improvement in precision. Today, the isotopic decays that are valuable in determining geologic age include not only uranium to lead, but also thorium to lead, rubidium to strontium, potassium to argon, and carbon to nitrogen.

RADIOCARBON DECAY

0 years – death of plant

5,570 years – 50% remains

11,140 years – 25% remains

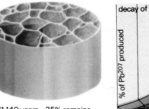

16,710 years – 12.5% remains

22,280 years 6.25% remains

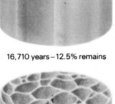

55,700 years – 0.1% remains

Above: The rate at which radioactive carbon isotopes (C^{14}) decay to nitrogen isotopes (N^{14}) is shown here. All living plants and animals absorb radiocarbon from the atmosphere. This decay rate is known and the approximate time of death can be calculated by measuring the amount of C^{14} remaining in a specimen.

Above right: The enormous Columbia ice fields in Jasper National Park in western Canada, an area where long sequences of glacial deposits allow a count going back thousands of years. Seasons of melting and freezing are clearly marked in the graded layers or varves (right) deposited in lake floors formed by melting ice.

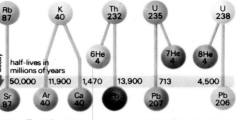
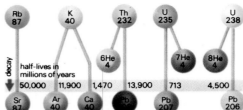

Above: These isotopes are used by geologists in absolute dating. The original radioactive materials are shown with their half-lives and end-products. As the half-lives are millions of years long, the decay rates are used to calculate the ages of rocks and fossils—and the earth's age, estimated to be 4,500 million years.

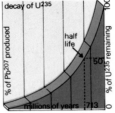

Above: Half-life decay follows the same curve, which can be plotted on a graph, for all radioactive materials. The curve remains constant although the rates vary considerably. Half the radioactive material decays quite early in the specimen's existence. The remainder decays by half again for each half-life period.

Right: The yearly growth of trees in spring is marked by a series of annual tree-rings in the wood. When counted these reveal the tree's age.

Below: The bristlecone pine, the world's oldest living thing, survives in the cold, dry White Mountains of California. Pines nearly 5,000 years old have been found.

Leonard Lee Rule/Bruce Coleman

Robert Harding

PRE-CAMBRIAN SHIELD

Artic Ocean

GREENLAND SHIELD

site where oldest
known rock found

CHURCHILL

Hudson
Bay

CORDILLERAN MOUNTAIN BELT

CENTRAL STABLE REGION

SUPERIOR

GRENVILLE

APPALACHIAN MOUNTAIN BELT

Atlantic Ocean

cific
ean

☐ CANADIAN SHIELD

Above: A Pre-Cambrian map of North America indicates the Canadian shield, the age of granite rocks and location of the oldest rock. Pre-Cambrian rocks form the core or shield area of all the continents. The three provinces of the Canadian shield are drawn on the basis of radioactive ages. The oldest is the Superior province where most rock ages are close to 2,500 million years. The average ages of the Churchill and Grenville provinces are about 1,700 and 900 million years respectively. Today they may be covered by glacial and other deposits.

Left: The oldest rock in the world was found in western Greenland, where this amitsoq gneiss crystallized some 3,800 million years ago.

Two isotopes of uranium, U^{235} and U^{238}, occur in minerals. The rate of decay of U^{235} to Pb^{207} (with a half-life of 713 million years) is much greater than that for U^{238}, which slowly decays to Pb^{206} with a half-life of 4,500 million years. Since the two are found together in minerals, this permits geologists to make a third measurement of age by comparing the ratio of Pb^{207} and Pb^{206}.

The element thorium also produces lead—changing from its single natural isotope Th^{232} to Pb^{208} with a half-life of 13,900 million years. As with uranium decay, the disintegration of thorium releases helium gas. The best of these methods is U^{238} decay, for Pb^{206} makes up 95 per cent of the lead developed by radioactive decay or *radiogenically* and hence can be determined with the best precision.

Even in carefully controlled experiments, the ages determined by the three decay processes may be different. One correction often required, though usually small, arises from the presence of 'common lead' not produced by the decay being measured. Unless allowed for in the calculation, this will inflate the value of Pb^{206} and Pb^{207} and the age of the sample.

The ratio of the abundances of uranium isotopes can be used to estimate roughly the age of the earth. The result given is 5,400 million years. From the ratios of lead isotopes in certain minerals, the composition of lead existing at the origin of the earth can be calculated and this leads to another estimate of the earth's age. Early calculations gave around 4,000 million years but higher figures have been obtained more recently.

Certain meteorites, rock masses which have fallen to earth from space, contain a mineral known as troilite which is virtually uranium-free. Any lead they contain is considered to represent the original mix or ratio in the planetary system, a ratio frozen through time since their creation. Using this primaeval lead isotope ratio and applying it to terrestrial rocks gives an age for the earth of 4,500 million years. Intensive analysis of meteorites also revealed none older than 4,500 million years.

The ages of moon rocks given by uranium-lead and other methods range from 3,100 to 4,500 million years. Some lunar rocks have given slightly greater ages, but probably these result from special processes operating on the moon. In contrast, the oldest rock on earth found so far is about 3,800 million years old. The fact that maximum ages for the earth, moon and meteorites give the same date—4,500 million years—suggests to scientists that a major event occurred at that time throughout the solar system.

Finding the ages of rocks

The lead isotope methods have not proved very useful for dating crustal rocks. The elements are relatively rare, only a few minerals being suitable for analysis. These include zircon, monazite, sphene, uranite and pitchblende, the first substance to be analysed by Rutherford in 1904. Other techniques have been more widely used. The value of the rubidium-strontium method is that it can be applied to several common rock-forming minerals. The rubidium isotope Rb^{87} decays to strontium isotope Sr^{87} with a half-life of about 50,000 million years, giving useful age data for the oldest rocks including the oldest meteorites and moon rocks.

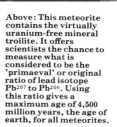

Above: This meteorite contains the virtually uranium-free mineral troilite. It offers scientists the chance to measure what is considered to be the 'primaeval' or original ratio of lead isotope Pb^{207} to Pb^{206}. Using this ratio gives a maximum age of 4,500 million years, the age of earth, for all meteorites.

Below: Information gathered from the face of the moon is immensely valuable in dating the rocks on earth. Moon rocks, which are as old as 4,500 million years, have escaped the weathering, erosion and transformation processes which occur on earth, where rocks older than 3,800 million years have probably all been lost.

This method is not so useful for younger rocks, but has provided valuable information on the source of igneous rocks, allowing a distinction to be made between igneous materials derived from the mantle and those from the crust. Extension of this idea has indicated to geologists the possibility that the crust has accumulated at a more or less consistent rate throughout geological time.

There are several factors that can cause dates derived from radioactive dating methods to be incorrect. On one hand, for example, the unnoticed presence of a 'common' or original isotope has exaggerated the findings. On the other, the escape of daughter elements may reset the 'clock' to zero or reduce the ages given. Argon is the gas given off in small amounts by decay of potassium isotope K^{40}, which has a half-life of 11,900 million years. The meaningfulness of results from this method is limited because the gaseous argon isotope Ar^{40} can be lost in some later, perhaps mild, heating of the rock. However, using carefully chosen materials, this method has yielded good results, and is applicable to a wide range of rocks and minerals containing sufficient potassium.

The long half-lives of all these radioactive elements restrict their use in dating to the distant past. This is exactly the period of the earth's history, however, about which relative dating methods can reveal little because of the lack of fossils. Pre-Cambrian rocks in which fossil evidence is rare form the cores of the continents, the so-called *shield areas*. Thousands of age determinations have been made, revealing provinces which are distinct in space and time. The Canadian shield, for example, contains three such provinces—Superior, Churchill and Grenville. Each is essentially the product of a cycle of sedimentation, volcanism, folding, metamorphism and igneous intrusion, and each took several hundred million years to complete. Provinces of comparable ages have been located on other continents, and geological maps drawn up which reveal the ancient history of the land masses.

In general, the most reliable radioactive dates are obtained from igneous and metamorphic rocks, in which the mineral crystallization provides a relatively sharp starting point in time.

Dating the recent past

For younger dates, much use has been made of the *radiocarbon* method, which measures the decay of carbon to nitrogen. All living plants and animals absorb the carbon isotope C^{14} in the form of carbon dioxide in their food cycles. The amount in organic bodies is the same as the small fixed proportion in the atmosphere, and remains constant through the life of the plant or animal. But when an organism dies, the intake of carbon ceases and the C^{14} slowly decays to nitrogen isotope N^{14}, starting a radioactive decay clock which can be applied to wood, peat, shells and certain limestones and bone materials.

The results can be subject to serious error. Contamination from other forms of carbon can upset the clock, and great care has to be exercised. One assumption which is basic to this method is that the concentration of C^{14} in the atmosphere, and thus in plants and animals, has remained constant through geological time. This assumption is now being questioned and corrections to some early radiocarbon dates have been made using age correlations with tree-ring dating.

Long-living trees like the bristlecone pine, found in California, Utah and Nevada in the United States, provide in their annual growth rings a precise method of dating for the last 8,000 years or so. Dates obtained by radiocarbon methods have been revised or *calibrated* both by tree-ring dating and by the yearly cycle of deposits left by melting ice. These deposits, called *varves*, mark the seasonal melting and freezing of ice as recorded in the debris deposited in lakes left behind by retreating ice sheets. The glaciers of the last ice age, in Scandinavia, for example, have created a time sequence of varves stretching back some 11,000 years.

One major contribution of radioactive methods has been to date the eras and periods included in the Geologic Column. This time-scale was constructed in the 19th century by correlating rock strata and fossil evidence, without any real idea of the dates of major earth events. Disputes as to the age of the earth are now substantially resolved and agreement exists that the earth's crust was created about 4,500 million years ago.

Man appears as no more than an afterthought, with an abruptly short record of existence. It has been calculated that if one thinks of the entire history of the earth as having occurred in one year, the first known living things would have appeared about 240 days before the end of the year. Early man would have appeared some 5 hours before the end of the very last day, and modern man some five minutes before midnight.

44

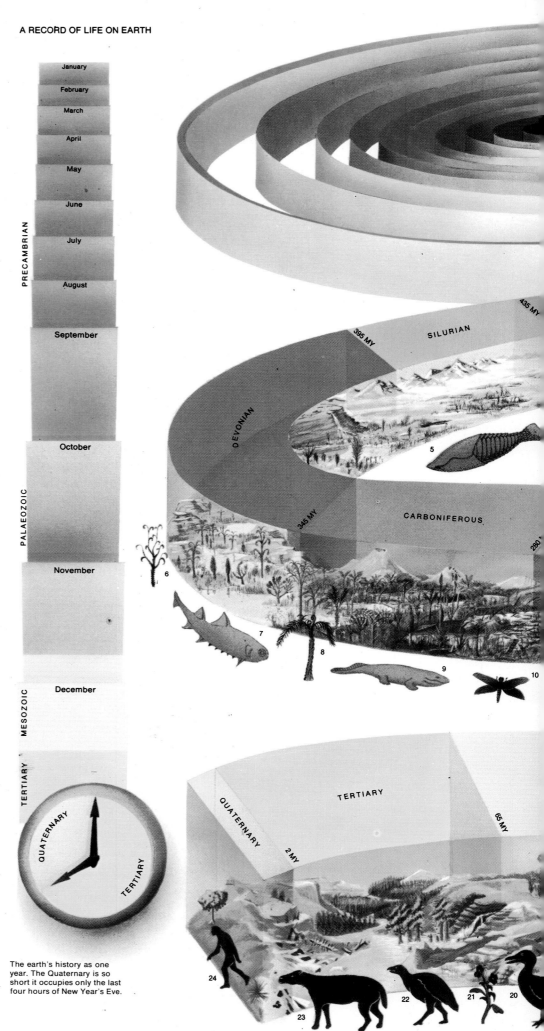

A RECORD OF LIFE ON EARTH

The earth's history as one year. The Quaternary is so short it occupies only the last four hours of New Year's Eve.

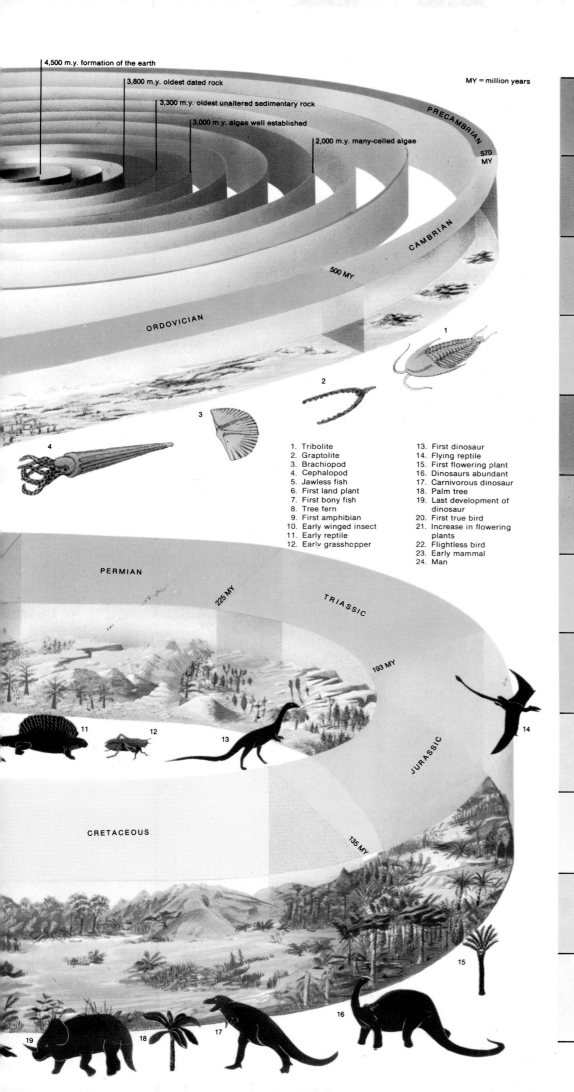

4,500 m.y. formation of the earth

3,800 m.y. oldest dated rock

3,300 m.y. oldest unaltered sedimentary rock

3,000 m.y. algae well established

2,000 m.y. many-celled algae

MY = million years

PRECAMBRIAN

570 MY

CAMBRIAN

500 MY

ORDOVICIAN

PERMIAN

225 MY

TRIASSIC

193 MY

JURASSIC

135 MY

CRETACEOUS

1. Tribolite
2. Graptolite
3. Brachiopod
4. Cephalopod
5. Jawless fish
6. First land plant
7. First bony fish
8. Tree fern
9. First amphibian
10. Early winged insect
11. Early reptile
12. Early grasshopper
13. First dinosaur
14. Flying reptile
15. First flowering plant
16. Dinosaurs abundant
17. Carnivorous dinosaur
18. Palm tree
19. Last development of dinosaur
20. First true bird
21. Increase in flowering plants
22. Flightless bird
23. Early mammal
24. Man

PRE-CAMBRIAN
The greatest part of geological time is represented by the Pre-Cambrian. The crust, land masses and seas formed and great volcanic activity occurred. Pre-Cambrian rocks form shield areas of all the continents. Traces of life are generally rare.

CAMBRIAN
The transition to the Cambrian is notable for the sudden appearance of abundant fossils. This marks the beginning of the Palaeozoic (ancient life) era. In the widespread shallow seas, early marine life proliferated. Tribolites were particularly common.

ORDOVICIAN
Much of the earth enjoyed a mild climate and seas still covered most of the surface. There was continuing sedimentation and important mountain-building occurred. Reef-building algae were notable and corals, sponges and molluscs such as cephalopods abundant.

SILURIAN
A dramatic development in earth's history came with the evolution of jawless fish, the first vertebrates (animals with backbones), which first appeared in the Ordovician. The late Silurian saw another important step — the growth of the first land plants.

DEVONIAN
Mountain-building movements reached a peak early in the Devonian but this was notably a period of explosive evolution. Land was colonized by the earliest seed plants. Fish grew in variety and size and the first land creatures — amphibians — evolved.

CARBONIFEROUS
Mountain building, folding and erosion continued. Richly forested swamps and deltas in North America and Europe were submerged and formed large coal measures. Extensive glaciation gripped the southern continents. Insects thrived. The first reptiles appeared.

PERMIAN
Desert conditions prevailed over much of Panagaea, the giant land mass made from all the drifting continents. The reptiles spread widely and modern insects evolved. Several marine creatures became extinct but new land flora, including conifers, developed.

TRIASSIC
As the Mesozoic era opened, Pangaea began breaking up. On land conifers became the dominant plants. This was a period of great diversity among the reptiles and the first dinosaurs and giant marine reptiles appeared. Small primitive mammals also evolved.

JURASSIC
Considerable volcanic activity was associated with the opening of the Atlantic Ocean. On land the dinosaurs reigned supreme and the air was first conquered by flying reptiles and later by primitive birds. There are traces of the earliest flowering plants.

CRETACEOUS
During the maximum extension of the seas of the world, great deposits of chalk formed in Britain. Dinosaurs remained dominant until they and many large reptiles became extinct at the end of the period. First true birds and early mammals became numerous.

TERTIARY
The opening of the Cainozoic (recent life) era heralded an explosive growth of mammals. Many large species evolved but some died out. Flowering plants increased rapidly and as climates later cooled grasslands appeared. Considerable uplift of land occurred.

QUATERNARY
This, the latest geological period, continues up to and including the present day. It is marked by climatic changes in which four major ice ages alternated with warmer intervals. Mammals increased and adapted and man evolved to dominate the earth.

Ancient Environments

Creating an image of the Earth's surface as it looked in the past requires information from all the many branches of geology. Occasionally, there is sufficient information to create a relatively clear picture and sometimes the evidence can be closely compared with present-day occurrences, all of which make it easier to envisage the environment of the past. Tlere are, however, some ancient environments which seem to bear no relation to the present, such as the Pre-Cambrian ironstone-forming lakes and the Cretaceous chalk-forming seas.

Some evidence can be read directly from the rocks. Volcanic bombs, for example, indicate the existence of an explosive volcano. Other evidence has to be read indirectly. Tracing the source of a particle in a sedimentary rock could give information on the nature of mountains and hills adjacent to the area of deposition. Indeed it is vital that the many lines of evidence should tell a consistent story and fit in to the overall picture.

Strictly, any image of an ancient environment can never be proved conclusively as the evidence can never be complete. In sediments the record provided by fossils is inevitably biased by the decay of soft-bodied organisms, such as marine worms, though they sometimes leave trace fossils as evidence of their activities. In addition, there may be a distortion or obliteration of the sedimentary record by later events such as earth movements, metamorphic or igneous activity, and erosion.

Despite these limitations, geologists have been able to make considerable advances in reconstructing ancient environments. As in any story of detection, the investigator relies on recognizable evidence which he must carefully select from a wealth of potential clues. Hutton's long-established geological axiom that 'the present is the key to the past' plays an important role, provided it is used cautiously.

On present-day coastal mud and sand flats, for example, it is possible to see features such as ripple marks, scour depressions and sun cracks forming. It is logical to assume that a similar environment and origin existed in the past if these features are found in old mudstones and sandstones. But if tree trunks, branches and twigs are found in the beds instead of marine shells then the deposits are more likely to be associated with an inland river system than a coastal flat.

Evidence from sea and land

Among the great variety of sediments some are more easily determined as marine beds than others. For instance, a collection of unworn, in-place fossil shells and algae resembling modern marine organisms in their morphology and ecology is usually taken as adequate evidence that the containing rock is marine. Certainly, a limestone body carrying a very rich fauna and flora of limey or *calcareous* corals, polyzoans and algae would be taken to be of marine origin. At present, extensive reef growth is

Left: Ripple marks are the undulations produced by the movement of water over sediments. They are not confined to marine conditions, and the information they give is substantial. Their size and shape indicate the speed of water across tidal flats or beaches. The orientation of the crests can often help in determining the approximate alignment of the nearby coastline or beach. This sample is a cast, formed when a layer of sediment was deposited on a lower bed in which traces of ripple marks and raindrops were sharp enough to leave imprints.

Below: Ripples forming on a present-day sandy beach exposed at low tide.

Heather Angel

Right: The abundance of these relatively thin-shelled molluscs from Lincolnshire indicates marine conditions there in the Jurassic period. The ironstone rock, coloured brown in parts from weathering, is formed of *chamosite* and *siderite* minerals, which are normally widely precipitated in marine environments. The climate is not indicated directly, but the presence of the minerals commonly suggests fairly warm currents.

Below: Fossil coral from Derbyshire. The presence of dense patches of coral in these very poorly bedded Carboniferous layers suggests clear, shallow seas—conditions required for coral reefs.

Dr. Peter Rawson

Dr. Basil Booth

Dr. John S. Shelton

Right: This map of the British Isles shows the environment in the Devonian period, about 375 million years ago. Freshwater deltas and swamps surrounded the hilly sandstone area covering much of the present-day Midlands. Northern Scotland was part of another large land mass.

Left: Mudcracks are formed by compression and drying, and usually indicate exposure of a lake or stream floor to the air.

Below: This freshwater plant debris has been carried by silt and sand-laden water from its position of growth. The distance was not far as the leaves are relatively unworn. This is evidence of terrestrial conditions.

THE BRITISH ISLES IN THE DEVONIAN PERIOD

NORTH ATLANTIC CONTINENT

Caledonian Mountains

SCOTLAND

freshwater (non-marine) facies

lowlands

volcanoes

volcanoes

ENGLAND

mountains and hills

IRELAND

OLD RED SANDSTONE CONTINENTAL FACIES

volcanoes

WALES

delta and swamps

non-marine facies

volcanoes

marine facies

DEVONIAN SEA

only possible in particular ecological circumstances which include relatively clear and shallow sea waters and warm currents. These requirements appear to have remained comparatively stable throughout large periods of geological time. Reef-building calcareous algae are known from late Pre-Cambrian times onwards, but reef corals have become important since Ordovician times. The suggestion is that those northern regions must have been located in much warmer latitudes with coral reefs. Continental drift explains how this occurred.

A different style of marine deposition, on a muddy sea floor, is indicated by a shale or clay carrying a marine fauna. Unfortunately, these kinds of rock rarely give evidence of how near they were to land, nor the depth of the water.

In general, fossil preservation on land is poor. Ancient non-marine or *terrestrial* deposits, such as were laid down in deserts, lakes, rivers and deltas, are more likely to be deficient in fossils than the bulk of marine deposits. This is because processes of weathering and biodegradation actually have a much more persistent effect on land than in seas and oceans. Major exceptions to this scarcity of fossils are found in plant-rich beds and certain fish and bone beds. A prime example is the extensive development of coal seams in Carboniferous and Tertiary deltas throughout the world. These seams represent the mass accumulation of land plant debris in marshy environments.

A lack of fossils alone is not sufficient evidence to suggest a non-marine origin. This is particularly true of deposits from Pre-Cambrian times when few organisms

with hard skeletal parts had evolved. Plants only began to adapt from a marine environment and colonize land areas in the Devonian period. For these and earlier periods, other techniques may have to be employed alone.

A characteristic property of clay minerals is the inclusion of certain elements such as boron in their crystal structures. Measuring the distribution of these *trace elements* provides a promising new technique which has shown, for example, that the proportion of very small amounts of boron is relatively high in some marine clay-rich deposits and relatively low in freshwater ones.

Ancient climates

Other techniques include analysis of soil varieties. Soils can be surprisingly well-preserved considering that they consist of an easily-eroded mixture of clay, carbonate and iron minerals. When they do survive, it is commonly as a consequence of land subsidence followed by gentle inundation either by river flood water or, in some instances, by sea water. The old soils found beneath many coal seams typify this style of preservation.

A more rapid form of preservation is burial under volcanic lava. For example, the upper surface of Carboniferous basalt lava flows in the Midland Valley of Scotland and Tertiary flows in Antrim in Nothern Ireland were frequently exposed long enough for bauxitic and lateritic soils to develop prior to very rapid burial by the next flood of lava.

Laterites and bauxites in ancient successions provide fascinating information about the climate of the times. It is likely

that they formed under wet sub-tropical conditions, as they do today. Other soils from the same area but of different age can be equally informative. In the Devonian rocks of northern Europe, including those in the Midland Valley of Scotland, there are certain varieties, known as *cornstones*, which are mostly carbonate-rich soils similar to those forming on the Russian steppes at present. These cornstones prove that a semi-arid, hot environment prevailed in Scotland over 50 million years before sub-tropical conditions.

The colour of some rock beds can also suggest an ancient environment. A red colour, caused by the iron oxide haematite, often pervades thicknesses of many metres of strata, including lava flows of comparable age, and may extend over vast regions. The creation of these rocks required oxidizing conditions over millions of years and could only be sustained on land areas subject to persistent semi-arid, and occasionally arid, climatic conditions. This deduction is supported by other evidence.

The lines of geological reasoning used to capture an image of ancient cold polar environments are basically no different from those adopted for deducing hotter climatic conditions. The distribution of animals and plants has to be assessed. Water temperature can be indicated in what are assumed to be the marine parts of sedimentary successions by oxygen isotope analysis of calcareous shells.

Areas once covered in great thicknesses of ice are revealed by such clues as boulder clay deposits and scratch marks on rock surfaces. Strong evidence for the

MAJOR GEOLOGICAL EVENTS IN EARTH'S HISTORY

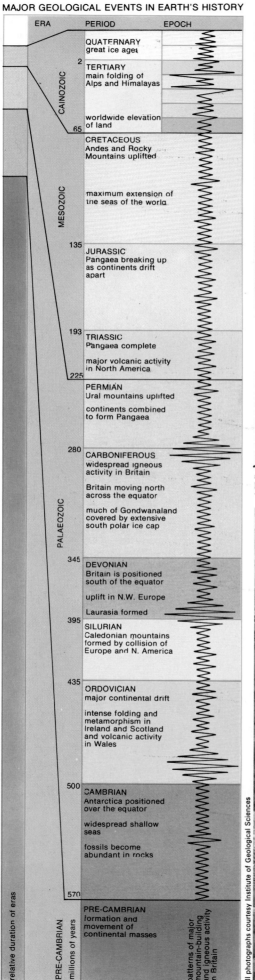

ERA	PERIOD	EPOCH
CAINOZOIC	QUATERNARY great ice ages	
	2	
	TERTIARY main folding of Alps and Himalayas	
	worldwide elevation of land	
	65	
MESOZOIC	CRETACEOUS Andes and Rocky Mountains uplifted	
	maximum extension of the seas of the world	
	135	
	JURASSIC Pangaea breaking up as continents drift apart	
	193	
	TRIASSIC Pangaea complete	
	major volcanic activity in North America	
	225	
PALAEOZOIC	PERMIAN Ural mountains uplifted	
	continents combined to form Pangaea	
	280	
	CARBONIFEROUS widespread igneous activity in Britain	
	Britain moving north across the equator	
	much of Gondwanaland covered by extensive south polar ice cap	
	345	
	DEVONIAN Britain is positioned south of the equator	
	uplift in N.W. Europe	
	Laurasia formed	
	395	
	SILURIAN Caledonian mountains formed by collision of Europe and N. America	
	435	
	ORDOVICIAN major continental drift	
	intense folding and metamorphism in Ireland and Scotland and volcanic activity in Wales	
	500	
	CAMBRIAN Antarctica positioned over the equator	
	widespread shallow seas	
	fossils become abundant in rocks	
	570	
PRE-CAMBRIAN	PRE-CAMBRIAN formation and movement of continental masses	
	millions of years	

relative duration of eras

patterns of major mountain-building and igneous activity in Britain

THE EDEN VALLEY THROUGH TIME

From Pre-Cambrian times until late in the Mesozoic era, what is now the British Isles lay near the heart of Pangaea, the super-continent composed of all the land masses. After the break-up of Pangaea, north-west Europe and Britain drifted over the changing earth's surface to reach their present position. These artist's reconstructions based on geological finds show the changes to one place—the Eden Valley in England's Lake District.

ORDOVICIAN PERIOD

Above: About 450 million years ago, the Eden Valley was the site of an open sea. The marine conditions are evident in the mud and sandstones deposited in the deeper parts of the sea. The growth of originally submarine volcanoes spread a considerable amount of debris into the adjacent seas. As the seas became shallower, the volcanoes eventually burst above the water level. The development of layers of volcanic ash and bombs, covering large areas at one time, is useful for correlation purposes. Many volcanoes were arranged in narrow zones. Much of the grand scenery of today's Lake District is a relic of this great period of volcanic activity. A long series of explosions poured out lavas and ashes to a thickness of many thousands of metres. Later, a shallow sea spread over the area, depositing in-shore sediments. The sea was probably warm at the time because there are rich deposits of organisms, such as crustaceans, molluscs and sea-urchins.

PERMIAN PERIOD
Left: 50 million years after the swampy Carboniferous, the Eden Valley was a hot desert. The contrast is illustrated clearly in the artist's reconstruction. Geologists have discovered several sources of evidence of the arid or semi-arid terrestrial conditions. For example, the process of oxidizing, when minerals react with oxygen, occurs on dry land. The record of this process is found in the weathered rocks in the background, whose red and brown colours indicate oxidizing conditions. The boulders, pebbles and sand produced by weathering occupy the middle and foreground. The sand dunes have wind-rippled surfaces and their shape indicates that prevailing wind probably blew from left to right at the time. Fossils generally are not well-preserved in terrestrial conditions, but the rocks from this period have a notable lack of fossils, suggesting that life in the Permian was minimal.

PLEISTOCENE TIMES
Below: One million years ago, the British Isles were in the grip of a great ice age. The painting shows how a record of glaciation was left behind. Glacial deposits and erratic boulders (transported by moving ice) are strewn over the denuded landscape. Boulders frozen into the underside of the ice left scratches on the rock surface, indicating the direction of ice-sheet movement.

CARBONIFEROUS PERIOD
Left: The Eden Valley of 300 million years ago was a tropical or sub-tropical swamp. The overall lack of red colours in the soil (instead greys, blacks and browns predominate) is evidence of wet conditions. Lush vegetation thrived in low-lying alluvial areas along valley bottoms and, closer to sea, between delta distributaries. In these complex, fertile soils, freshwater plants grew. As the plants died, they fell onto the forest floors or into the swamps, to accumulate as peat. At times of rapid subsidence, submergence of this area by fresh or salt water buried the plants beneath mud and sand. The beds of peat were compacted to form seams of coal, from which geologists have been able to identify the original plants. Giant club-mosses, tree-ferns and horse-tail plants thrived in the moist, mild, humid climate. The *Lepidodendron* and *Sigillaria* trees grew to a height of 30 metres. While the Eden Valley enjoyed an equatorial climate, much of the southern continents that then made up Gondwanaland lay around the South Pole and were covered in extensive ice-sheets.

THE PRESENT DAY
Right: The Eden Valley as it appears today. Clearly the interpreting and reconstruction of ancient environments is a slow process requiring the sorting and detailed examination of a variety of evidence.

theory of continental drift has been collected by proving that during the Permo-Carboniferous age, ice sheets covered parts of the modern warm temperature zones in South America, South Africa, India and Australia.

Creating a picture of the past

Putting together the jig-saw of evidence to build a picture of an ancient environment begins with the fine details of rocks. Once these are pieced together, the groups of related, interbedded rocks on a larger scale are examined until, finally, the extent of their distribution over very large regions can be considered.

For this broad environmental picture it is important to ensure that the rocks are of the same age. The age-equivalence, or *correlation*, of rocks is most reliable with beds laid down under uniform marine conditions. The Cretaceous Chalk series in Britain is a good example of this, although there is not a great deal of evidence to indicate that the depths of seas were uniform. However, towards Scotland the Chalk series becomes more sandy, probably indicating the nearness of land. This change is known as a facies change. The term *facies* encompasses all the physical, chemical and biological properties shown by a single bed or group of beds.

The correlation of different marine facies can be troublesome if certain of the rocks lack fossils. But the greatest problems arise when correlating marine and terrestrial facies. It is possible to radiogenically date volcanic ash which, by chance, may fall on both the land and in the sea. This would establish a reference level, yet such ash falls are rare.

Facies changes in rocks are usually deduced by tracing the rocks of comparable age from one area to another. The succession of rocks in Britain from the Devonian age illuminates quite well the lessons learnt from the long-established principles of correlation. Because of the presence of such fossils as cephalopods, trilobites and brachiopods, the Devonian succession of south-west England appears to be predominantly marine in origin.

The mixed successions represent sand and mud laid down in shallow, turbid seas with occasional shallows of clearer water where reefs grew. Submarine volcanoes were also active. As the marine facies is traced northwards towards Wales, marine fossils become scarce and the rocks become thickly bedded, and sometimes red-coloured sandstones and siltstones occur, with many features typical of coastal deposition.

In the Welsh borderland, and indeed as far north as the Orkney Islands of Scotland, rocks believed to be of the same age are called the Old Red Sandstone facies. There is no doubt of their land origin as they are extensively red-coloured, contain land plant beds, calcareous soils, river and lake deposits, and are associated with volcanic larvas and ashes, and weathered by terrestrial conditions. The overall picture is of a northern land mass, semi-arid and volcanic in nature. It was sparsely vegetated except near spasmodic water-courses, which contained a few fish. This land mass abutted a rather shallow, turbid sea supporting relatively little life except in clearer water where reef faunas could proliferate.

The Fossil Record

The term *fossil* originally referred to any object dug from the ground, but its use is now limited to the remains of once-living animals and plants. Although the study of the fossil record often seems of distant relevance to the practicalities of modern life, it does in fact have great importance. One outstanding example is the use of fossil evidence by geologists in their search for sources of fuel. Most importantly, however, its study provides us with a fascinating glimpse of the colourful assortment of life on earth during its long history. 'Glimpse' is, unfortunately, the most appropriate word, for the fossil record is far from complete and much of the existing record remains poorly explored by *palaeontologists*, the scientists who study fossils.

The fossil record depends on how much has survived the ravages of time. Only the hard parts, such as the bones and shells of animals, the tree trunks or leaf cuticle of plants, are normally preserved in the rocks. Consequently, information about the function of the hard and soft parts has to be deduced from the skeletal remains.

Completely soft-bodied animals usually leave little or no direct evidence of their former existence. However, certain 'freak' sediments, such as the Burgess Shale (Cambrian) of British Columbia, preserve such creatures and give a fleeting impression of the real diversity of life hundreds of millions of years ago. In addition, many animals burrowed into sediment, or briefly rested on it, or bored into a hard sea floor. The traces of these activities are preserved surprisingly often as *trace fossils*.

Even fossil excreta are found and can sometimes be attributed to a particular kind of animal living long ago. Evidence of damage during life, or of disease, are also often visible. Palaeontologists have found such examples as ammonites that have patched up tears in their shell and dinosaurs that suffered rheumatoid arthritis.

The fossil record is biased towards the marine realm because the seas and oceans have always been the main area of deposition of sediment. Because land areas are essentially regions of weathering and erosion, even those animals with backbones, the *vertebrates*, may have been poorly preserved on land. The remains of many vertebrates—amphibians, reptiles, mammals and many birds—are rare except at certain limited geological levels or *horizons* where non-marine deposits have been preserved.

Fossils can provide an immense amount of information. Historically, it is their role in the correlation of rock strata that was first appreciated, but they are also used in the interpretation of past environments, in studying the rates, processes and paths of evolution, and in testing alternative models of plate movement and continental drift. The correlation of rocks by the fossils they contain—a key principle in *stratigraphy*, the study of rock strata—reflects the evolution of life through time. The stratigrapher collects

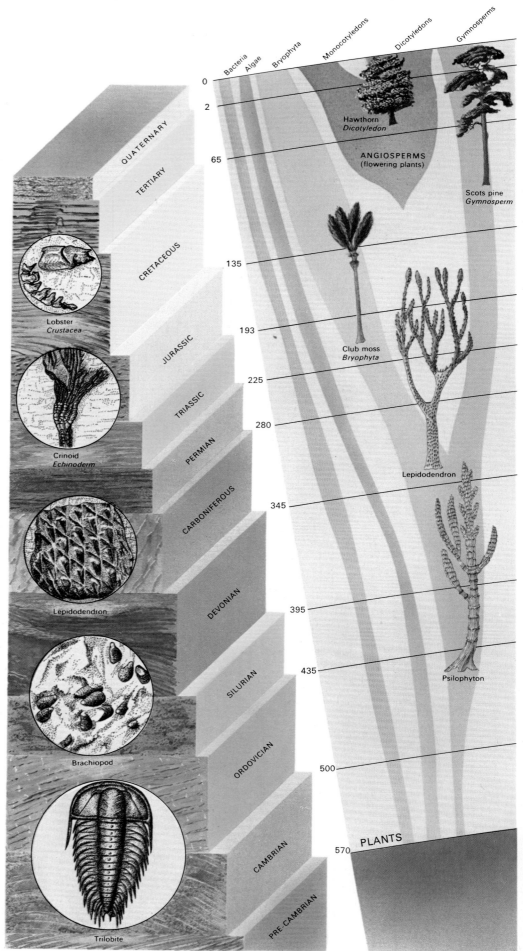

REPRESENTATIVE FOSSILS

million years ago

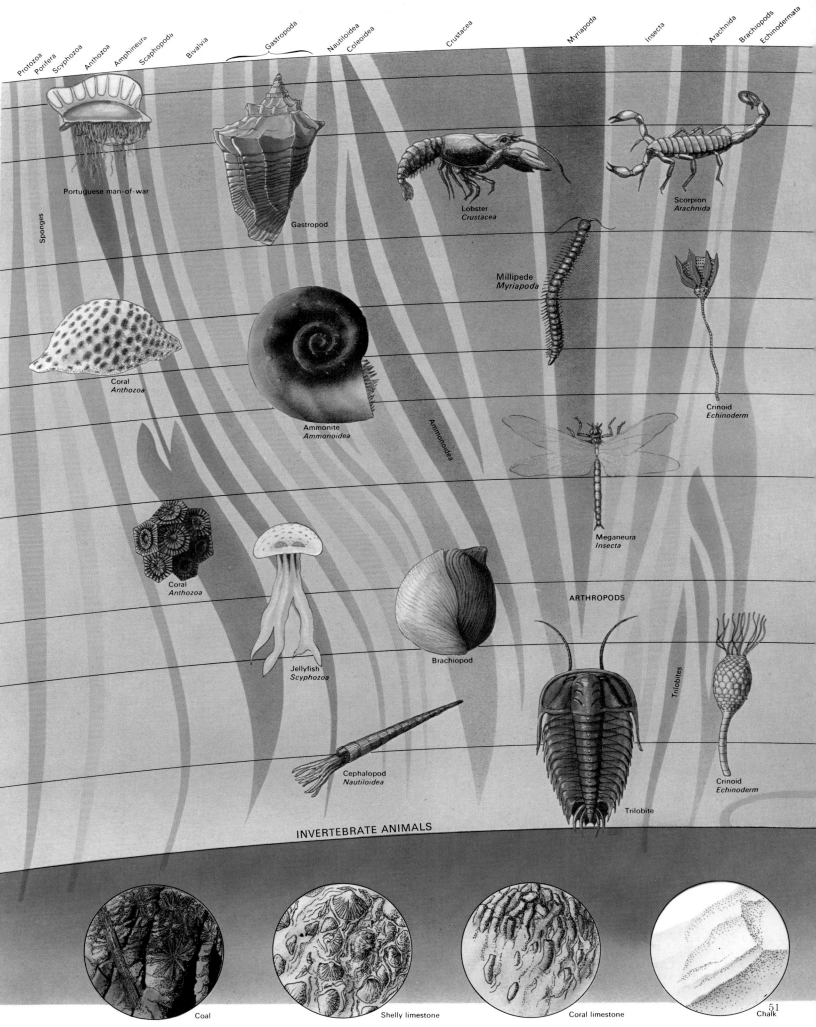

Protozoa
Porifera
Scyphozoa
Anthozoa
Amphineura
Scaphopoda
Bivalvia
Gastropoda
Nautiloidea
Coleoidea
Crustacea
Myriapoda
Insecta
Arachnida
Brachiopods
Echinodermata

Sponges

Portuguese man-of-war

Gastropod

Lobster
Crustacea

Scorpion
Arachnida

Millipede
Myriapoda

Coral
Anthozoa

Ammonite
Ammonoidea

Ammonoidea

Crinoid
Echinoderm

Coral
Anthozoa

Jellyfish
Scyphozoa

Brachiopod

Meganeura
Insecta

ARTHROPODS

Cephalopod
Nautiloidea

Trilobites

Trilobite

Crinoid
Echinoderm

INVERTEBRATE ANIMALS

Coal

Shelly limestone

Coral limestone

Chalk

51

ROCKS FORMED PREDOMINANTLY FROM FOSSILS

Hemichordata Urochordata Cephalochordata Cyclostomes Elasmobranchs Cephalochordata Teleosts Crossopterygii Lung fishes Urodeles Apoda Anura Chelonia Crocodilia Ophidia Aves

Acorn worms

Herring
Teleost

Newts

Turtles

Legless lizards

Birds

Rays

Bony fishes

Snakes

Lizards

Archaeopteryx
Aves

Sharks

Turtle
Chelonia

Ornithopods

Acorn worm

Coelacanth
Crossopterygii

Sauropoda

Theropods

Ichthyosauria

Holosteans

Protosuchus
Crocodilia

Lungfish
Dipterus

Chondrosteans

Shark
Elasmobranch

REPTILES

Acanthodires

Sea squirt
Urochordata

Rachitomes

Ichthyostega

Ichthyosaur
Icthyosauria

Lepospondyls

Agnatha

Ostracoderms

Dipterus

Cheirolepis
Chondrostean

Pterosaur	
Ceratopsian	
Sauropod	
Carnosaur	
Ichthyosaur	
Plesiosaur	
Pliosaur	

Pteraspidomorph
Ostracoderm

Amphioxus
Cephalochordata

Acanthodes
Acanthodire

CHORDATES

Dominant reptiles of
the age of Dinosaurs

VERTEBRATE ANIMALS

Nautiloid dies

Sediment settles

Earth Movements

Erosion exposes fossil

52

THE STORY OF A FOSSIL

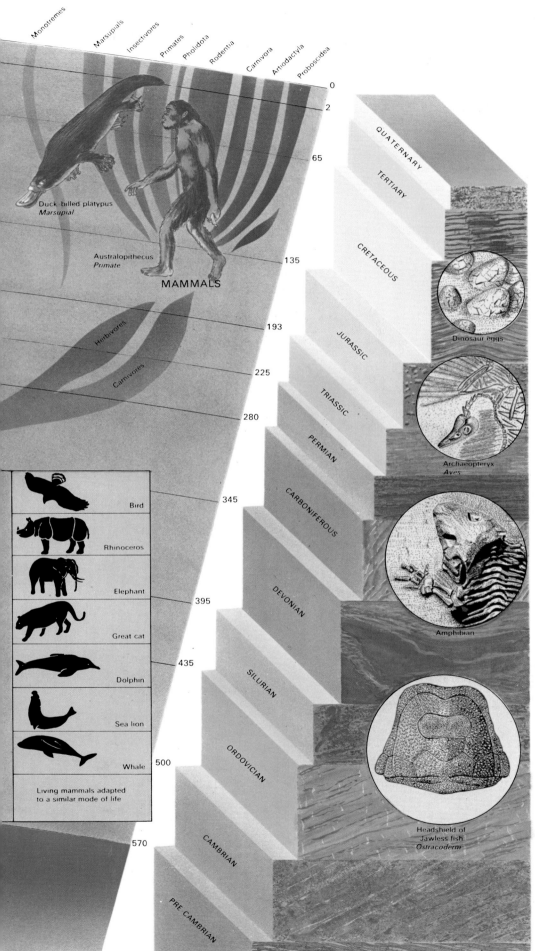

Monotremes
Marsupials
Insectivores
Primates
Pholidota
Rodentia
Carnivora
Artiodactyla
Proboscidea

0
2

Duck-billed platypus
Marsupial

65

Australopithecus
Primate

135

MAMMALS

Herbivores

193

Carnivores

225

280

QUATERNARY
TERTIARY
CRETACEOUS
JURASSIC
TRIASSIC
PERMIAN
CARBONIFEROUS
DEVONIAN
SILURIAN
ORDOVICIAN
CAMBRIAN
PRE CAMBRIAN

Dinosaur eggs

Archaeopteryx
Aves

Amphibian

Headshield of
Jawless fish
Ostracoderm

Bird
Rhinoceros
Elephant
Great cat
Dolphin
Sea lion
Whale

345
395
435
500
570

Living mammals adapted
to a similar mode of life

million years ago

REPRESENTATIVE FOSSILS

fossils layer by layer to establish the time-sequence of the various forms, and then recognizes that any rock succession containing the same sequence of species spans the same period of geological time —no matter how different the rock types themselves may be. In this way the relative geological time scale was built up.

The *palaeoecologist* studies the relationship of a fossil animal or plant to the environment in which it lived. Study of whole *fossil assemblages*, the complete entity or number of fossils in an area, can indicate differing depths of sea water, while research into the geographical distribution of fossil organisms, the study of *palaeobiogeography*, sheds light on ancient climates or geography.

Fossils and evolution

The present is simply a brief cross-section of geological time. Biologists build up much of their understanding of the processes and result of evolution by studies in such fields as the comparative morphology, embryology, genetics and biochemistry of living forms. But present-day life represents only the culmination of over 3,500 million years of evolution, the direct evidence of which is locked into our fossil record. Charles Darwin (1809-82), in his celebrated work *The Origin of Species*, was fully aware of the potential importance of fossils in testing his evolutionary theories, but he stressed the many imperfections of the record. Since Darwin's day our knowledge has vastly expanded and a more rigorous approach has demonstrated definite patterns in evolutionary processes, though these are certainly not to be regarded as 'laws' of evolution.

The most spectacular pattern is that of *explosive evolution*. On several occasions through geological time there have been relatively sudden bursts in the evolution of major groups of animals and plants. One instance is the rapid diversification or *radiation* of fish during the Devonian period nearly 400 million years ago. Such bursts interrupted the more usual, slow or *progressive evolution* within individual groups, and often seem to be associated either with periods of major extinctions or with significant environmental changes such as the flooding of extensive areas of continental margins to form shallow shelf seas.

Explosive evolution often affected unrelated groups of animals or plants at the same time. The sudden diversification of a group to exploit an environmental change is called an *adaptive radiation* because it usually results in a great variety of new forms evolving. Some of these prove to be successfully adapted to live in the new environment, but others quickly become extinct.

For periods of more normal, progressive evolution, *rates of evolution* can be worked out. Although absolute rates have rarely been calculated, there has long been tacit recognition among palaeontologists that some fossil groups evolved faster than others. The most rapidly changing groups have always been used as *zone fossils*, those fossil species which are used to characterize a particular horizon and are restricted to it in time.

Rates of evolution can apparently vary considerably within any division of the animal kingdom, or *phylum*. Some bivalve species, for example, apparently lasted at least six times as long as contemporaneous

53

Above: These extinct ammonites date from the Jurassic. Some species lived for less than half a million years before evolving into another species and their sequence gives an accurate relative time scale for Jurassic and Cretaceous rocks.

Left: Trilobites are extinct marine arthropods which superficially resemble woodlice. They are zone fossils, used in the age correlation of rocks, for the Cambrian and Ordovician periods.

Below: These shellfish are brachiopods. Living examples are quite rare but they are significant as zone fossils from the Ordovician period to the Permian.

ammonites during the Cretaceous, yet both belong to the phylum *Mollusca*. However, some authorities point out that the rate of evolution of some groups may appear faster simply because they have more characters which can vary and are therefore more readily divided into chronological 'species'. This reflects the problem that affects every palaeontologist. He is dealing not with a single slice of time but with a continuum, and therefore has to distinguish both contemporaneous and chronological species.

Evolutionary convergence is known from both the fossil and modern records. It is the tendency of completely unrelated groups to give rise to similar looking forms, usually reflecting a similar mode of life. Thus the fossil plesiosaur developed into a form very much like a fish although it was a reptile. Repeated or *iterative*

evolution is a similar tendency which occurs in related organisms. Many different ammonites, for example, give rise to tightly coiled shells at the end of their evolutionary lineages.

Extinction of fossil species

While many fossil species became 'extinct' simply by evolving into another species, there were periods when whole groups disappeared. Such wholesale extinctions are quite common in the geological record and, as explained earlier, their occurrences have been linked with bursts of explosive evolution. Indeed, the boundaries between our major divisions of Phanerozoic time—the Palaeozoic, Mesozoic and Cainozoic eras—and to a lesser extent the boundaries between the geological periods were based essentially on the recognition of major periods of extinction followed by bursts of evolution.

Some of the extinctions were spectacular. Some were so impressive, as for example the disappearance of the giant reptiles about 65 million years ago at the end of the Cretaceous period, that external catastrophies, such as changes in the sun's radiation or collision with a huge meteorite, have been invoked. However, more thorough study has demonstrated that most extinctions and evolutionary radiations actually occurred over a period of time, though accelerated in relation to more normal periods of evolution and extinction. The changes probably reflect major but progressive changes in the environment, such as extensive marine retreats or advances, or significant changes in the world's climate.

The progress of life through time

Despite its major imperfections, the fossil record, when properly interpreted, provides an immense amount of information on the progression of life through geological time. The record starts very early in the earth's history. Indeed, so-called *chemofossils*, minute agglomerations of organic acids possibly of living origin, are known from rocks almost 4,000 million years old, and algae were well established by 3,000 million years ago. Much more advanced, though soft-bodied, animals are known from a variety of late Pre-Cambrian rocks and trace fossils of this age are common. All are *invertebrates*, animals without a backbone, but some are difficult to assign to their correct phylum.

Invertebrate fossils are common from the beginning of the Cambrian period (some 570 million years ago) onward. This resulted from the development of hard shells, initially often chitinous but soon mainly calcareous, by most invertebrate phyla at that time. With one exception—the *Archaeocyatha*, a group of extinct marine forms—all the phyla which had appeared by the end of the Cambrian still flourish today, though many of the early forms look very different from their modern descendants.

The phylum *Arthropoda* probably originated in the Pre-Cambrian and is represented at first by marine creatures called *trilobites*. These became extinct during the Permian period of 280 to 225 million years ago, but the phylum is by then represented by many other forms including abundant crustaceans—a group represented today by such creatures as crabs, lobsters and shrimps. 'Modern' crabs originated some 100 million years later during the Jurassic. To the palaeon-

tologist some of the most important crustacean arthropods are the microscopic *ostracods* which originated late in the Cambrian and are of importance as zone fossils in the correlation of rock strata of Silurian and later age. An equally important group for this purpose are the *foraminifera*, a division of the single-celled phylum *Protozoa*. The phylum must have had a long Pre-Cambrian history, and foraminifera appeared early in the Cambrian.

The phylum, *Coelenterata*, which includes present-day corals, sea-anemones and jelly-fish, is represented in the Pre-Cambrian by the traces of jelly-fish and in many later systems by the skeletons of fossil corals. The latter often formed reefs in ancient tropical areas. The phylum *Mollusca* has reached its peak today, but its fossil record is varied and impressive. The *cephalopod* molluscs, forms with chambered shells, appeared at the end of the Cambrian and radiated rapidly at the beginning of the Ordovician 500 million years ago. They gave rise during the Devonian, 100 million years later, to the *ammonoid* cephalopods, whose shells are so common in some Mesozoic sediments.

Another cephalopod group, the *belemnites*, appeared in the Carboniferous and are ancestral to the modern squid and cuttlefish. Other molluscan groups include the *bivalves*, which are rare until the Silurian, 400 million years ago, but then become increasingly common to achieve enormous diversity today, where they include the common cockles, mussels and scallops. The *gastropod* molluscs, common today as snails, slugs and whelks, have coiled shells and a geological history similar to that of the bivalves.

The phylum *Brachiopoda* is another shellfish group. In contrast to the Mollusca they are relatively insignificant now, although their geological record, especially from Ordovician to Permian times, was much more important. The phylum *Echinodermata* also originated in the Cambrian or earlier, and its two major fossil groups are the *Crinoidea* (sea lilies) and the *Echinoidea* (sea urchins). The former were most important in the distant Palaeozoic where their skeletal remains are sometimes important rock builders, while the latter diversified during the Mesozoic to reach a peak in the Cretaceous.

The *graptolites* appeared in the Ordovician and became extinct 200 million years later in the Carboniferous. They are colonial organisms that were once classified with the Coelenterata but are now placed among the most primitive members of the phylum *Chordata*, which includes the vertebrates. The first true vertebrates, the fish, evolved in the Ordovician. Land was first colonized in the Devonian, when amphibians as well as the first land plants appeared, to be followed by reptiles in the early Carboniferous.

The conquest of land left only one realm to be fully occupied—the air. Flying insects were well established by the Carboniferous, and the first flying reptiles are of Triassic age (over 200 million years ago). Some 50 million years later, true birds appeared in the late Jurassic, by which time many forms of life were taking on a modern appearance while the land was roamed by the dinosaurs, now long extinct. Man appeared only about 2.5 million years ago, at about the beginning of the Pleistocene epoch.

In fossilised wood (as here, in the Petrified Forest National Park, East Arizona) the wood fibres have been replaced, through the action of hot, silica bearing waters, by opal or chalcedony.

Life in Ancient Waters

In tracing the evolution of life on earth, the story of the first vertebrate animals is of vital importance. In fact the first vertebrates were fish and during the Devonian period—which is often known as the 'Age of Fish'—there is evidence of the origins of both modern fish and many other fish-like animals which have long since become extinct. Moreover, from fish evolved the first amphibious creatures which could live on land. And from them, ultimately, evolved all the reptiles, birds and mammals that now inhabit this planet.

Jawless fish

The earliest evidence of vertebrate animals is found in sandstones of middle Ordovician age, about 465 million years old. It consists of small plates of bone-like material, and the animal that possessed these plates was a fish-like vertebrate belonging to a group that includes the modern eel-shaped lamprey. This group is distinguished from other vertebrates by its lack of true jaws or teeth. It is called *agnatha*, meaning 'without jaws'.

Unlike the modern lamprey, the Palaeozoic agnathans were covered with bony plates and scales and are consequently called *ostracoderms*, 'shell-skinned'.

Most ostracoderms lived in lakes, rivers and lagoons during the late Silurian and the Devonian periods, 400-350 million years ago. It is probable that they were rather idle, spending much of their time resting on the bottom, only occasionally darting from place to place feeding on organic debris which accumulated on the bottom sediments. The end of the Devonian witnessed the extinction of ostracoderms, but the agnathan lineage continued with the lamprey.

The advantages of jaws

The appearance of upper and lower jaws with associated teeth was a major step forward in vertebrate evolution. It transformed the rather weak, circular mouth of ostracoderms into a long, powerful organ potentially capable of grabbing active prey. However, in order to realize this potential there had to be improvements in mobility to aid the pursuit of likely victims. Not surprisingly, therefore, the development of jaws is accompanied by the development of true paired fins—the *pectoral* or breast fins, one on each side behind the head, and *pelvic* fins, on either side of the lower surface of the body. These helped control the movement of the fish through the water.

One of the early groups to exploit the advantages of jaws was the *placoderm* fish, sometimes called the 'armoured fish'. The head was encased in a bony shield and this *articulated* or moved by means of a ball and socket neck-joint, with another bony shield covering the foremost part of the trunk. The neck-joint was an interesting innovation. It allowed the front part of the skull to be raised at the same time as the lower jaw was lowered. Effectively, therefore, this considerably increased the size of the mouth opening.

Despite the great variety of placoderm

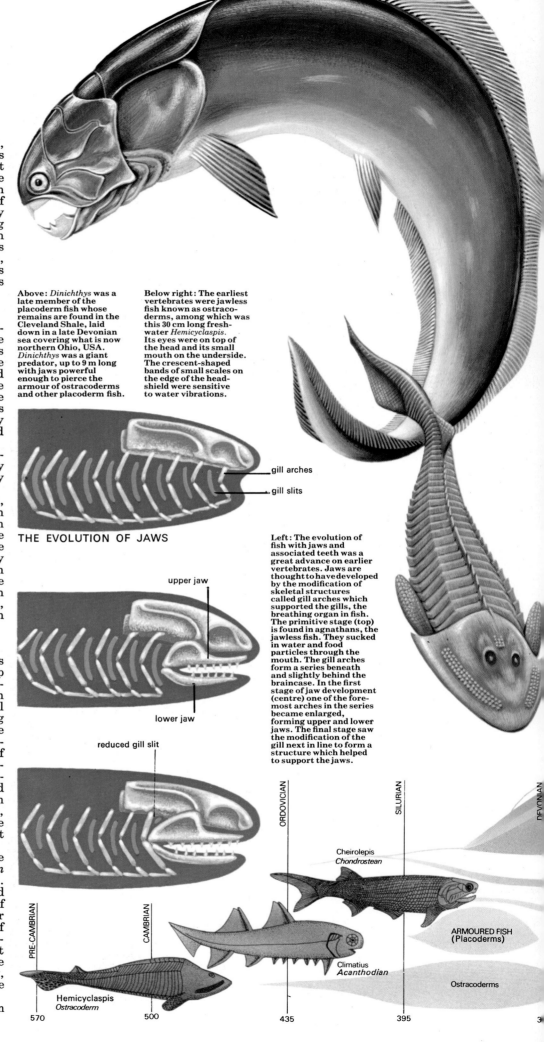

Above: *Dinichthys* was a late member of the placoderm fish whose remains are found in the Cleveland Shale, laid down in a late Devonian sea covering what is now northern Ohio, USA. *Dinichthys* was a giant predator, up to 9 m long with jaws powerful enough to pierce the armour of ostracoderms and other placoderm fish.

Below right: The earliest vertebrates were jawless fish known as ostracoderms, among which was this 30 cm long fresh-water *Hemicyclaspis*. Its eyes were on top of the head and its small mouth on the underside. The crescent-shaped bands of small scales on the edge of the head-shield were sensitive to water vibrations.

gill arches

gill slits

THE EVOLUTION OF JAWS

upper jaw

lower jaw

reduced gill slit

Left: The evolution of fish with jaws and associated teeth was a great advance on earlier vertebrates. Jaws are thought to have developed by the modification of skeletal structures called gill arches which supported the gills, the breathing organ in fish. The primitive stage (top) is found in agnathans, the jawless fish. They sucked in water and food particles through the mouth. The gill arches form a series beneath and slightly behind the braincase. In the first stage of jaw development (centre) one of the foremost arches in the series became enlarged, forming upper and lower jaws. The final stage saw the modification of the gill next in line to form a structure which helped to support the jaws.

PRE-CAMBRIAN

CAMBRIAN

ORDOVICIAN

SILURIAN

DEVONIAN

Cheirolepis
Chondrostean

Climatius
Acanthodian

ARMOURED FISH
(Placoderms)

Hemicyclaspis
Ostracoderm

Ostracoderms

570

500

435

395

56

fish, particularly in late Devonian times, all had become extinct by the end of that period. This fact is difficult to explain but two factors may have been important. The solid head shields may have imposed restrictions on breathing, and hence on activity; also the bony shearing blades were not replaceable once they had been worn down. Perhaps these limitations became too great at a time when fish with more efficient breathing mechanisms and methods of tooth replacement were making their appearance.

Cartilaginous fish

The cartilaginous fish are today represented by the sharks, rays and the deep-sea ratfishes. This group is characterized by an internal skeleton made of cartilage and a body covering of tiny denticles or scales. Throughout their history, cartilaginous fish have been a predominantly marine group. Unfortunately, the fossil record is rather poor since, with a few exceptions, only the isolated denticles, teeth and fin spines are preserved.

From their appearance in the middle Devonian the cartilaginous fish were a group which became adapted to an active swimming, predatory existence. There is no restrictive bony shield covering the head and the teeth are hard-wearing, being composed of dentine with a tough coat of enamel, and replaceable.

Sharks of truly modern form appeared by the late Jurassic, some 150 million years ago. This period also marks the appearance of modern rays which, in all probability, evolved from a shark-like ancestor. The rays became adapted to life on the sea floor. They became flattened with enormously expanded pectoral fins.

Bony fish

The dominant group of modern fish are the *bony fish*, such as salmon, cod, herring, perch and angel fish. They are numerous as fossils, particularly in deposits of late Mesozoic and Cainozoic age. As the group name suggests, the skeleton, both internally and externally, is composed of strongly calcified bone. An important internal structure that was developed in early bony fish is the paired lung. In one group of bony fish, the fleshy-finned fish, the lung retained its original form and function—that of gaseous exchange—but in the ray-finned fish the lung became modified to form a swim-bladder and took on the function of a buoyancy tank. This was an important energy saving development. It provided the fish with neutral buoyancy and eliminated the need for constant swimming in order to stay at one level.

The ray-finned group of bony-fish were numerous and have shown great variation throughout their geological history. The first ray-fins were found in freshwater Devonian deposits but by the end of that period a few had taken up life in the sea and this has remained their principal environment. In the late Mesozoic and the Cainozoic several kinds of ray-fin fish re-invaded freshwater and formed most of the freshwater fish fauna of today.

The earliest, most primitive of the ray-fins were members of a group called the *chondrosteans*. This was essentially a Palaeozoic group although a few members, such as the sturgeon, survive today.

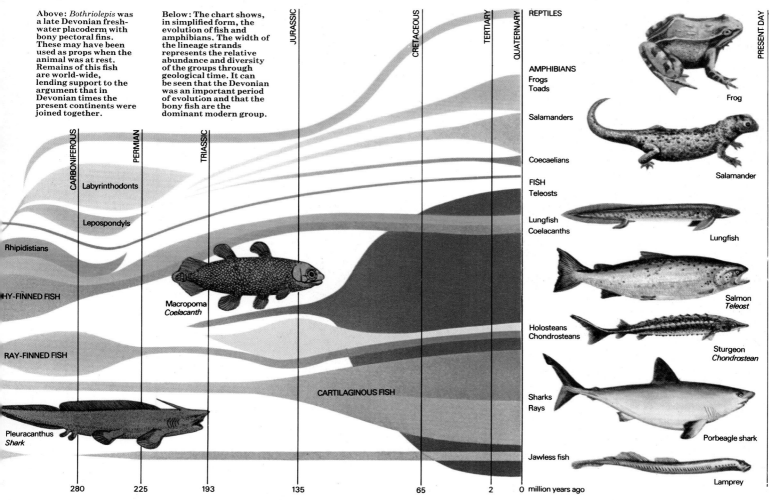

Above: *Bothriolepis* was a late Devonian fresh-water placoderm with bony pectoral fins. These may have been used as props when the animal was at rest. Remains of this fish are world-wide, lending support to the argument that in Devonian times the present continents were joined together.

Below: The chart shows, in simplified form, the evolution of fish and amphibians. The width of the lineage strands represents the relative abundance and diversity of the groups through geological time. It can be seen that the Devonian was an important period of evolution and that the bony fish are the dominant modern group.

Another more advanced level of ray-fin evolution is represented by the *holosteans*. This was essentially a Mesozoic group, and only two types have survived.

At the top of the ray-fin evolutionary ladder stand the *teleosts*. This group first appeared in the Triassic but became particularly important in the late Mesozoic and the Cainozoic when they show a great variety of body forms. The evolution of ray-fin fish is marked by repeated improvements in feeding methods and mobility.

Ray-finned differ from another group of bony fish, the fleshy-fin fish, in the structure of the paired fins. In fleshy-fin fish, the skeleton and muscles, which support and move the paired fins, extend outside the body and give the fin a fleshy lobe at the base.

Of the three groups of fleshy-fin fish, lungfish are a very specialized group. They possess solidly constructed skulls and large grinding plates which are adapted for crushing molluscs and plant material. Lungfish are so-called because the primitive lung has been retained and can be used for ·obtaining oxygen in unfavourable climatic conditions. Structurally, the lungfishes have remained relatively unchanged since their appearance in middle Devonian times.

Another structually conservative group of fleshy-fin fish are the *coelacanths*. The Palaeozoic coelacanths inhabited freshwater but they migrated to the sea in the Mesozoic. They were thought to have been extinct for 65 million years until one was caught in 1938 off the coast of Africa.

In contrast to the lungfish and coelacanths, the *rhipidistians*, the third fleshy-fin group, were short-lived. They were, however, a very important group since it is likely that the first animals to exist on land, the amphibians, arose from rhipidistian stock. During the Devonian, most lived in freshwater where they must have been voracious carnivores.

Many of the rhipidistian features foreshadowed those in early amphibians. Not only was the backbone composed of strong vertebrae, but also the skeleton of the pectoral and pelvic fins was comparable with that of the fore and hind limbs of amphibians. Perhaps more importantly, the arrangement of limb muscles allowed for multi-directional movement of limbs. Rhipidistians also possessed internal nostrils which opened through the roof of the mouth. This totally unfish like feature is precisely that found in amphibians and is an adaptation to air breathing. Such air breathing might have been very impor-

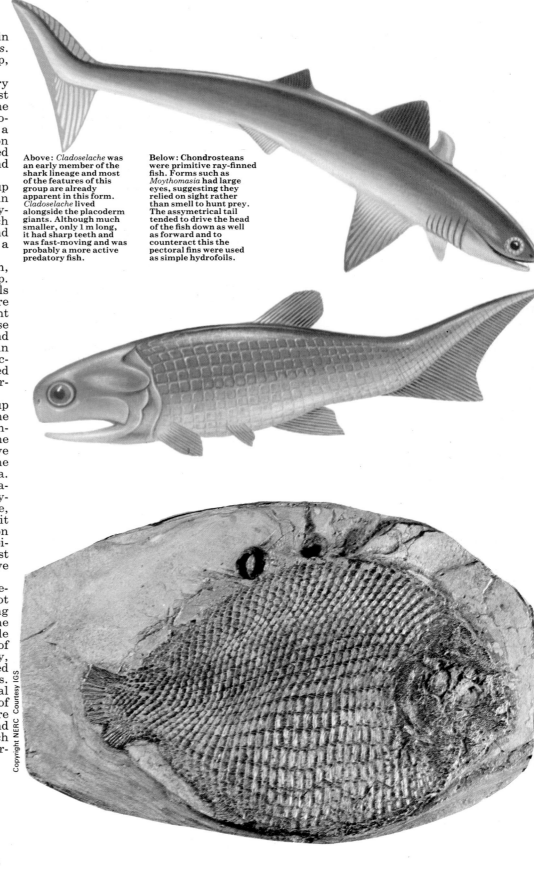

Above: *Cladoselache* was an early member of the shark lineage and most of the features of this group are already apparent in this form. *Cladoselache* lived alongside the placoderm giants. Although much smaller, only 1 m long, it had sharp teeth and was fast-moving and was probably a more active predatory fish.

Below: Chondrosteans were primitive ray-finned fish. Forms such as *Moythomasia* had large eyes, suggesting they relied on sight rather than smell to hunt prey. The assymetrical tail tended to drive the head of the fish down as well as forward and to counteract this the pectoral fins were used as simple hydrofoils.

Below: Life in certain late Devonian pools may have been rather harsh with times of drought and stagnant water. Early lungfish, such as *Dipterus* (left), probably gulped air and may even have had the ability to 'hibernate' in the mud during droughts. Rhipidistians such as *Eusthenopteron* (centre) were capable of walking out on land to seek new pools. *Ichthyostega* (right) was better at walking with much stouter limbs with fingers and toes. This early amphibian shows some terrestrial adaptations but it probably spent most of its time in the water since there was very little animal food on land in the Devonian.

P. Morris/Ardea

tant as geological evidence suggests that at least some of the Devonian freshwaters were periodically subject to low oxygen levels.

From water to land

About 350 million years ago, some rhipidistian fish probably left the water for brief periods. The reasons for these temporary excursions on to land are not clear but the late Professor A. S. Romer, an eminent American palaeontologist, suggested that it may have been to escape from oxygen-depleted pools which were drying up to more favourable bodies of water. Whatever the reason, it is from a land-venturing rhipidistian that the first amphibians are descended.

On land the early amphibians made an attempt to raise the body off the ground on to four legs. Fossil remains reveal that both the shoulder and pelvic girdles were large, and that the pelvic girdle was rigidly anchored to the backbone. These primitive land-venturers needed to travel more efficiently in their new environment and there was modification of the rhipidistian paired fins to form the first kind of fore and hind limbs with fingers and toes.

The first amphibian, *Ichthyostega*, lived in late Devonian times. Ichthyostega was structurally intermediate between rhipidistians and later amphibians and belongs to a large group of fossil amphibians called the *labyrinthodonts*.

Labyrinthodonts reached the peak of their radiation about 300 million years ago in the late Palaeozoic, but 100 million years later by the end of the Triassic period they had become extinct.

Another Palaeozoic group of amphibians were the *lepospondyls*. Most were small aquatic forms. Some became eel-like while others had highly flattened heads that were extended on each side.

The amphibians living today are the frogs and toads (anurans), the salamanders (urodeles) and the coecaelians. The frogs are known as fossils from the Triassic, 200 million years ago, and the salamanders from the Jurassic, about 50 million years later. However, when they appear in the fossil record they are already very similar to their modern-day counterparts and their ancestry from older Palaeozoic amphibians is obscure.

But this was only the beginning, for from the early amphibians many new forms of life were to evolve, animals that severed completely any connections with the sea. These animals were the reptiles, birds, mammals and, ultimately, man.

Above: In teleost fish the tail is fully symmetrical and this produces a horizontal thrust. This example, *Acanthonemus*, was found in Eocene marine deposits in Italy. The fish fauna of this area, rich in teleosts, is very similar to that found in lagoons and shallow seas of the Indo-Pacific region today.

Left: Holostean fish were the dominant ray-fins of the Mesozoic era. *Dapedium* was a Jurassic form with a deep body about 60 cm long and a small mouth with a profusion of sharp peg-like teeth. The teeth indicate that this fish may have lived around coral reefs feeding on hard-shelled invertebrates.

P. Morris/Ardea

Left: Coelacanths had been known as fossils for a long time but were thought to have become extinct in the late Cretaceous, 65 million years ago. However, in 1938 a local fisherman hauled up a rather unfamiliar fish off the coast of East London, South Africa. Tremendous excitement was aroused in the scientific community when it was realized that the fish was a coelacanth, named *Latimeria*. Since then about 80 more specimens of this 'living fossil' have been recovered from the deep waters around the Comoro Islands. The coelacanth is very important for it is the nearest living relative of the amphibians.

Left: *Eryops* was a Permian amphibian which reached a large size of about 1.5 m. No doubt its powerful jaws made it an aggressive carnivore. It appears capable of spending much of its time on land but it probably returned to the water to feed. Its prey were fish and other amphibians.

Fossil Reptiles and Mammals

The key to successful life on land seems to have lain in the development of the reptilian egg. Apparently simple, it gave the reptiles a distinct advantage over their ancestors, the amphibians. The egg contains a complex set of adaptations to allow the unborn or *embryonic* reptile to develop with its own enclosed supply of food and water, while at the same time allowing it access to the life-giving air around it. The evolution of this egg made it possible for reptiles to dispense with the vulnerable, aquatic *larval* stage—characteristic of amphibian reproduction.

The reptilian egg probably evolved over 300 million years ago, in the Carboniferous period. But reptiles were not immediately able to evolve into a complete range of land animals. The first reptiles were small and lizard-like, for the only other land animals available as food were small invertebrates—insects, spiders and snails. As larger reptiles evolved, each in turn was potential food for yet larger *carnivores* or flesh-eating animals.

Even more complex problems had to be overcome before *herbivorous* or plant-eating reptiles could evolve. This is not only because the digestion of plant material takes a long time—and therefore requires a bulky body—but also because, like most animals, reptiles cannot digest that material unaided. They first had to develop a special bacterial flora which, living within the digestive passage or *alimentary canal*, could carry out the preliminary stages of digestion. When herbivorous reptiles did evolve, they in turn provided yet more food for larger carnivores, forming new links in the increasingly complex community of plant and animal land life.

The earliest major group of successful reptiles are called *mammal-like reptiles*, for it was from them that the mammals eventually evolved. The mammal-like reptiles seem to have originated in a continent made up of what is now North America and Europe. Their remains are common in early Permian deposits, about 270 million years old, laid down in a great river delta which lay in what is now northern Texas. These animals, both herbivores and carnivores, were still slow and clumsy, but more active mammal-like reptiles evolved later in the Permian.

The first mammals evolved from advanced mammal-like reptiles about 200 million years ago. But their eventual success was still far in the future, for alongside them there also evolved the first of those reptiles which were to dominate the world for the next 135 million years—the dinosaurs.

The massive dinosaurs
Some dinosaurs were surprisingly small; one called *Compsognathus* was only the size of a chicken. But most were large and some were enormous. As always, the largest were the herbivores, especially the great four-footed, long-necked types known as *Sauropods*. It was long thought that these animals could only support the weight of their massive bodies if they spent most of their time in lakes or

Right: The strange 'sail' of the mammal-like reptile Dimetrodon may have been a device to keep its body temperature constant. If it was cold, it would have basked broadside to the sun, with a network of blood-vessels circulating the heat to its body. When it was warm enough, it would have faced the sun or retired to the shade.

Below: Cynognathus lived about 220 million years ago. It was about the size of a pig and was probably close to the line of ancestry of the mammals. Whether it had a covering of hair is not certain, but it was doubtless an active predator, with teeth capable of biting, stabbing and chewing like those of living mammals.

Above: The egg of both a reptile and a bird looks deceptively simple. But it contains a complex system of blood-vessels and membranes which allow the embryo to obtain the nourishment from the yolk, to get rid of its waste products and to breathe air. The air passes through pores in the shell, which protects the embryo from damage.

THE LATE CRETACEOUS

EQUATOR

land mass
shallow sea
fossil find

P. Morris/Ardea

Right: The chart shows, in simplified form, the evolution of reptiles, mammals and birds. The width of the strands represents the relative abundance and diversity of groups through geological time. Most notable is the sudden extinction of all the dinosaurs at the end of the Cretaceous and the evolutionary explosion of mammals.

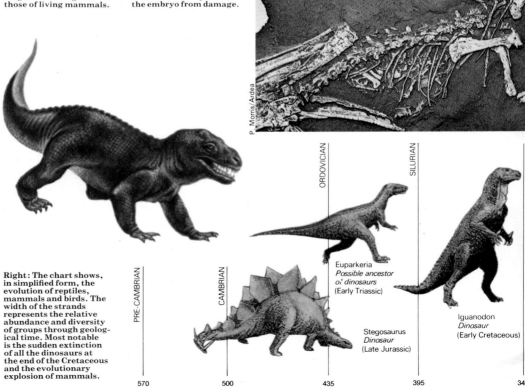

PRE-CAMBRIAN

CAMBRIAN

ORDOVICIAN

SILURIAN

DEVONIAN

Euparkeria
Possible ancestor of dinosaurs
(Early Triassic)

Stegosaurus
Dinosaur
(Late Jurassic)

Iguanodon
Dinosaur
(Early Cretaceous)

570   500   435   395   345

Below and left: A plesiosaur skeleton, 3.5 m long, was found at Fletton in England when a bed of clay was being excavated. Around it lay the remains of other sea creatures. Such fossils provide a wealth of evidence on the anatomy and way of life of ancient animals, on which artists can base reconstructions (left).

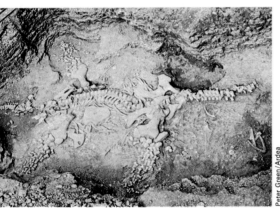

swamps. But many scientists now believe that they were dry-land animals, using their long necks to reach high vegetation.

Some herbivores, such as *Stegosaurus* or the Certopians, were protected from their enemies by bony plates, frills or spikes. Some such protection was certainly necessary. For some of the carnivorous dinosaurs were fearsome animals, with great heads bearing dagger-like teeth, armed also with sharp, ripping claws on their limbs.

The dinosaurs inhabited the world at a time when the great supercontinent of Pangaea was breaking up. Separated continents drifted apart and some became partly covered by shallow seas. Though scientists are still uncertain, it is even possible that this process was the cause of the extinction of the dinosaurs.

The spectacular extinction of dinosaurs occurred at the end of the Cretaceous period, 65 million years ago. At that time

continental drift was slowing down and the shallow seas were withdrawing from the continents. This would have led to the climate becoming colder and more variable, perhaps causing serious physiological problems for the dinosaurs, which were adapted to a more genial and uniform climate. Whatever may have been the reason, they all died out and their only surviving relatives today are the lumbering, aquatic crocodiles.

While the dinosaurs were dominant on land, the surrounding seas were dominated by other reptiles. Some, the *ichthyosaurs*, swam by powerful strokes of their tails which bore a large fin. They would have found it difficult to move on land and there is evidence that they gave birth to live young in the water, as whales do today.

Other marine reptiles, the *plesiosaurs*, swam like turtles, by strokes of their enlarged, paddle-like limbs. They were probably able to haul themselves ashore to lay their eggs. Some of the plesiosaurs had long, thin necks, flexible enough to allow them to catch agile, darting fish. Others, with great powerful heads and jaws, had turned to prey on their own reptilian relatives.

The main flying animals in Jurassic and Cretaceous skies were the *pterosaurs*, related to the dinosaurs. They were like bats in many ways, with a leathery flight membrane supported on their fourth finger and with tiny hind limbs which must have made it impossible for them to walk on land. There is even evidence that, more like a mammal than a reptile, pterosaurs had an insulatory covering of hair so that their body temperature and

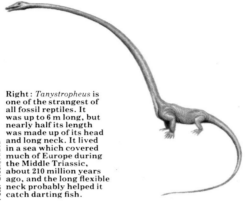

Right: *Tanystropheus* is one of the strangest of all fossil reptiles. It was up to 6 m long, but nearly half its length was made up of its head and long neck. It lived in a sea which covered much of Europe during the Middle Triassic, about 210 million years ago, and the long flexible neck probably helped it catch darting fish.

Peter Green/Ardea

Left: *Coelophysis* was one of the first of the small carnivorous dinosaurs. Only about 2.5 m long, it probably ran on its hind limbs and grasped its prey with its forelimbs. Within this fossil can be seen traces of its food which seems to include the remains of some young individuals of its own species.

Above left: The world inhabited by dinosaurs about 70 million years ago was very different from today's. Eastern N. America and Europe were still connected to one another but seaways across North America and Asia separated this land area from another which included Asia and western N. America. Fossil dinosaur finds are marked.

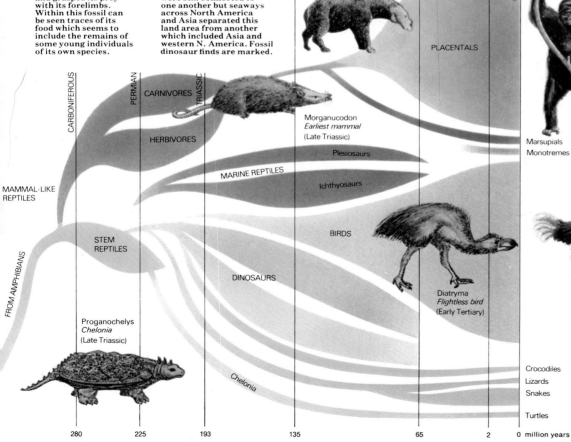

activity did not vary if the daily or seasonal temperature increased or decreased.

Prehistoric birds

The bones are usually all that remains of a fossil animal. Occasionally, however, impressions of softer structures are preserved. In at least one case, this has given us vital clues about the course of evolution. In late Jurassic rocks from southern Germany, a few specimens that might well have been thought to be merely skeletons of small dinosaurs have been preserved in very fine-grained sediments. However, around the skeletons these showed the clear impressions of feathers, proving that these animals, called *Archaeopteryx*, were really almost perfect intermediates between a reptile and a bird.

Archaeopteryx is the oldest known bird. There is a great gap in time, over 75 million years, between the Jurassic *Archaeopteryx* and the next birds in the fossil record. But specimens from late Cretaceous deposits show a high degree of specialization and by the early Tertiary, 60 million years ago, many modern kinds of bird were represented.

Like ostriches and emus today, some fossil birds lost the power of flight and became large, fast-running birds. The powerful beaks and claws of such extinct creatures as *Diatryma* or *Phororhachos*, with a head the size of that of a horse, must have deterred even the most savage predatory mammal.

Mammals themselves evolved in the late Triassic from advanced, active mammal-like reptiles rather like *Cynognathus*. Mammals, including birds, are 'warm-blooded', able to maintain a constant body temperature. This adaptation was an advance over 'cold-blooded' reptiles, whose body temperature is determined by the outside temperature. Though a number of different types of little mammals evolved during the next 135 million years, the real burst of adaptive radiation of mammals only became possible after the dinosaurs became extinct at the end of the Cretaceous period.

Early in their evolutionary history, the mammals divided into two stocks. The young of the *placental* mammals are born at an advanced stage of development, whereas those of the *marsupials* are born more prematurely but continue their development in the mother's pouch. The marsupials may have evolved in the great southern land mass, Gondwanaland, made up of South America, Antarctica and Australia. The marsupials also colonized North America and Europe, but soon became extinct there due to competition from the placental mammals. These evolved in Asia, but soon spread all over the northern hemisphere.

At the beginning of the Tertiary, 65 million years ago, Africa was still isolated from the northern continents by the Mediterranean Sea which then extended

Below: The great sauropod dinosaurs such as this *Barosaurus* were the largest land animals ever to exist. They were up to 30 m long. To provide enough energy for their gigantic bodies, these herbivores must have spent much of their time eating. The size of the head seems remarkably small in comparison with that of the body.

Below: This reconstruction of what life was like in both Asia and western North America about 70 million years ago gives some idea of the diversity of dinosaur life. The largest known carnivorous land animal is the *Tyrannosaurus*. It is shown attacking a hadrosaur, the head of which bears a strange bony crest, of uncertain function. Though these animals had no defence —except perhaps speed— the ceratopian *Triceratops* had bony rhino-like horns on its head, and *Anklyosaurus* had protective plates and spikes of bone on its body and tail. Overhead swoops *Pteranodon*. These flying reptiles, which had a wingspan of up to 13 m, are known as pterosaurs and were closely related to the dinosaurs. The diversity of giant reptiles, just before their final extinction, indicates that they were not gradually dwindling in numbers or importance. Instead, they seem to have reached a peak of dominance, making their sudden and complete disappearance from land, sea and air 65 million years ago very puzzling.

LATE JURASSIC

LATE CRETACEOUS

eastwards into Arabia. A few types of placental mammal did, however, reach Africa. There some of them became the ancestors of the elephants which, when dry land later connected Africa to Eurasia, eventually spread over most of the rest of the world. Only the Indian and African elephants survive today.

Evolution of superior mammals

In the great connected landmass of Eurasia, Africa and North America, placental mammals continued to evolve and compete throughout the Cainozoic era. As a result of this evolutionary competition, even more efficient types had evolved by the Miocene epoch, about 25 million years ago. These included the ancestors of not only the great cats, wolves and other carnivores, but also such browsing and grazing herbivores as cattle and deer.

The superiority of these new types of placental mammals became dramatically apparent at the end of the Pliocene epoch. At that time, about two million years ago, a continuous land bridge connected North and South America for the first time. For the previous 60 million years South America had been almost totally isolated from the rest of the world. Apart from

monkeys and rodents, which had later found their way across the surrounding ocean barriers, its only mammals had been marsupials and some early, primitive types of herbivorous placental. A variety of strange mammals had evolved such as the giant ground-sloth *Megatherium* and the giant armadillo-like *Glyptodon*.

But these once-isolated stocks were no match for the new placental mammals which poured across the Panama isthmus from the north. A great wave of extinction of the South American mammals took place. All the less advanced herbivorous placentals died out and the opossums are almost the only marsupials that survived there.

As a result, another island-continent—Australia—became the last refuge of the marsupials. There they evolved undisturbed into a great diversity of animals, including types similar in appearance and habits to many of the placentals, and also such unique types as the kangaroos.

Man and climate have also had a great effect on the mammals of the rest of the world, together or separately causing the extinction of many. During the last two million years, a series of ice ages brought vast sheets of ice and snow southwards over enormous areas of Eurasia and North America. Some mammals were able to adapt to these conditions. Both elephants and rhinoceroses, for example, evolved types with thick, warm coats of hair. But many others became extinct, either when the ice ages arrived or later, when the ice was receding and the climate changed once more. Also, at this time man was becoming an increasingly numerous and skilled hunter.

Below: *Baluchitherium*, about 7 m tall, is the largest known land mammal. It lived in Asia about 25 million years ago and it became extinct soon after elephants spread there from Africa. It seems likely that the long trunk and great grinding teeth of elephants provided a more economic way of reaching high foliage.

Below: Yet another way of feeding on the leaves of trees is shown by *Megatherium*, the 6 m long ground sloth that lived in South America until a few thousand years ago when it became extinct. *Megatherium* probably reared up on its haunches and used its clawed forelimbs to pull the branches down to its mouth.

EARLY TERTIARY

LATE TERTIARY

Cave painting at Altimira, northern Spain. Inside the cave, 270 metres long, have been found remains from the upper Solutrian and middle Magdalanian periods (between approximately 30,000 and 10,000 B.C.).

The Emergence of Man

Man belongs to a major group of mammals known as the *primates*. Two sub-groups are recognized. These are the *anthropoids* (man-like forms including the monkeys, apes and man himself) and *prosimians* (early monkeys or pre-monkeys, including the tree-shrews, lemurs, lorises and bush-babies and tarsiers) and they jointly form man's living relatives. The primates also include a range of extinct ancestral forms known only as fossils.

The earliest prototype primates, resembling modern tree-shrews, were long-snouted, insect-eating tree dwellers which flourished over 65 million years ago. They differed little from other groups of ancestral mammals.

The prosimian descendants of these primates flourished until 45 million years ago. They were also small, tree dwelling forms, leading retiring and often largely nocturnal lives. The characteristic large eyes, grasping hands and stereoscopic vision—needed for well-judged movement through the trees and found in such forms as the fossil primate *Adapis*—suggest that they lived in a similar manner to prosimians of today.

Many of the prosimians have now been replaced by the 'higher' primates. However, some survive in isolated parts of the world—the only surviving lemurs, for example, live on the island of Madagascar, where they were free from competition with other more advanced primates until the arrival of man there 10,000 years ago.

Fossil monkeys and apes

The living monkeys are distributed in two major groups, inhabiting respectively the Old World of Asia and Africa and the New World of the Americas but sharing a common ancestry. This common stock dates from a period before the separation of South America and Eurasia by continental drift. From the period of separation the two monkey groups evolved along independent but parallel lines.

The way of life, and death, of monkeys, and the fact that the forest floor provides poor conditions for preserving bones, result in a scanty fossil record of monkeys. However there is sufficient material to show that two major groups of Old World monkeys—the Cercopithecine and Colobine monkeys—were already well differentiated at least 20 million years ago.

More than 30 million years ago small, unspecialized ancestors of the modern great apes (chimpanzee, gorilla and orang) are known as fossils. The best preserved find dating from this time is a skull of *Aegyptopithecus* from the Fayum area of Egypt.

The fossil evidence becomes much more abundant by about 20 million years ago. It shows that ancestral gorilla-like forms (*Dryopithecus* (*Proconsul*) *major*) were already markedly different in appearance from ancestral chimpanzee-like forms (*Dryopithecus* (*Proconsul*) *africanus*). Over 400 specimens of these two forms have been collected from Kenya. Other fossil Dryopithecines, or 'oak apes', are known from various localities in Europe and Asia.

Above left: The lemurs are a surviving prosimian group which found refuge from competition with higher primates on the island of Madagascar. The slow loris (above) is another prosimian. The chimpanzee (left) and gorilla (below left) found in equatorial Africa are man's closest living relatives.

Below: The cast of the skull of *Dryopithecus* (*Proconsul*) *major* (top), an 18 M.Y. old fossil ape from east Uganda. It represents a creature resembling, and ancestral to, the modern gorilla. The smaller cast (bottom) is of the skull of *Dryopithecus* (*Proconsul*) *africanus*, a chimpanzee-like form found in Kenya by Dr. Mary Leakey and dating from about the same time.

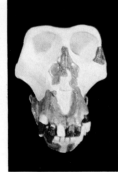

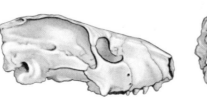

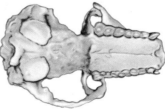

Left: The skull of the fossil *Adapis*, a four-footed, squirrel-like animal. Abundant in Eurasia from 55 to 45 M.Y. ago, it probably moved by clinging and leaping between nearly vertical branches—similar to the way modern bushbabies move. *Adapis* resembled the stock from which the later primates developed.

The earliest hominids

It has been claimed that signs of the earliest hominids can be detected in some of the specimens from this collection of 20 million year old unspecialized ape-like ancestors. The *hominid* family is the one which includes all forms of true fossil men and also modern man. However, this is a speculation and a 20 million year old origin for the hominids is not generally accepted.

Instead, it is a creature called *Ramapithecus* which is generally thought to represent the first recognizable hominid. Originally discovered in the Siwalik Hills in northern India, *Ramapithecus* also includes a fossil hominid known as *Kenyapithecus wickeri* which was found in Kenya. The oldest fossil specimens of this group are dated to about 14 million years ago.

There is a major gap in the trail of fossil evidence from between 14 million years ago and about 5 million years ago. Only two separate molar teeth (one about 10 million years old and the other about 6.5 million years old), both from Kenya, provide slender evidence of the forms that one day may be found to close this gap.

In 1925 Professor Raymond Dart, an Australian anatomist, discovered in Taung in southern Africa the fossil skull of a child aged about 7 years. This was the first discovery of what was to become an important and large group of fossils, the *Australopithecines* or southern apes. Numerous fossils have since been recovered from deposits infilling three former caves in the area between Pretoria and Johannesburg in South Africa. The three infilled caves all lie virtually in line and about a mile apart in a broad valley cut in limestone. Investigation has been carried out by combining careful excavation with diligent detective work by the noted palaeontologist Dr. Robert Broom and numerous later workers.

Detection and reconstruction of former conditions were necessary because quarry workers extracting limestone had been active at all the sites before the palaeontologists arrived on the scene. Large numbers of good fossil hominid specimens had been torn from their matrix of cave fill and thrown onto the quarry dumps still in rough hewn blocks. Over the years this material has been carefully sorted and many fossils have been retrieved from the dumps to add to the excavated specimens. Other specimens have been found at another cave in the northern Transvaal.

The fossils consist mainly of two different species of Australopithecine. One is the sturdy form *Australopithecus robustus* and the other a more lightly built creature *Australopithecus africanus*, which includes the original Taung infant. A few other specimens from the caves represent the genus *Homo*, the same genus as modern man.

Unfortunately, it has not been possible to accurately date the South African cave deposits with the use of radioactive 'clocks'. The fossil mammals that they contain allow a broad assignment of age to a period between 3 and 1 million years ago. Statistical analysis of 111 Australopithecine specimens from one site does, however, reveal something about their life expectancy—27 per cent of the individuals died before reaching the age of 10 years; a total of 88% had died before reaching the age of 25 years, and only one was more than 35 at the time of death.

The East African Rift Valley

In 1959 two British anthropologists, Dr Louis Leakey and his wife Mary, announced the discovery of the first important Australopithecine find from East Africa. This was the skull of *Australopithecus boisei*, or 'Zinj', from Olduvai Gorge in Tanzania. It is interesting that this discovery was made just 100 years after Darwin published *The Origin of Species*. Although in 1859 there was almost no evidence of fossil man, and none from Africa, Darwin suggested that Africa was the place where such evidence would be found. He argued that this was because man's closest living relatives, the chimpanzee and the gorilla, are found there.

Following the Leakeys' breakthrough, the focus in fossil 'head hunting' switched to East Africa. The discovery of 'Zinj' (East African Man or 'Nutcracker' as he was nicknamed because of his large molar teeth) was the first of more than 400 hominid fossils recovered from Tanzania, Kenya and Ethiopia. They are all from the flanks of or within the great East African Rift Valley. This wealth of fossil remains has been of outstanding value in providing evidence of man's evolution.

A further 50 hominid fossils have been found from Olduvai Gorge. Since 1969, 125 fossils have come to light from the east of Lake Turkana (formerly Lake Rudolf) in Kenya, and 180 have been found since 1967 in the Omo Valley in southern Ethiopia. Rich finds have been made recently in northern Ethiopia.

The Rift Valley situation not only favours the preservation of bone and tooth, but its well exposed, layered sequences of fossil-bearing rocks are also highly suitable for accurate dating by

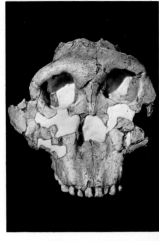

Left: The late Dr. Louis Leakey working at Olduvai gorge in Tanzania. His discovery of fossils of the 'near man' known as *Australopithecus* made a significant contribution to understanding man's evolution.

Below left: The Olduvai Gorge, a dry valley for most of the year, is about 100 m deep and numerous fossil hominids have been discovered in its well-stratified deposits. This has enabled most of the finds to be accurately dated.

Above right: The skull of *Australopithecus (Zinjanthropus) boisei*, a robust fossil of a 'near man' who was contemporary with some of the early 'true men' about 1.75 M.Y. ago. Found in 1959 in Olduvai Gorge, it is known as 'nutcracker' because of the large molar teeth.

Right: A more lightly-built hominid, *Australopithecus africanus*. This fossil, thought to be a female and nicknamed 'Mrs Ples', was excavated from the infill of a former cave near Johannesburg in South Africa. This was one of first fossils of *Australopithecus* to be found.

Below: The map of Africa shows the main areas yielding fossils of early man. The earliest finds of *Australopithecus* came from South Africa, but the wealth of fossils— different forms of Australopithecines, and the earliest men *Homo habilis* and '1470' man— has come from the Rift Valley area of East Africa.

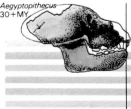

Right: Our present knowledge of man's emergence is shown in this generalized chart. Important skull finds reveal the evolution of the hominid family, but the story remains incomplete. One notable discovery was that the Australopithecines and the early *Homo*, known as '1470 man', were contemporaries.

Aegyptopithecus 30+MY

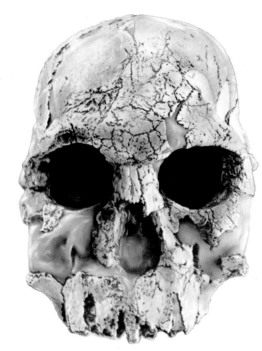

Left: Deposits east of Lake Turkana (formerly Rudolf) have proved to be a rich source of remains of fossil man and of his early stone tool kits. Richard Leakey and his team made their dramatic discovery of '1470 man' to the east of the lake in 1972.

Right: The skull of '1470' man. It is thought to represent the genus *Homo*, and the fossil has been given an age of almost 3 million years.

Below right: A skull of modern *Homo sapiens* gazes towards those of some of his fossil ancestors. These are grouped in order of increasing antiquity, with Cro-Magnon man, who had many features in common with modern man, at the top. Both Neanderthal man and Java man had heavy brow ridges. The bottom cast is believed to be an Australopithecine skull.

Below: Stone tools are useful indicators of man's former presence. These tools illustrate the range of types fashioned by early man. (1) Two very early tools of Oldowan type (named after Olduvai Gorge) showing a core and a primitive chopper, up to 2 M.Y. old. (2) Two very early bifaces. These were later to develop into neatly shaped hand axes. (3) The tools of Acheulian culture (named after St. Acheul in France) include hand axes and cleavers made from quartz, flint and a variety of lavas. (4) Various evolved types of tool including points, spearheads, arrowheads and polished stone axe.

Douglas Botting

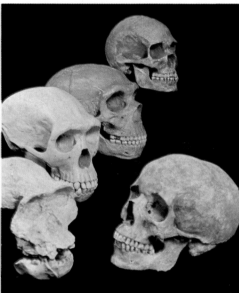

radioactive methods. For example, decay of potassium-40 to produce the gas argon-40 is used to date rift valley lavas and other strata rich in potassium that occur interbedded with fossil-bearing sediments.

The dates may then be compared with the ages obtained by using the fossils themselves as in classical geology. The result is that the Rift contains an exceptional sequence of rocks and fossils dated more firmly than has previously been possible. This makes it quite unique for the study of the nature and rate of evolutionary change in fossil man over the last 3 or 4 million years.

The fossil evidence shows that Australopithecines, both *robustus* and *africanus* forms as in South Africa, were living virtually side-by-side throughout the Rift area. Contemporary with these 'near men' are remains of 'true men' that have been assigned to the genus *Homo*.

Evidence of man

The first *Homo* specimen was from Olduvai Gorge and dates from about 1.75 million years ago—almost the same level that yielded 'Zinj'. This was *Homo habilis* (or handy man) who was named because the fossil hand bones revealed his capability of using the precision grip thought necessary in order to be a successful tool maker.

Other evidence of the *Homo* line has now been found by Richard Leakey, the son of the late Dr. Louis Leakey, in the form of various fossils from east of Lake Turkana. These include the specimen numbered '1470'. This fossil startled the scientific world by having a brain capacity of 800 cc (the Australopithecenes range around 500 cc) and by dating back to almost

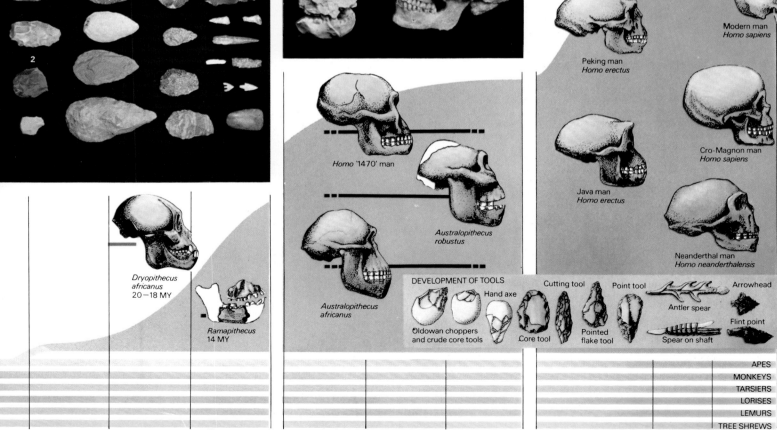

Dryopithecus africanus 20–18 MY

Ramapithecus 14 MY

Homo '1470' man

Australopithecus robustus

Australopithecus africanus

MAN

Peking man
Homo erectus

Modern man
Homo sapiens

Java man
Homo erectus

Cro-Magnon man
Homo sapiens

Neanderthal man
Homo neanderthalensis

DEVELOPMENT OF TOOLS

Hand axe   Cutting tool   Point tool   Arrowhead

Oldowan choppers and crude core tools   Core tool   Pointed flake tool   Antler spear   Flint point   Spear on shaft   Missile

APES
MONKEYS
TARSIERS
LORISES
LEMURS
TREE SHREWS

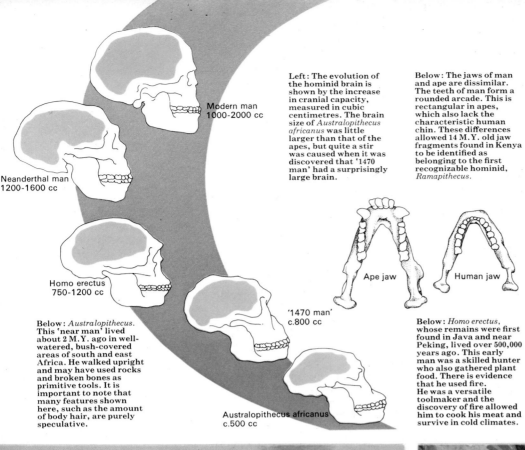

Modern man
1000-2000 cc

Neanderthal man
1200-1600 cc

Homo erectus
750-1200 cc

Left: The evolution of the hominid brain is shown by the increase in cranial capacity, measured in cubic centimetres. The brain size of *Australopithecus africanus* was little larger than that of the apes, but quite a stir was caused when it was discovered that '1470 man' had a surprisingly large brain.

Below: The jaws of man and ape are dissimilar. The teeth of man form a rounded arcade. This is rectangular in apes, which also lack the characteristic human chin. These differences allowed 14 M.Y. old jaw fragments found in Kenya to be identified as belonging to the first recognizable hominid, *Ramapithecus*.

Ape jaw

Human jaw

'1470 man'
c.800 cc

Below: *Australopithecus*. This 'near man' lived about 2 M.Y. ago in well-watered, bush-covered areas of south and east Africa. He walked upright and may have used rocks and broken bones as primitive tools. It is important to note that many features shown here, such as the amount of body hair, are purely speculative.

Below: *Homo erectus*, whose remains were first found in Java and near Peking, lived over 500,000 years ago. This early man was a skilled hunter who also gathered plant food. There is evidence that he used fire. He was a versatile toolmaker and the discovery of fire allowed him to cook his meat and survive in cold climates.

Australopithecus africanus
c.500 cc

3 million years ago. Still older material probably representing *Homo* has now been found in the extreme northern part of the Rift, the Afar region of Ethiopia.

Thus there is evidence of at least three, and possibly more, different types of 'near men' and early man living as contemporaries in the Rift Valley area from about 3.5 million years ago to 1.5 million years ago.

Having seen the origins of the genus *Homo* traced back to such an early date, it remains only to note that three other species are known spanning the last million years. These are *Homo erectus*, *Homo neanderthalensis* and *Homo sapiens*.

Evidence of *Homo erectus* came first from south-east Asia when the original find of this heavy-browed man with a shallow vault to the top of his skull was made in Java at the end of the last century. Other similar finds have since been made from the same area, from caves near Peking in China and from other parts of the world, including East Africa. Although, the finds from the river terrace gravels in Java and from the Peking cave have proved impossible to date with accuracy, and the African finds are not yet dated, *Homo erectus* is generally thought of as belonging in the range between 1,000,000 and 500,000 years ago.

AUSTRALOPITHECUS about 2 million years ago

HOMO ERECTUS about 1 million years ago

The fossils of *Homo neanderthalensis* (Neanderthal man, named from the Neander River in Germany) are much more recent and a great deal of evidence has been found in Europe from deposits broadly equivalent in age to part of the last Ice Age (100,000 to 50,000 years ago). This is shown by the fossil remains of cold climate animals such as the woolly rhinoceros, mammoth and reindeer from the rock-shelters where Neanderthal man has been found. The Neanderthals also lived in places such as Africa.

By this time man had learned the use of fire and his brain capacity was in some cases as large as that of modern man. Despite his rather heavy-browed and massive skull form, Neanderthal man was close to *Homo sapiens* (modern 'thinking' man) in both time and evolutionary development. Indeed he is sometimes classified as a sub-species (*Homo sapiens neanderthalensis*).

The features of the group characterized by the fossils of Cro-Magnon man (*Homo sapiens*) are very similar to those of ourselves and are of no great antiquity. And from this point on, it is early man's tool-making abilities rather than his fossils which provide evidence of his development.

Below: *Neanderthal man.* The rather brutish-looking Neanderthal man first appeared over 100,000 years ago. Fossils have been found in many parts of Europe, Asia and Africa. He survived the last Pleistocene ice age by living in caves, building fires and wearing skin clothes. There is even evidence that he buried his dead.

Below: *Cro-Magnon man.* The last fossil man was also the first true *Homo sapiens*. The 30,000 year old remains from many sites in Europe show these early stone-age people, with advanced tools and weapons, were skilled hunter-gatherers who were becoming more settled. Their fine cave paintings reveal a developed culture.

NEANDERTHAL MAN about 100,000 years ago

CRO-MAGNON MAN about 30,000 years ago

The Land

Cedar Brakes Canyon, Utah. In arid regions crossed by rivers whose water sources are elsewhere, deep valleys are cut into the rocks. These channels are also shaped by weathering of the valley sides and by mass movement of the resulting debris.

Landforms

Every day, physical and chemical processes are at work, changing the apparently solid face of the earth. *Geomorphology* is the study of these processes and of the landforms shaped by them. *Weathering*, which is the breakdown or decay of rocks, is perhaps the most fundamental of all geomorphic processes, for without it landforms created by structural movements of the earth's crust, such as rift valleys and mountains, would undergo very little subsequent alteration.

Mechanical weathering or physical disintegration is distinguished from *chemical weathering*, in which rock decomposition is achieved by such agents as acid contained in water. In turn, a distinction is generally drawn between weathering and *erosion*, which is the process of destruction by those agents—wind, moving ice and running water—which carry away the debris at the same time. Indeed, the development of erosional landforms by wind-blasting, glacial abrasion or stream action depends on the production of coarse particles by weather-

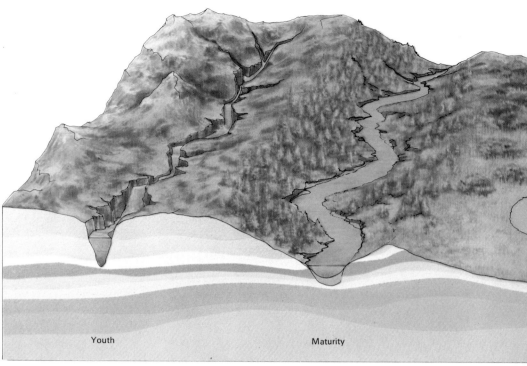

Youth

Maturity

72

Left: A spectacular example of the effect of underground water. Limestone, like all porous rock, stores water but, being composed of calcium carbonate, it is soluble. This cave in France was opened up by the solvent action of underground water. Water seeped down the joints, dissolving the calcium carbonate. As it dripped from the cave roof, partial evaporation caused it to deposit some of the calcium carbonate. This grew downwards as a *stalactite*. Water landing on the floor formed a similar deposit, producing a *stalagmite*.

Below: A river in the Northern Territory of Australia has reached its 'old age' stage. The river, in the last stage of development, is close to *base level* (usually sea-level), the point at which it cannot cut its bed down any deeper. The curves of a river always tend to become exaggerated because of the effect of centrifugal force. This causes the current to swing against the outer bank of a curve and wear it away, a process called *lateral erosion*. In the middle distance is a meander soon to be cut off by lateral erosion.

Right: This section across the Weald of southern England shows clearly a landscape in old age. The contrast with the 'ideal type' as advanced by Davis is striking. Instead of a flat peneplain, the Weald is an irregular landscape of hills and vales from the English Channel to the River Thames. It was originally uplifted as a large anticline, but rivers flowing off the dome cut through the chalk to expose the underlying layers, leaving the resistant ridges forming the North and South Downs.

CYCLE OF EROSION

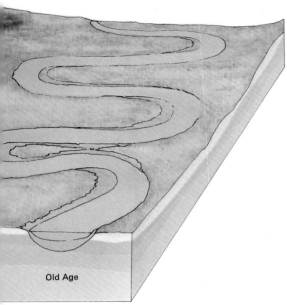

Old Age

Left: A theoretical 'cycle of erosion' was advanced by the American geomorphologist W. M. Davis. His theory was based on an 'ideal case' of a block of sea-floor being uplifted to form land. The first or *youthful* stage is characterized by fast-flowing rivers which cut steep valleys into the land. In the *mature* stage, the original surface has been eroded away by the enlargement of the valleys, now broader and more open, and the curves of the rivers are more developed. By the *old age* stage, the valleys have broad, flat floors, only a little above sea-level, over which the sluggish rivers meander. This final stage Davis termed a *peneplain*, the lowest level of reduction.

Right: Ingleton Falls in Yorkshire, a river in its youthful stage causing vigorous downwards erosion. Most erosion happens when a river is in flood—at that time it has sufficient velocity to carry large rock fragments which wear away the river bed. The boulders seen here will be rolled downstream next time the river is in flood.

THE WEALD OF SOUTHERN ENGLAND

Beachy Head on English Channel

THE WEALD

SOUTH DOWNS

Ashdown Forest

River Medway

Sevenoaks

NORTH DOWNS

River Thames

Eocene rocks

Chalk

Upper Greensand and Gault

Lower Greensand

Weald Clay

Hastings sands

Jurassic rocks

Palaeozoic rocks

---

ing to provide the weapons of erosion and landform sculpture.

Some of the first explanations of landforms were derived from a blend of geology and theology. As late as the nineteenth century, thinking was shaped by an effort to link the age of the earth with the Creation, and landforms with such supernatural catastrophes as the Biblical flood. After 1900, however, English-speaking geomorphologists were encouraged to explain the land surface in terms of 'youth', 'maturity' and 'old age' after the pioneering work of W. M. Davis. An American, whom many call 'the father of geomorphology', he postulated an ideal *Cycle of Erosion* to account for landforms which proceeded with a gradual flattening of relief by weathering and erosion, until the levelling was nearly complete and a *peneplain* (meaning 'almost a plain') was achieved at the 'old age' stage.

The scope of geomorphology
Currently, there is no neat framework into which landforms can be realistically placed. But there is little doubt about the scientific ingredients of a modern geomorphological explanation. These are drawn from a study of geomorphological *processes*, a study which in turn depends on a working knowledge of a wide range of sciences. These include geology as the indispensable, basic science concerned with the properties of the raw materials of landforms.

But to understand the geomorphological processes which sculpture rocks, transport debris and which modify geological structures, information is essential from other sciences, including *climatology*, *hydrology* (the study of water), *pedology* (the science of soils) and *ecology* (the study of organisms in relation to their environment). Furthermore, an appreciation of the physical motions of water, wind and ice and the nature of their role as transportation agents may be deepened by an understanding of physics.

Chemistry and biology are also important, since much of rock weathering, particularly in tropical areas, is a biochemical process. Chemical reactions are involved that are difficult to simulate in the laboratory but which depend on the vital biological contribution of carbon dioxide to the soil from plant and animal respiration. Carbon dioxide concentration in soil is commonly between 10 and 100 times greater than the 0.03 per cent found in the atmosphere. The intensified carbonic acid dissolved in soil water accounts, for example, for the impressive *solutional* weathering associated with limestones.

Biophysical processes are also at work, shaping the landforms around us. The rate of reworking of soils by animals has been known since the late nineteenth century to be impressive. In 1880, the English naturalist Charles Darwin calculated that earthworms annually bring to the ground surface about 25 tonnes of soil per hectare (10 tons per acre). Equally noteworthy is the varying effectiveness of a given vegetation cover in protecting soil from erosion. Even the social sciences are involved here since many of man's activities, such as agriculture and engineering, have an important, and often underestimated, influence on the nature and rate of some contemporary processes.

At the outset, however, the influence of geology on landforms is fundamental. The disposition of rocks at the earth's surface is determined by earth movements and expressed in structures like folds or faults. Moreover, the characteristic properties of rocks are important in relation to their resistance to erosion.

Controversy exists about the influence of climate on landforms, but some of the processes which lead to rock breakdown and the subsequent movement of the fragments or *detritus* are most distinctive in a given climatic zone. Particularly instructive in this context are studies of the processes operating in arid and semi-arid areas, such as the waterless deserts of Africa and the inhospitable 'badlands' of North America. The scant vegetation cover in these areas leaves the actual shapes of landforms starkly obvious. Such areas also show clearly the physical breakdown of rocks and the implications of a sparse vegetation cover when an occasional downpour of rain beats upon unprotected earth.

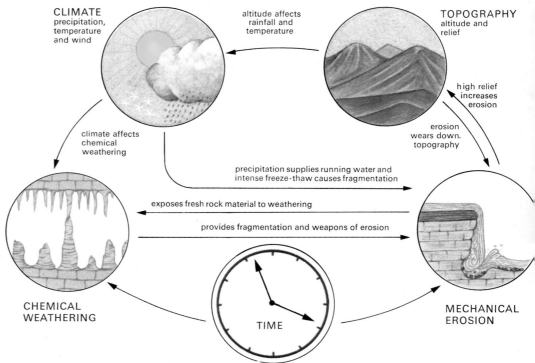

CLIMATE
precipitation,
temperature
and wind

altitude affects
rainfall and
temperature

TOPOGRAPHY
altitude and
relief

high relief
increases
erosion

climate affects
chemical
weathering

erosion
wears down.
topography

precipitation supplies running water and
intense freeze-thaw causes fragmentation

exposes fresh rock material to weathering

provides fragmentation and weapons of erosion

**CHEMICAL
WEATHERING**

TIME

**MECHANICAL
EROSION**

Marc Riboud/Magnum

Water at work

Water, flowing down to the oceans over
the land surface, is the dominant agent of
erosion. In upland areas with moist
climates, fast-moving rivers may flow
with sufficient volume to shift enormous,
abrasive loads of sand, pebbles and even
boulders. Erosion by stream action tends
to broaden and deepen a valley floor,
particularly if undercutting leads to land-
sliding. There is, however, a theoretical
base level, or lowest point, below which
most *fluvial*, or river, processes cease to
be effective.

In the lowland reaches of a river, opposite valley slopes may be wide apart,
separated by a broad plain made up of
stream-deposited sediments, termed *alluvium*. Rivers usually wind across
alluvial plains in sweeping loops or
meanders, but there are interesting
exceptions. In Arctic environments, for
example, innumerable interlinking channel branches meet and diverge to form a
braided channel pattern. The characteristics of river mouths or *estuaries* also
vary greatly, in part depending on the
amount of silt that may be deposited in
tidal reaches of rivers. One finding from
this area of research is that such deposition or *siltation* has increased notably
within historic times.

Not only river waters come under close
scrutiny. Geomorphology also includes
the study of lakes, swamps and underground water. Only a portion of the
precipitation (rain, snow, hail, fog and
dew) that falls on to a soil runs off as a
surface stream. For instance, only about
25% of the 1500 mm (about 60 in) of annual
precipitation in the Congo basin enters
the river, due to the intense *evapotran-*

Aerofilms

Above: River estuary on
the Isle of Wight. An
estuary occurs at the
mouth of a river where
fresh water and sea
water mix. Sediment is
both brought down by the
river and carried in by the
tides, hence an estuary
tends to become silted up.
The light-coloured areas
seen here in the rivers
are the sediment below
water level.

Right: The steep chalk
cliffs of Flamborough
Head in Yorkshire are the
result of wave erosion
cutting away at the base.
As the cliffs are worn
back a shallow platform
is left behind, indicated
by the zone of breaking
waves. All the inlets and
caves are eroded along
the main joints in the
rock—the usual pattern
of marine erosion.

Above: Rocks in Saudi Arabia show how *exfoliation* (the splitting of successive layers from the rock surface) can create dramatic shapes.

Below: A natural arch in Utah (USA). Wind erosion has cut along vertical joint planes, leaving columns of rock isolated, and has carved an arch in the process.

Right: Two glaciers flow like rivers of ice into the sea at Spitzbergen in the Arctic. They have carved steep-sided, U-shaped valleys, with floors well below sea-level. Stresses within the moving glaciers cause cracks and crevasses in the surface. The tops of the mountains show the sharply fretted shapes created by frost.

spiration (the total loss of moisture in the form of water vapour) typical of tropical areas: Much of such *effective* precipitation infiltrates the soil.

Usually, water percolates vertically through soil, then down through the pores and joints of the underlying rock, where it increases the store of underground water. This water slowly continues to attack the deep rock, termed *deep-weathering*, an action which, in tropical areas, may extend down to 100 m (over 300 ft) below the land surface. Such effects on landforms are most thoroughly investigated in limestone terrains.

Regions of ice and snow

In the higher latitudes and at higher altitudes, an important concept may be the *snowline*, often defined as the lower limit of perennial snow. Snow becomes consolidated beneath accumulations which are at least 30 m thick and it recrystallizes into granular snow or *firn* and finally into ice. The observation, measurement and understanding of the physical mechanisms by which ice begins to flow downvalley as a *glacier* are an exceptional challenge to all the skills of the glaciologist. Although glacier-flow velocities range from a few millimetres to a few metres each year, large volumes of soil, frost-shattered debris and deep-weathered materials are pushed forward by the glacier's advance.

The land surfaces of glaciated uplands are thus areas of gaunt, bare-rock outcrops. By contrast, after the ice has retreated, lowland areas of glacial deposition are often paved smooth by a thick layer of *ground moraine*, composed of the debris dragged along at the base or *sole* of the glacier.

A significant portion of the debris moved by ice is initially loosened and transported by *periglaciation*. This term refers to a set of processes associated with the repetitive fluctuation between intense freezing and thawing characteristic of zones marginal to ice-caps, or, indeed, of any bare ground where the annual temperature is at or below freezing point. The ground of such areas is usually permanently frozen, a condition termed *permafrost*. However, the top metre or so often melts in summer and periglaciation includes the rapid downslope debris movements termed *solifluction* that then occur in this thawed or 'active' layer above the permafrost.

A compelling fascination about landforms is to enquire how long they have been there or perhaps how they may have changed with the passage of time. However, it is no longer thought realistic to confine consideration of the stages in the evolution of a land surface within an over-idealized framework. One reason is the number of quite extraordinary and rapid oscillations in ice volumes and in areas covered by ice that occurred in the high latitudes during the Ice Age of the Pleistocene epoch. Moreover, there were repeated oscillations of climate from rainy periods or *pluvials* to dry phases or *inter-pluvials* in lower latitudes.

Geomorphology includes the study of the narrow zone where land meets sea. Somewhere within that zone, geomorphology hands over to oceanography, but along the coast itself the influence of geological control and the nature and role of processes of rock breakdown, transport and deposition are as obvious as anywhere inland.

The Grand Canyon in northwest Arizona is one of the most magnificent sections of the great gorge of the Colorado river. The Canyon is 217 miles (349km) long and between 4 and 18 miles (6-29km) wide.

Rocks and Landscapes

The hills, valleys, plains and bays that form the landscape we see around us are sculptured by the processes of weathering, and then shaped by the erosion and deposition of rivers, glaciers, wind and sea. Nevertheless, these relief features depend on geology, for both the nature or *lithology* of the rocks and their structures are fundamental to visible landforms.

Igneous and metamorphic rocks, because of their interlocking crystalline texture, are usually resistant to erosion and tend to stand up as high ground. This resistance, however, also depends upon the chemical stability of the minerals making up the rocks.

Some minerals resist chemical weathering better than others. For example, quartz and white mica, which form a large part of granite, are relatively stable. But feldspar, the most common mineral in most igneous and metamorphic rocks, is less stable and tends to break down to form clay. Silicates of iron and magnesium, abundant in *basic* (low silica content) igneous rocks like basalt and dolerite, decompose still more readily under weathering.

Granite therefore usually forms high ground, as in Dartmoor in south-western England and the Cheviot Hills between England and Scotland. Basalt, dolerite and gabbro, on the other hand, may or may not form high ground, depending upon how active chemical weathering is. This in turn depends mainly upon the climate.

Young volcanoes usually form steep hills of lava and volcanic ash, but are eroded comparatively quickly. Volcanic *necks* (the pipes of old volcanoes, from which the surrounding deposits of lava and ash have been eroded away) often form sharp hills. A familiar example is Edinburgh's Castle Rock, the remains of the Arthur's Seat volcano which was active 325 million years ago.

Metamorphic rocks are sometimes more resistant than igneous rocks, as they have been intensely compressed. And sedimentary rocks vary still more in their resistance to erosion. Clay rocks are chemically stable, but are physically very unstable. They tend to 'flow' downhill and collapse along slip planes and so will stand at only a very low angle. This means that any hillside slopes formed of clay or shale will necessarily be gentle and the side view or transverse *profile* of a valley eroded in such rocks will appear wide and low-angled.

Sandstones and limestones do not have this tendency to flow and usually stand at a high angle with consequently steeper slopes. When alternated with clays, the sandstones or limestones often stand out as steep, bare edges, separated by gentler, grassy slopes on the clays. However, this arrangement is obviously dependent upon the extent of rock consolidation. In the case of sandstones this is determined by the degree of cementation; in limestones it depends on the degree of crystallization. Unconsolidated sand, for example, will stand in steeper faces than clay, but not as steep as a well-cemented sandstone.

Chalk country is characterized by

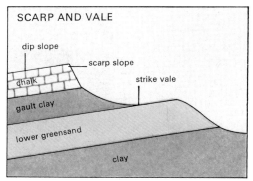

SCARP AND VALE

dip slope
scarp slope
chalk
strike vale
gault clay
lower greensand
clay

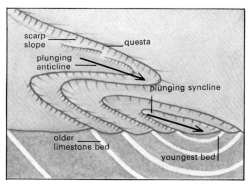

scarp slope
questa
plunging anticline
plunging syncline
older limestone bed
youngest bed

Above: The scarp at the Devil's Dyke in Sussex.

Left: The section shows that the hills, formed of chalk, are dipping to the left, with a steep scarp slope facing north. Beneath the chalk is the Gault Clay which has been eroded to form a strike vale. The Lower Greensand forms a ridge further north.

Below: A section taken through a rift valley bounded by successive fault scarps. The faults have thrown the strata down on both sides, so that a low strip of land runs along the centre, often the site of a river. Most rift valleys have one dominating pair of faults, but some, like this one, are formed by a number of small faults.

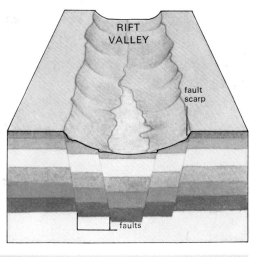

RIFT VALLEY

fault scarp

faults

Right: The view from the summit of St Victor in south-west France, an area of much folding. The anticline (upfold) and syncline (downfold) share an axis of folding (as shown above) which is plunging to the right. Resistant limestones, interbedded with less resistant strata, form ridges or cuestas. These curve round the plunging folds and are bare of covering vegetation. On the anticline the oldest beds come to the surface in the centre and are surrounded on three sides by the steep scarp slopes of the limestones. As the limestones are dipping away from the crest of the anticline, their dip-slopes stretch away from the outcrop of the oldest beds. On the syncline the youngest beds appear in the centre.

gently rounded hills with no steep slopes. The Salisbury Plain and the Chilterns of England, for example, are wide areas of grassy downs and smooth, rolling hills where the occasional chalk pit unveils the underlying rock. Chalk is an example of a poorly-crystallized limestone which is liable to flow downhill, especially under the influence of alternate freezing and thawing of the water it contains. On the other hand, a thoroughly crystalline limestone, as in the Pennines or the Niagara Limestone over which the Niagara Falls plunge, will easily stand in resistant, vertical faces.

The steepness of the slopes of a valley-side depends upon the relationship between the rate of erosion by the river running through the valley and the rate of movement downhill of rock material weathered from the sides of the valley. Anything which gives the river an advantage over the downhill movement will produce a steeper profile. Downhill movement may be inhibited by resistant rocks, or the energy of the river may be increased by recent uplift of the area. Conversely, the nature of clay gives the advantage to downhill movement and a gentler profile will result.

The influence of rock structure

The famous six-sided columns of basalt at the Giants' Causeway in Northern Ireland show how the shape of a landscape is influenced by the structure of the rocks, and not just by their nature. Structure is primarily important in opening the rocks to attack from rain, ice and streams along joints and faults. *Joints* are fractures in the rock along which there has been little or none of the movement associated with faults. But both these features act as planes of weakness where weathering and erosion can work effectively. The pattern of a river system is often found to be guided by joints and faults and this confirms that running water finds it easiest to erode the rocks along such planes.

When a fault has recently taken place—'recently' in a geological sense can, of course, extend to two or three million years—the fault plane is visible as a steep slope or *fault scarp*. A *rift valley*, for example, is a strip of country let down between two fault scarps, like the East African Rift Valley and the Rhine valley between Basel and Bingen. The opposite is a *block mountain*, a block of land pushed up between two fault scarps.

Eventually a primary fault scarp will become eroded away. More resistant rocks may, however, have been thrown by the fault against less resistant rocks. In that case the more resistant rocks, whether they are on the upthrown or the downthrown side of the fault, will be less affected by erosion and will stand up parallel to the outcrop of the fault as a *fault-line scarp*. The edge of the Ochil Hills near Stirling in Scotland and the northern front of the Harz Mountains in Germany are good examples.

Where inclined or *dipping* rock beds are being eroded, the more resistant strata will stand up as ridges, or *cuestas*, while the less resistant ones are eroded to form strips of lowland or *strike vales* between the ridges. In the scarp and vale landscape of the Weald in southern England, the Chalk and the Lower Greensand form cuestas separated by the vale of the Gault Clay. Another very good example can be seen further north in Shropshire, where

limestones form the cuestas of Wenlock Edge and View Edge, with the strike vale of Hope Dale on shales between them.

A different, but equally distinctive, landscape is found in regions subjected to folding. In the simplest case, the *anticlines* of the folds form hills and the *synclines* appear as valleys. Such simple correspondence is rare, but good examples are found in the Jura Mountains of eastern France and Switzerland. Here resistant limestones have preserved the anticlines from erosion.

It is much more usual for anticlines to have been breached by erosion. When this happens, the more resistant beds form cuestas which slope in opposite directions on the two sides of the fold, with the scarp slopes facing towards each other in an anticline and facing away from each other in a syncline. For example, the scarp slopes of the South Downs and the North Downs, both formed by chalk, face each other across the Weald. In fact, it is common to find that anticlines have been hollowed out to form valleys while synclines stand up to form hills, so that the topography is opposite to the structure. Although this is known as *inverted relief*, it is in fact the more usual case in an area where the rocks have been folded.

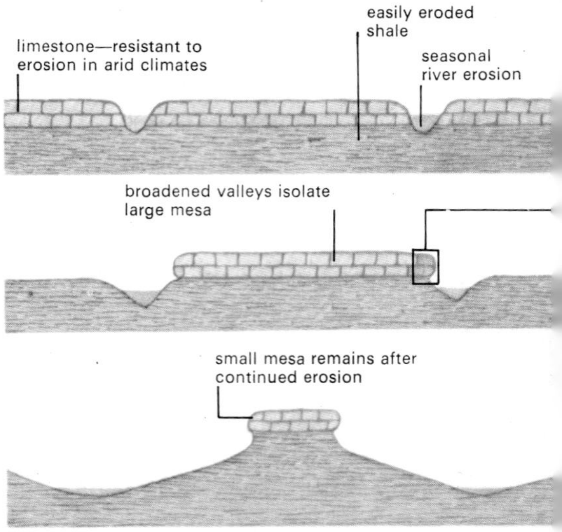

Above: How a mesa is formed: where resistant rocks are horizontal and lie over less resistant beds, weathering and erosion tend to work down the main joints until the soft rock is exposed. This is then easily eroded, leaving a remnant of the resistant bed as an isolated table which becomes steadily reduced in size.

Below: Monument Valley in Utah (USA) is famous for its sculptured mesas. In this arid region, wind has probably done most of the erosion. The steep angle of slopes on the resistant sandstones contrasts sharply with the more gentle slopes formed by the debris eroded from the less resistant shales.

[diagram labels:]
limestone—resistant to erosion in arid climates
easily eroded shale
seasonal river erosion
broadened valleys isolate large mesa
small mesa remains after continued erosion

Picturepoint

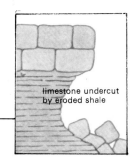

Below: The spectacular Giants' Causeway in Antrim, Northern Ireland. The regular six-sided columns of basalt were formed long ago by rapidly cooling volcanic lava flowing into the sea. Today, these joints act as planes of weakness where weathering and erosion by water, sea and ice are constantly wearing away the columns.

Spectrum

Right: The spectacular Niagara Falls interrupt the flow of water from Lake Erie to Lake Ontario. At the Falls, the massive, resistant and almost horizontal Niagara Limestone caps less resistant shale. The shale is being rapidly eroded into a deep plunge pool (left) beneath the falls and, as this is enlarged, the undercut limestone collapses along its main joints. Large limestone blocks can be seen in the foreground of the photograph. These will eventually become broken up by weathering and carried away by the river. In this way, the limestone edge is being cut back and the falls are retreating upstream towards Lake Erie by about 1m each year.

istant estone

undercut rock is likely to collapse

less resistant shale

plunge pool

ROCKS AND THEIR ORIGINS

There are three kinds of rocks. **Igneous** rocks have cooled and solidified from molten rock material or *magma* produced by heating deep in the earth. The magma is squeezed upwards through the earth's crust and may be forced in among the pre-existing rocks where it solidifies as *intrusive* igneous rock. Granite is a well-known example. Alternatively, magma may reach the surface at a volcano and flow out as *lava* to solidify as *extrusive* igneous rock, of which basalt is a common example.

During cooling the constituent minerals crystallize out from the molten mass, in approximately the reverse order of their melting points (the temperature at which minerals become molten). Consequently, an igneous rock is composed of interlocking crystals.

Sedimentary rocks are composed of fragments derived from weathering of pre-existing rocks. The fragments are commonly transported by wind, water or ice and deposited, usually in water and especially on the sea-floor, where the sediments become compacted to form rocks. There are again three main types of sedimentary rocks. First, there are those in which the fragments are recognizable pebbles of pre-existing rocks (*conglomerates*) or grains of identifiable minerals (*sandstones*). These rocks become consolidated when mineral matter becomes deposited between the particles to act as a cement. The second type is *clay*, in which the particles are extremely minute crystals of clay minerals formed from the chemical breakdown of other minerals during weathering.

Chemical deposits form the third main type of sedimentary rock. These are composed of material dissolved out of pre-existing rocks during weathering. The most important of this type is limestone, often formed of calcium carbonate from the shells and skeletal remains of dead animals accumulated on the sea-floor. Recrystallization takes place and the calcium carbonate consolidates to form limestone.

Metamorphic rocks were originally either igneous or sedimentary rocks which were thoroughly altered or *metamorphosed* by heat and pressure within the crust of the earth without being completely melted. In its original form marble, for example, was limestone.

IGS

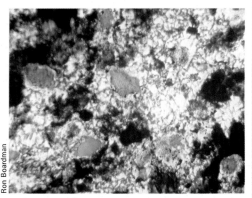

Ron Boardman

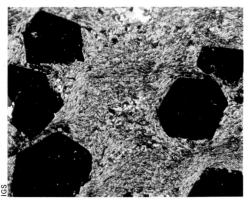

IGS

Above: Examples of the three main types of rock photographed under a microscope between crossed-polarizing lenses. This process gives distinctive colours to minerals. The igneous *gabbro* (top) is made up of intimately interlocking crystals of feldspar (black and white stripes) and silicates of iron and magnesium. The sedimentary *sandstone* (centre) is composed of grains of quartz (bright blue) cemented together by chert (fine-grained silica). The *schist* (bottom) is mainly composed of mica, but the large black crystals of garnet grew in the rock during its metamorphism.

Canadian High Commission

Climate and Landforms

In 1883, Albrecht Penck, a German, became the first geomorphologist to consider the possible relationship between distinctive climates and landform development. Later, in 1910, he suggested that five separate landform groupings could be recognized in the world from their correspondence to climatic regions. The five regions were *humid* (moist) and *sub-humid* areas, where precipitation exceeds evaporation; *arid* (dry) and *semi-arid* areas, where evaporation exceeds precipitation; and *glacial* areas, where the land surface is shaped by a mass of moving ice.

At the same time W. M. Davis, an American whom many call the 'father of geomorphology', put forward his theory of the *geographical cycle of erosion*. He suggested that, depending on the rock structure, landforms develop in stages through a 'normal' cycle of erosion in which running water is the dominant process. 'Landscape', he said, 'is a function of structure, process and stage.'

Davis's cycle, which really described the evolution of steep slopes (young landscapes) to a level surface or *peneplain* (old landscapes), was based upon humid, temperate conditions which he considered as 'normal'. In these 'normal' areas, slope angles vary, but are usually *convex* (bulging) on their upper parts and *concave* (hollowed) on their lower parts and have a relatively uniform covering of rock debris. Landforms which developed in extremely cold or hot areas, he considered climatic accidents or interruptions to the 'normal' development. Later, however, he too recognized special cycles for arid and glacial areas.

Differences of opinion

The ideas of Penck and Davis were the beginnings of *climatic geomorphology*, the study of climatic influence on landforms. Although their notions are now thought to be gross over-simplifications, both men were very influential at the time. After Penck, other Germans such as Carl Troll and Julius Budel, and the Frenchmen Jean Tricart and André Cailleux, have developed the concepts of climatic control of landforms, whereas in the US and Britain the idea has diminished in popularity. Most English-speaking geomorphologists either assume climate to be of secondary importance or neglect it altogether. Instead, emphasis has been placed more on the processes of weathering and erosion themselves.

This difference may be attributed to the emphasis given by the German scientists to detailed landform description rather than explanation. Or it may have been due to the language barrier, which enabled British and American workers to criticize and reappraise Davis's theories of landform evolution whilst overlooking the ideas of climatic influences developed by Penck.

There are some processes, such as the action of ice, which are limited to certain climatic areas. Glaciated areas at high latitudes, and elsewhere in mountainous regions, produce unique landforms, such as deposited *moraines* and U-shaped

D. H. Teuffen/ZEFA

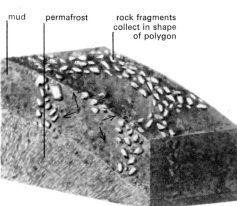

mud permafrost rock fragments collect in shape of polygon

STONE POLYGONS AND STRIPES

Above: A typical U-shaped valley created by glacial erosion in the Swiss Alps. Glaciers and frost shattering shape landforms unique to very cold, wet climates; but similar features exist in more temperate areas which were once glaciated. England's Duddon Valley (above centre) derives its primary shape from Ice Age glaciation, but the rounded hilltops and slopes are typical of humid, temperate areas.

Left and below: Some distinctive ground patterns only occur in periglacial regions. Repeated freezing and thawing force coarser rock fragments through the mud to collect in curious shapes, which depend on the angle of slope as shown below.

Right: A world map drawn by Büdel in 1970 to show the relations of climate to general patterns of existing landforms (high mountains are excluded). Büdel recognized the importance of past as well as present climates, and his regions do not coincide with those on a world climate map.

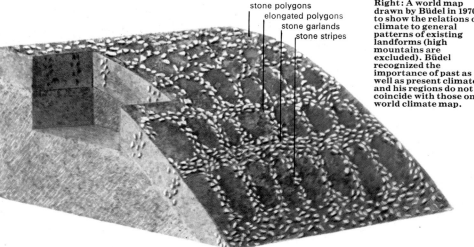

stone polygons
elongated polygons
stone garlands
stone stripes

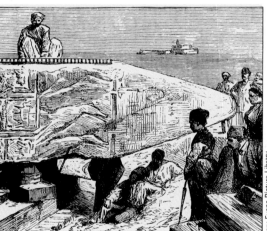

Above: In extremely arid areas like the Namib desert, climate affects landforms largely by inhibiting the growth of vegetation. There is little or nothing to bind the unconsolidated surface materials and strong winds can then sweep the loose particles into giant sand dunes.

Left and right: Cleopatra's Needle, an Egyptian obelisk of granite, was presented to the British people in 1878. It now stands on the Thames Embankment (right). However, after only a century of exposure to the humid, temperate atmosphere of London, it has weathered more extensively than after 3,500 years of exposure in Egypt's arid environment.

valleys. On the margins of glacial areas, in *periglacial* regions, where mean annual temperatures are still low but the temperature range is greater, other distinctive forms are found.

Here *mechanical weathering* or physical disintegration is more important than *chemical weathering*, in which rock decomposition is achieved by agents such as water, carbon dioxide or organic acids. In cold, moist periglacial conditions, the lack of vegetation and the low temperatures retard chemical reactions, but abundant moisture and frequent freezing and thawing of ice and snow in rock joints and below ground is highly conducive to mechanical disintegration.

Mechanical weathering by frost-shattering is most important in high mountain or *alpine* areas and in the vast, treeless plains known as *tundra* in North America and Siberia. As a result, the debris produced there is typically angular in shape. Because water increases its volume by nine per cent on freezing, its presence in rock joints and pores can easily shatter rocks. Low temperatures alone are not sufficient but prolonged temperature fluctuations around 0°C will cause severe breakage if water is available. In addition, the daily freezing and thawing of the 'active layer' above the permanently frozen subsoil or *permafrost* may create a mobile surface of mud and rock fragments. In such climates wind action is strong but water removal is sporadic and weak as most water is frozen.

The topography created as a result is unique. Steep rocky cliffs tower over layers of frost-shattered debris known as *scree* or *talus*. On gentler slopes, slow downhill flow or *solifluction* of saturated

- glacial zone
- periglacial zone of deep rectangular valleys
- temperate zone of broad rounded valley formation
- semi-arid zone of mixed pediments and valleys
- arid zone of pediment formation
- tropical zone of flat planation surfaces
- equatorial zone with some planation surfaces

BUDEL'S MORPHOGENETIC REGIONS

81

rock decomposed by chemical weathering

solid rock

George Hall/Susan Griggs

Colorific !

Left: Climate rarely acts alone in shaping landforms. Ayer's Rock in Australia is a giant dome of sandstone and conglomerates. Earth movements tipped the strata into a vertical position and erosion removed less resistant rocks to form an almost level erosion plain or *pediplain*. Present-day erosion processes have rounded the surface, but the rock structure is mainly responsible for this feature.

Above right: How an inselberg is formed: (1) With high temperatures and seasonal abundance of surface and ground water, chemical weathering may penetrate to great depths. (2) An irregular weathering 'floor' in the rocks often forms due to local differences in rock resistance and jointing. Subsurface domes are produced. (3) When erosion removes the weathered surface rock, the domes are exposed. Subsequent disintegration of the outcrops produces *inselbergs* 'island mounds' typical of arid and tropical areas.

Right: Isolated inselbergs found in Iran.

Left: A reef of coral fringing the Society Is. in the Pacific. Coral reefs are an indisputable example of landform determined by climate— they grow only in seas where temperature never falls below 18°C.

Below: The gaunt topography of dry regions is shown in this view of Dead Horse Point, Utah.

rock fragments and mud often occurs, giving rise to huge valley-side lobes, and mass movements such as *rockfalls* and *landslides* are common in the unconsolidated surface materials. On level ground occur plateaux of frost-shattered boulders, known as *blockfields*, and poorly-drained plains covered with curious ice-formed patterns and hollows. Braided river channels interweave through wide, rock-choked alluvial valleys.

By contrast, landforms in arid and semi-arid areas are quite different. These dry landscapes take many forms, from the deeply-dissected plateau blocks of the south-western USA to the flat, eroded plains of Africa and Australia; from stony deserts to sandy dunes. Two essential features are apparent in arid and semi-arid landscapes. Firstly, the existence of broad, gently-sloping surfaces known as *pediments* descending from steep slopes distinguishes dry climate landscapes from all others. Secondly, the angularity and sharpness of the landform profiles are impressive: the slightest change in rock type is at once reflected by a sharp break in slope.

A wide 24-hour temperature range, small but critical water supply, strong winds, lack of vegetation and the occurence of flash floods are the factors controlling landform development in arid climates. One of the major causes of rock decay is mechanical weathering by *insolation* (expansion and contraction of rock minerals by rapid heating and cooling); other causes are *salt crystal growth* and very active chemical weathering induced by high temperatures acting with small amounts of rainfall and dew.

ZEFA

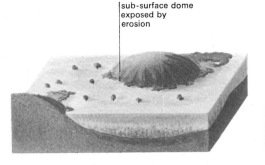

sub-surface dome
exposed by
erosion

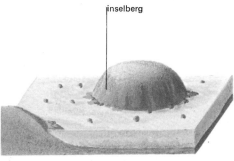

inselberg

C. Weaver/Ardea

valleys is determined by the typically 'convexo-concave' shaped hillslopes. Both mechanical and chemical weathering processes occur but the relative importance of each depends upon local conditions such as rock type, exposure, temperature and the amount of water present. Neither process acts as intensely as in polar or tropical climates.

Transportation of debris in river systems is most effective in this area because the amount of sediment supplied is roughly equal to the ability of the stream to transport it. As a result, the channel is not overloaded with coarse debris as in periglacial areas, nor is it laden with fine silt and dissolved material as in tropical areas.

Mapping the effects of climate

In 1948, Julius Büdel devised a world map showing the distribution of nine *morphogenetic regions*, in which distinctive individual landforms and physical landscapes are found, and in which the same geomorphic processes are supposed to predominate. The variations between these regions, however, do not arise because processes are operating there which do not occur elsewhere. Rather, the landforms are shaped by the way in which 'universal' geomorphic processes operate in different climates.

Several geomorphologists have tried to map the distribution of such large-scale regions. For example, one French scientist, Louis Peltier, even used measurements of temperature and precipitation to define his morphogenetic regions. None of these classifications, however, accurately shows the world distribution of landforms as it presently exists. There are a number of reasons why this is so.

The detailed form of most landscapes reflects past as well as present climatic effects. In *polygenetic* landscapes, several types of climatic conditions have left their imprint. This is especially so in middle-latitude, temperate areas which have experienced many fluctuating cycles of glacial and periglacial conditions. Many parts of Britain, for instance, have glacial valleys. Similarly many of the blockfields of present periglacial regions, and dry river channels or *wadis* in deserts, are due to former climates when conditions were very different.

Many so-called distinctive climatic landforms occur in widely differing climatic zones. Inselbergs, for example, occur in both arid and humid areas. Similar forms often develop in different rock types from a different set of processes and in different climates. Moreover, when landforms over small areas are considered, no clear relationship with climate emerges.

Today, geomorphologists do not agree on the relative importance of climate in landform development. It is possible that the influence of climate is felt most directly through the effect of vegetation. Certainly vegetation greatly affects the nature of the processes operating. It also seems that many landforms are influenced more by infrequent climatic events than they are by average or typical events. This is the case with rivers where the shape of the channel is generally adjusted to the maximum flow rather than the average, and in deserts where the most important landform modifications are brought about by the occasional flash flood.

HUMID TEMPERATE LANDSCAPE

harder rock eroded down

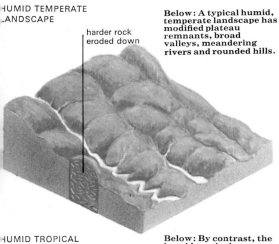

Below: A typical humid, temperate landscape has modified plateau remnants, broad valleys, meandering rivers and rounded hills.

HUMID TROPICAL LANDSCAPE

harder rock forms prominent hill

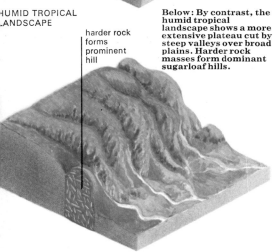

Below: By contrast, the humid tropical landscape shows a more extensive plateau cut by steep valleys over broad plains. Harder rock masses form dominant sugarloaf hills.

In the drier parts, combined mechanical and chemical weathering affects only rock cracks. Intervening grains are loosened to produce mostly granular sands. With sparse vegetation and strong winds these are soon removed or used to carve wind-blasted stones. Residual hills known as *mesas* or *buttes* are often left isolated due to the protection of more resistant cap rock.

In semi-arid climates, increased water leads to a more extensive penetration of rock joints and the production of rounded boulders from joint blocks. Active erosion by *sheet wash*, a broad flood of rainwater, in wet periods easily removes the surrounding weathered mantle, leaving only isolated hills called *inselbergs* or piles of rocky boulders, *castle koppies*, rising above a flat surface.

In humid, tropical climates chemical weathering is extremely intense. Soluble products of weathering such as calcium bicarbonate are removed by rainwater into the river system. On slopes, however, rock decomposition is generally faster than the transport of slope material. Consequently, deep soils are formed of the abundant clays produced by chemical weathering aided by intense biochemical activity. It is the balance between the products of weathering and the effects of heavy tropical rain which controls slope evolution in this zone. Rounded hillslopes, sugarloaf-shaped hills, and silty rivers are the typical landforms of tropical regions.

The highly variable landforms of temperate areas show forms intermediate between those of arid and humid, cold and tropical areas. As has been observed, a rolling landscape of hills and broad

Desert Landscapes

Approximately one-third of the earth's land surface has a scarcity of water. Some of these arid (dry) and semi-arid regions, like the Sahara and Kalahari of Africa, the Thar in India and Pakistan, and the great Australian desert, are vast, hot deserts, created mainly by the global pattern of climate. Other arid zones, such as the Great Basin and Mohave deserts of the United States and the Gobi desert in Mongolia, are sheltered from rain by mountain ranges or vast continental expanses.

Dry regions may be broadly described as deserts or semi-deserts, but not all of them are hot. Patagonia in South America and the Siberian steppes, for example, are seasonally very cold. But in all deserts the amount of moisture that can be lost through evaporation exceeds the amount of water received as precipitation.

As a result of this deficiency of water, vegetation is either totally lacking or very sparse, and consists of remarkable drought-resistant species of plants such as the American cacti. Despite the wide range of rock types and topographies found in arid areas, certain very distinctive landforms are produced. These are the result of the predominance of bare ground, and the effects of infrequent, and often violent, rainfall and high *insolation* (radiation received from the sun).

Wind and sand

Deserts are often thought of as vast expanses of drifting sands. Yet, no more than 30 per cent of the Arabian desert, for example, is sandy terrain, and only 11 per cent of the Sahara and two per cent of North America's arid lands are sand deserts. These wastes are dominated by seas of sand (known as *ergs* in the Sahara) which are swept by the wind into ripples, dunes and sand ridges, some of which are 450 m (1,500 ft) high. The distance between adjacent crests, the *wavelength* of these features, tends to grow when the dominant wind speed increases.

Wind is a major agent of removal and transportation in deserts. The process by which unconsolidated sand and dust is caught up and swept away by wind is termed *deflation*. Eventually, such material is deposited to form ripples, dunes, sand ridges and sheets of loess.

Ripples form transversely to the wind direction. Some are *aerodynamic ripples*, created by regular patterns of turbulence in the moving air. Others are *ballistic ripples*, formed by the bouncing motion or *saltation* of most wind-blown sands. When a saltating grain lands, it ejects several other grains into the airstream. In their turn, these grains land downwind

Photri

Left: The effect of weathering is clearly visible in deserts. This rock in Death Valley, California, was attacked at its base by chemical and mechanical weathering and the wind has removed the debris to reveal its shape.

Right: A satellite photograph of the Namib Desert, SW Africa. This view, covering about 40,000 sq km, shows a series of enormous dunes (lower left) which were swept into parallel lines by off-shore winds. North of the Kuiseb River, an eroded landscape of Pre-Cambrian rocks is partially veneered by sand. The large sand-bar in the middle part of the Atlantic coast forms Walvis Bay, the largest settlement in this thinly-populated but diamond-rich desert.

Below: The Bad Lands of South Dakota give their name to badly gullied, semi-arid areas. Once natural vegetation is removed by man, short but violent flash floods erode weak and unprotected sediments into an intricate pattern of gullies. More resistant beds form ledges and benches.

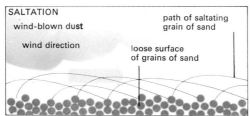

SALTATION
wind-blown dust
path of saltating grain of sand
wind direction
loose surface of grains of sand

Left: This illustration shows the bouncing movement or *saltation* of wind-blown grains over a sandy surface.

Right: The alignment of long, narrow sharp-crested dunes, known in the Sahara as *seifs*, is the result of the combined effect of winds blowing in different directions.

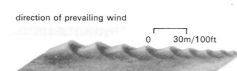

SEIF DUNE

direction of prevailing wind

0   30m/100ft

sand blown up windward slope

at a distance equivalent to one bounce, dislodge more grains, and so perpetuate a regular spacing between the ripples created in the sand.

Dunes come in a wide range of shapes, sizes and patterns. The classic crescent-shaped *barchan* is only found on hard desert surfaces which have little sand covering. A barchan has a gentle wind-ward face and a steep leeward or slip face. Sand is swept over the crest and slides and slumps until it reaches its angle of rest (typically 34°). As a result of this transfer of sand, the dune slowly advances. The margins of the original mound, being lower, move more quickly and so develop into the characteristic horns.

Sand ridges and dunes occur also in long, narrow lines. These linear types may be parallel, diagonal or transverse to the dominant winds, and their align-ments can sometimes be traced over tens, or even hundreds, of kilometres. The alignment of some of the long and narrow sharp-crested dunes known as *siefs* results from the combined effect of all the local winds which are capable of moving sand. Others arise from the interaction between a dominant wind and a cross wind. Even more complex wind patterns are thought to account for intersecting linear dunes and for sand mountains called *rhourds*.

Large sand grains are said to 'creep' when rolled by the wind or nudged along by saltating particles. Those which are fine enough to be held aloft in suspension by the wind may be carried far afield. The 'blood rains' occasionally experienced in Italy and other parts of Europe, for example, are coloured by red Saharan sand blown across the Mediterranean Sea. Extensive sheets of such fine dust, or silt, laid down by the wind are called *loess*. They resist further wind displacement because the particles tend to stick together to form a protective *silt crust*. But once the surface is broken up—perhaps by animal hooves, ploughs or traffic—defla-tion readily follows. This has created disastrous results in areas such as the North American prairies. In the 1930s, for example, the 'dust bowl' of the Midwest was created by the ploughing up of prairie lands—devastating dust storms resulted which removed vast amounts of soil.

Despite both the spectacular nature of dust storms, however, and the likelihood that the breakage of colliding sand grains is constantly producing additional particles, the volume of dust generated by deserts appears to be inadequate to account for any of the world's major loess deposits. The loess of the Huang Ho valley in China, for example, is usually traced to the Gobi Desert. However, it is more likely that it consists of silt produced by the grinding action of mountain glaciers from the Pleistocene epoch.

Where deflation removes sand and dust, basin-like depressions are left behind. However, it seems unlikely that this process alone could account for some of

Above right: An approaching sandstorm in the Sahara. The finer particles in sand deserts are swept up and kept in suspension by air turbulence. If the winds are strong enough, sand as well as dust is blown along and threatens unwary travellers with burial.

Right: These hillocks in the Sarazac area of northern Chad are called *yardangs*. Ancient lake beds were weakened by salt weathering and then carved by sand-laden winds into streamlined, undercut hillocks. The ridges are roughly parallel and lie in the direction of the dominant wind.

Right: Tall sharp-crested sand dunes tower over the palm trees at an oasis in the Sahara. Plant roots bind the sand and help prevent it being carried away by the wind. However, dunes may gradually encroach on an oasis and bury it.

Below: How a *barchan* is formed. These crescent-shaped dunes generally develop over hard, poorly-sanded desert surfaces. Having accumulated, the sand moves forward as grains blown up the windward side fall over the lee side to form a slip face. The sides of the mound, being lower, move faster.

BARCHAN

slip face

0   3m/10ft

horns of dune

Right: Unlike the barchan sand dune, this *parabolic dune* travels with its points trailing behind. Also known as a 'blow out', this type of 'hollow' dune may be the result of upsetting the delicate balance between vegetation and sand, exposing loose, finely-grained sand which is easily carried forward by the wind.

PARABOLIC DUNE

0   6m/20ft

blow out hollow

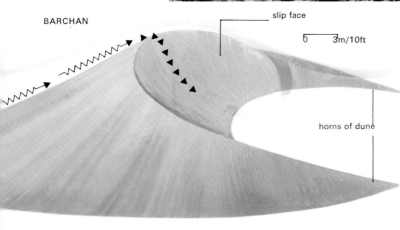

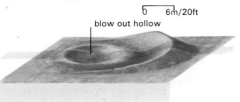

the giant hollows, such as the Qattara Depression of Egypt, which are found on arid plains. The Qattara Depression is over 160 km (100 miles) wide, and the soft shale floor lies over 300 m (100 ft) below the level of the surrounding limestone plateau.

Wind is very ineffective in eroding solid rock. Unless armed with abrasive particles, it lacks 'teeth' and even when suitably equipped for erosion its action is confined to within a few metres above the ground. The only landforms definitely shaped by wind erosion are streamlined, undercut hillocks called *yardangs*, carved from soft deposits such as lake clays. Some major channels cut into the rock in the Sahara are thought to be of similar origin, but they could well have been scoured out by glaciation of the area some 450 million years ago.

Rocky deserts

Most of the world's arid landscapes, both lowlying and mountainous, have rocky surfaces. Rock breakdown is performed by a variety of agents. At high altitudes, and in the cold, continental deserts, frost weathering produces coarse, angular debris. Elsewhere, salts—brought to the surface by high evaporation— enlarge cracks and pores in the rocks when they crystallize, or when the crystals themselves expand on combining with water and on being heated by the sun.

The extent to which temperature fluctuations cause rock breakdown remains controversial. Some geologists attribute mysterious 'shots' heard in the desert to the collapse of stressed rocks, and others explain them as pistol shots. On the other hand, it is clear that plant roots, lichens, and the cycles of wetting and drying created by dew formation, are all effective agents of breakdown.

Fluctuations in temperature, as well as chemical changes, promote the distinctive onion-like peeling called *exfoliation* of granitic and other rocks. Similarly, hollows or *tafoni* worn in rock faces by weathering promote their own expansion by harbouring moisture. Eventually, a striking honeycomb effect is produced.

On some desert floors, the stones fit closely together as though deliberately laid down in a mosaic. These gravelly *desert pavements* are produced by the removal of fine debris by wind and water and the upward migration of stones through mixed ground deposits, following repeated cycles of wetting and drying or of freezing and thawing. Local names for this feature include *gibber plain* in Australia and *hammada* in North Africa. The stones are commonly coated with dark 'desert varnish' composed of iron and manganese oxides. Desert varnish also occurs on rock faces, and iron oxide coatings account for the characteristic redness of many desert sands. In this sense the colourfulness of arid landscapes is only 'skin deep'.

In semi-arid areas, the landscape features may be capped by pale crusts of calcium carbonate or of gypsum. These minerals are either derived from waters drawn to the surface by capillary flow and brought in by rare floods, or have formed beneath the surface and been subsequently exposed by the erosion of the overlying material. These crusts are often very resistant to erosion and tend to fossilize the topographies on which they have developed.

Above: This steep-sided ravine in Tunisia is a *wadi*. The violent floods that occasionally sweep down rocky desert wadis carry a heavy load and can achieve a great deal of erosion during their brief lives. In addition, the flood waters carry away rock material loosened by weathering, leaving behind the more resistant rock strata. The sharp, angular landscape is typical of many arid areas.

Below: Death Valley in California exhibits a variety of arid landforms. In some places, great dunes have formed from drifting sand. This view of another part of the valley from Zabriskie Point shows the dramatic effect of desert floods. Deep gullies have been eroded and the valley floor is choked by the heavy load of sediments washed down by the flood-waters from distant mountains. The exposed sediments reveal the lines of flow and their colour and composition are in marked contrast to those of the local rocks.

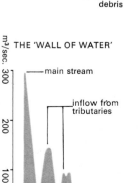

band of resistant rock

accumulated debris

m³/sec. THE 'WALL OF WATER'

main stream

inflow from tributaries

0 4 8 12 16 20 24 hours

Below: The landscape of arid and semi-arid regions is distinctive. Steep cliffs rise above shattered rock debris and flat areas of alluvium. When the infrequent downpours follow the same course, they cut deep, wide channels, leaving wadis and residual mesas and buttes. Dry conditions help to maintain the steep sides. Where the wadis open onto a plain, the streams dump their loads and build up alluvial fans. A series of such fans is termed a *bahada*. If the flow is sufficient to sweep away all the products of weathering, a broad, gently-sloping *pediment* of bedrock is formed. The water itself often flows into saline lakes and evaporates, creating a salt pan.

Above: Prehistoric rock drawings in the Tibesti Mountains of the Sahara. The surfaces of long-exposed rocks and pebbles sometimes gain a coating of iron and manganese oxides and other minerals. The red, brown or black crusts protect the underlying rock. Prehistoric inhabitants of the Sahara scratched out drawings of familiar animals on this 'desert varnish'. The fact that these animals once lived in what is now a barren desert is often cited as evidence of former wet climates in the Sahara.

sa
butte
wadi
run-off channel
gently sloping pediment —sheet wash carries fine debris to the basin
alluvial fan
salt lake
salt pan
note: vertical scale is exaggerated
alluvial fans unite to form a bahada

The spectacular effect of water

When water does flow through desert regions, the effects are dramatic. The great drainage networks characteristic of many arid landscapes have often been explained as relics of wetter climates in the past. But anyone who has witnessed the violence of a desert flood will have little difficulty in accepting that such features are still forming today, albeit in a random fashion.

Dry desert gullies which contain running water only after heavy rainfall are called *wadis* or *arroyos*. The walls of these ravines are typically steep and irregular, and they undermine residual mesas and buttes. Regions which are scored with numerous ravines and gullies carved into alluvium and other weak rocks are called *bad lands*, named after the inhospitable Bad Lands of South Dakota, USA.

In arid regions crossed by rivers which gain their waters elsewhere and manage to maintain a regular flow, very deep valleys or *canyons* are cut into the rocks. The most dramatic of all is the Grand Canyon in the western United States. Carved by the Colorado River on its way from the Rocky Mountains to the Gulf of California, the Grand Canyon extends more than 350 km (217 miles), reaches a depth of over 2,000 m (6,550 ft) and varies from 6.5 km (4 miles) to 21 km (13 miles) wide.

The growth of drainage channels, however, does not depend on water erosion alone. The channels are also shaped by weathering of the valley sides and by mass movement of the resulting debris. This sediment is ultimately carried out of the wadis and gullies to be dumped at the mouths in alluvial fans which, when joined together, produce aprons of alluvium termed *bahadas*. In the absence of fans and bahadas, weathering may act with the spreading floodwaters to produce very gently sloping, broad, rock-cut surfaces termed *pediments*.

Many arid-zone drainage systems fail to reach the sea and are termed *endoreic*. They either fall prey to evaporation and infiltration, or are confined within closed basins. In endoreic systems, the salts carried by run-off gradually accumulate on the floors of temporary lakes to form a salt pan, known as *playa* or *salina* in North America.

Salt pans may be bordered by swamps, as in the Lop Nor basin in China. Saline lakes which increase in size or perhaps only come into being during wet periods sometimes occupy the floor of such desert basins.

Left: Violent downpours on bare desert terrain lead to rapid run-off and flash floods. This graph of the volume of water rushing through a wadi, which was totally dry only a few minutes earlier, plots the sudden flood—described by desert travellers as a 'wall of water'—and the gradual decline after the peak has passed.

Right: A salt pan in the cold, arid region of the Bolivian altiplano, an elevated plateau in the Andes of South America. This salt pan, known locally as *salar*, was deposited when rare flood waters evaporated leaving an accumulation of salts, which are often economically valuable, at the base of an extinct volcano.

Dr. C. Vita-Finzi

87

Slopes and Landslides

Slopes occur in almost all landscapes and, apart from providing variety in the scenery, more significantly they give the geomorphologist clues to the evolution of that landscape. In addition, it is important to understand the processes whereby slopes are formed and changed, since most of man's activities take place on the surface. Soil erosion, damage to property, roads and railways, and even loss of life, may all be avoided to some extent if these processes are understood.

Previously the study of slopes involved the use of simple, descriptive words, such as steep and gentle, feral (uncultivated) and non-feral. Recent research, however, has become more mathematical and slopes are now the subject of careful measurement. One method of gauging the rate of downward movement on a slope, for instance, is to follow the change in position of stakes hammered into the ground. Deeper movements are measured by the use of buried nails or wooden pins, although these can be difficult to retrieve. These two methods are among the easiest and least expensive.

Quantification has revealed the fascinating complexity of slopes. Research topics include, for example, investigation of the angle of inclination at which different soils and rocks tend to remain stable without slipping. One discovery

Dr. Lauri Wright

Above: This island in Fiji in the Pacific presents a panorama of rugged relief composed entirely of slopes. This type of landscape occurs in areas of infrequent but high intensity rainfall. Various processes —such as surface wash, rain splash and chemical weathering—are at work, stripping the slopes of their soil covering.

Robert Harding

Spectrum

Dr. Lauri Wright

Above: In many areas of the world, man has now interrupted the natural slope-forming processes. The most obvious example is terracing, as here in Peru. But deforestation and ploughing have also helped to speed up some processes and initiated others. In extreme cases an accelerated rate of erosion creates severe problems for land use and water supply.

Left: Middle Tongue in the Yorkshire Dales. Smooth, long slopes characterize many of the world's temperate areas, like the British Isles, where the consistent rainfall is of low intensity. Slope processes are usually slow-acting, and solutional weathering and soil creep are important though barely perceptible. Many slopes in these areas originated under a different climate from that occurring today.

Right: Many landslides require a trigger action, such as an earthquake, before movement occurs. This relatively small slide in Buller Gorge, New Zealand, is one of many initiated by the 1968 Murchison earthquake.

pressure of buildings on ground

soaking and drying out of soil
by precipitation and evaporation
loosens grains

movement by animals and humans
disturbs the soil

surface wash carries
soil and stones
down stream

channel flow widens
and deepens streams
bearing away more debris

soil movement
hindered by
vegetation cover

fluctuations in
upper level of
saturated rock

ground
water
infiltration

sub-surface
seepage of
water

soil movement

river erodes
the base
of slopes

expansion and contraction
of soil due to freezing
and thawing

**Above: A landslide
occurs when some
force upsets the
delicate balance between
the stress on a slope
and the resistance of
the soil or rock.**

**Right: A scree slope
looms over the dark
waters of Loch Aire in
Scotland. Screes are a
frequent result of the
destruction of slopes
by frost action. The
loosened material falls
downslope under the pull
of gravity and
accumulates at the base.
The angle of rest is
closely related to the
size and shape of the
fragments. The slope is
often so steep that a
slight disturbance—
perhaps by sheep, whose
tracks can be seen across
the face of this slope—
may send the whole mass
sliding downwards.**

Heather Angel

is that most slope angles fall into two or three groups, 25°-29° slopes predominating in sandstones and shales, for example, while 8°-12° slopes are typical of clays.

Landslides

It has long been known that slopes do change, but attention has previously been focused on the more spectacular events. Among recent ones, these include the landslide which fell into the Vaiont reservoir in Italy in 1963, washing a great wave of water over the dam and causing a flood which killed 3,000 people, and the 1970 Huascaran disaster in Peru of which more than 20,000 people were victims.

Events of this magnitude have occurred from time to time throughout history and evidence of catastrophic landslides goes back into the distant geological past. However, the processes responsible for such devastations are also those which create movements on a much smaller scale, and which affect all slopes to a greater or lesser degree. It is the study of these processes with which much modern research is concerned.

The downward movement of material under the influence of gravity is termed *mass movement* or *mass wasting*. Such movement generally occurs when the force of the weight of rock and soil (and of the water it contains) along with the pull of gravity exceeds the forces of resistance within the rock and soil mass itself. In essence, movement occurs when the balance between *stress* and *resistance* is shifted sufficiently in favour of stress. This effect can be achieved either by an increase in stress or by a reduction in resistance.

Increase in stress can be brought about in a number of ways. Under natural conditions, undercutting by a river or the sea at the base of a slope leaves the slope unsupported, thereby placing greater stress on those parts of the slope lying immediately above. An increased load on the slope, possibly through the addition of rainwater or the deposition of a *moraine* by a glacier would have the same effect. The tilting of an area by geological forces could also be responsible.

Similar effects are often produced by man. The cutting of a road into a hillside effectively undermines the slope, while the dumping of spoil from mines at the top of valley sides increases the load on the slope. These changes in applied stress, as in the construction of a road, are often clearly visible. However, decreases in the internal strength of rock and soil masses caused by weathering can go largely unobserved.

For example, underground caves may be opened up in limestone when the calcium and magnesium are dissolved by water. No indication of this would appear on the surface, but if enlargement of the caves continued there would come a point when the ground above, being insufficiently supported, would collapse. Nearly all minerals can, in fact, be taken into solution. Although this would happen at a much slower rate than with calcium and might not form caves, the rocks would become progressively weaker and progressively less able to withstand the stress.

Slope failure, nevertheless, does not occur immediately whenever stress exceeds resistance. If it did, slopes would be showing continual adjustment and this does not happen. In reality, many slopes are inherently unstable and slippage may

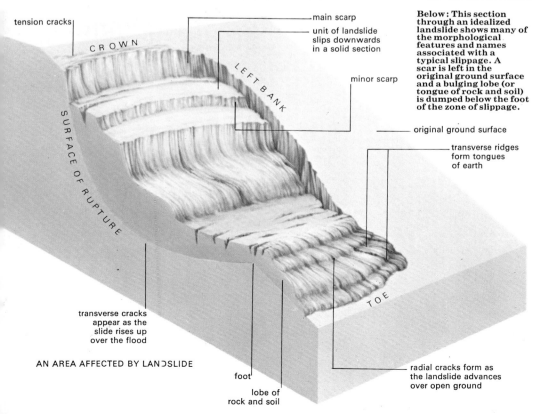

tension cracks

CROWN

LEFT BANK

SURFACE OF RUPTURE

main scarp

unit of landslide
slips downwards
in a solid section

minor scarp

**Below: This section
through an idealized
landslide shows many of
the morphological
features and names
associated with a
typical slippage. A
scar is left in the
original ground surface
and a bulging lobe (or
tongue of rock and soil)
is dumped below the foot
of the zone of slippage.**

original ground surface

transverse ridges
form tongues
of earth

transverse cracks
appear as the
slide rises up
over the flood

TOE

AN AREA AFFECTED BY LANDSLIDE

foot

lobe of
rock and soil

radial cracks form as
the landslide advances
over open ground

89

occur at any time, given the appropriate stimulus.

Among the factors contributing to mass movement are the angle of rest of the soil and waste material, and the looseness or lack of consolidation of the soil or rock. But water is certainly one of the chief agents. Most sudden mass movement is, in fact, associated with heavy or prolonged rain or snow melt. Water acts in several ways. It can, for example, provide an additional weight on the slope. More importantly, it can enter the pore spaces within the rock and soil and weaken the bonds between mineral grains. Rarely, if ever, does the passage of water through the rock and soil cause movement by lubrication; in many cases water actually increases the friction between particles and so acts against movement.

Melting snow plays its part, too. It produces its own moisture and a surface on which it can slide, creating avalanches which carry boulders and rock fragments along in their path. The spring thaw is the time for avalanches, which may be caused by an exceptional rise in temperature (and thus an uneven but rapid thaw), or triggered off by the smallest vibration. Avalanches usually flow at great speeds.

Types of mass movement
Many attempts have been made to classify the different types of mass movement and their causes, and a number of names have been coined. Among the more common are rock fall, soil creep, mud flows, earth flows, rain splash action and surface wash. The term landslide is noticeably missing from this list. This is because it is often used in a general sense to cover any sudden movement on a slope.

Rock fall, a rapid mass movement in which rocks slide down along a plane of weakness, is intermittent and typically produces uneven, irregular slopes. Rock fall activity can produce a *scree* or *talus*, accumulations of rock fragments which pile up at the bottom of slopes. The fragments are dislodged by the action of frost and weathering from the face of a slope. Screes are unstable, and material continues to slide downwards, while new material is constantly added from above. Normally, a scree will lie at a fairly steep angle of rest, but heavy rain or melting snow can upset this situation. The entire scree may be cemented by ice and, when the ice thaws, it may slip downhill, burying the slopes below under rocks and stones.

In contrast to rock fall, *soil creep* is gradual, operating more or less continually, and only detectable by careful measurement. It is caused by the expansion and contraction of soil particles due to wetting and drying, freezing and thawing, or even heating and cooling. Downslope movement occurs because expansion tends to be at 90° to the angle of the slope, while contraction tends to be vertical and unrelated to the slope angle. Following a zig-zag path, the soil slowly moves downhill, often no faster than a centimetre (0.39 in) a decade. If this increases to between 5 and 10 cm a year, as can happen on steep slopes subject to repeated frost action and a marked spring snowmelt, the surface may crack to produce a series of steps known as *terracettes*. Similar features can also be produced by the tramping and burrowing

Dr. Lauri Wright

Below left: Not all slopes are affected by water. Sand on this dune in the Namib Desert was built up by wind to an unstable angle before collapsing.

Below: How 'piping' develops. This type of slope-forming process, particularly important in regions where periods of drought alternate with heavy rainfall, affects only a small area. Below the surface, a cemented layer of soil, often consisting of clay, or an abrupt change from soil to the weathered rock, prevents the seepage of soil water down into the ground. The existence of a pipe is revealed only when the overlying soil collapses.

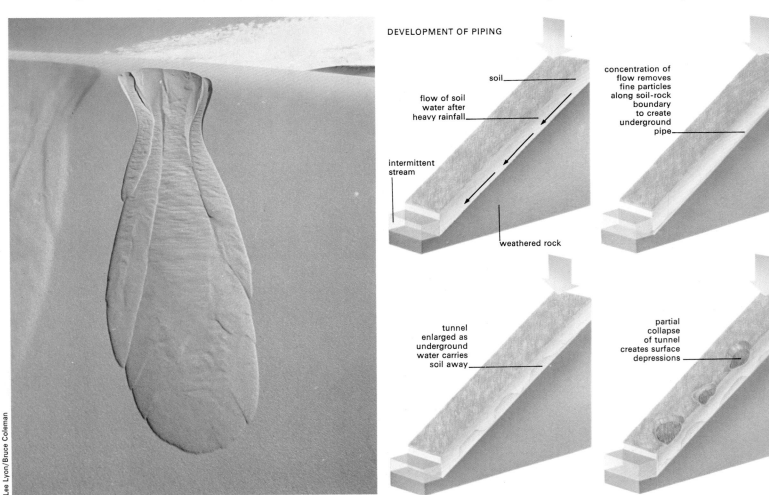

DEVELOPMENT OF PIPING

soil

flow of soil water after heavy rainfall

intermittent stream

weathered rock

concentration of flow removes fine particles along soil-rock boundary to create underground pipe

tunnel enlarged as underground water carries soil away

partial collapse of tunnel creates surface depressions

Lee Lyon/Bruce Coleman

MASS MOVEMENTS

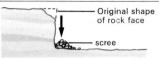

ROCK FALL rapid collapse of rock from top of coastal cliff or steep mountain side creates scree at foot of slope.

Original shape of rock face — scree

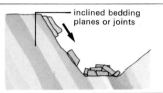

ROCK SLIDE occurs when beds or joints of cliff are steeply inclined. Depending on the height and angle of slope, large chunks may break away. Occurs in high mountains and on coasts.

inclined bedding planes or joints

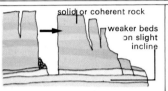

BLOCK GLIDE large blocks of solid or coherent rocks glide on a very gently inclined floor or more sensitive beds. Movement is mainly sideways and is often considerable.

solid or coherent rock — weaker beds on slight incline

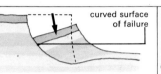

SINGLE ROTATIONAL SLIP ground rotates by both slipping down and forward on a curved surface of failure. Often occurs in silts, clays and shales.

curved surface of failure

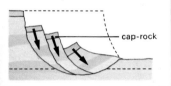

MULTIPLE ROTATIONAL SLIPS several blocks all rotate backwards on a shared, curved surface of failure. Slippage of this kind occurs in clays with a caprock and very sensitive clays.

cap-rock

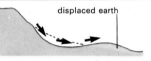

EARTH FLOW occurs in saturated shale or clay which is disturbed by vibration. Movement is usually small.

displaced earth

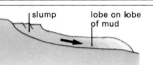

MUDFLOW often occurs in arid regions where fine deposits slump or slide when saturated with water. Usually long and shallow.

slump — lobe on lobe of mud

of animals along a hillside.

Earth flows are movements involving finely grained material, such as clay or shale. These materials can sometimes become so saturated with water that the slightest vibration causes the whole hillside to flow downwards. One of the most disastrous examples of an earth flow was the Aberfan landslide in October 1966. Undermined by heavy rains, a man-made hill of pit waste collapsed, engulfing part of the village and killing 144 people, including 116 children.

Similar to earth flows, but occurring in dry, sloping valleys of arid and semi-arid areas, are *mud flows*. Quantities of sand and dust accumulate in these valleys and after a heavy rainfall are mixed with the rainwater to form a thick mud. This then flows downwards, sweeping away everything in its path.

Lahars are a type of mud flow which occurs on the slopes of volcanoes, and are thought to cause greater loss of life than volcanic explosions or flows of hot lava. Fine ash, sand and dust accumulate on volcanic cones and are transformed into liquid mud by the addition of water. This water can come from volcanic steam or melting snow or ice, but most frequently its origin is seasonal rainfall. Probably the most famous lahar occurred in 79 AD, when a river of hot mud flowed over the Roman town of Herculaneum.

Slopes bare of vegetation

In semi-arid regions, slopes are largely unprotected by vegetation cover. When not affected by rock fall, they are often subjected to the action of rainwater, which removes individual particles from the surface rather than disturbing soil or rock masses. The impact of the drops of water or *rain splash* dislodges particles in all directions, although those directed downwards tend to move furthest. Rain splash is most effective at the beginning of rainstorms and on the crests of hills. In the absence of other activity, a convex slope is produced, in practice only clearly visible on hill crests.

Surface wash occurs when water can no longer percolate into the ground and flows over the surface. In areas of heavy but occasional rainfall this is not uncommon and, acting under the same forces as river water, the process tends to produce smooth, slightly concave slopes. Contrary to what its name implies, surface wash does not occur in the form of a flowing sheet of water. Rather, myriads of tiny streams or *rills* are created. These fill up as their sides collapse between rainstorms, so that with further rain new rills are formed in a slightly different position. The overall effect is as if sheet erosion were taking place.

The clearing of natural vegetation on slopes in order to plant crops can be counter-productive, as once vegetation cover is removed, the soil can be eroded. Only strict measures to limit the area cleared at any one time and to direct the flow of water into concrete culverts can prevent severe erosion, particularly in regions with high rainfall. Alternatively, erosion can be allowed to continue, and the eroded debris collected and spread out behind long walls at a lower level. This creates flatter fields, which are easier to farm than the steep slopes and are less susceptible to erosion.

Right: An avalanche on the flanks of Mt Nuptse in the Himalayas. On steep slopes, snow may start to slide when its own weight or a sudden thaw makes it unstable. Once under way, an avalanche tends to pick up speed and may sweep up thousands of tonnes of soil, rock and vegetation before finally reaching a halt.

Below: Movements include not only such spectacular events as avalanches, but also slow, barely perceptible processes such as soil creep. One of the common indications of creep is a series of terracettes, often formed (like these in New Zealand) by the tramping of animals across the face of a hillside.

Rivers at Work

Until the late seventeenth century, the continuous flow of water from the earth to rivers was thought to be magical. Then two Frenchmen, Pierre Perrault and Edmé Mariotte, measured the flow of the River Seine, which runs from the hills of Burgundy through Paris to the English Channel. They concluded that there was more than enough rain and other precipitation falling on the *catchment area*, the entire region drained by a river, to account for the flow of the river. The first step had been taken into *hydrology*, the science dealing with the many properties of water.

Recent research into the total world stock of water has revealed some unexpected facts. In 1960, R. L. Nace, an American hydrologist, calculated the amount of water in storage and in transit in the various parts of the *hydrological cycle*, the continuous process in which water evaporates from the seas, is precipitated on to the land, and eventually runs back to the seas. It may not be surprising that the oceans contain 97 per cent of all the water in the world, but what is surprising is that the amount stored in the atmosphere is no more than one-thousandth of one per cent. Yet it is this small percentage that provides water to sustain vegetation and ultimately to flow in the rivers of the world.

The quantity of water to be found both in and on the continents is only three per cent of all the earth's stock. Of this, over 77 per cent is locked up in the ice caps and glaciers and another 22.5 per cent lies under the ground. This leaves a mere one half of one per cent of the waters in and on land to flow in the world's rivers, streams and lakes.

Nevertheless, running water is the most widespread and effective agent of landscape sculpture, continually carving deep valleys and broad plains and altering the surface features of the earth. In general, work starts with the rainfall and other forms of precipitation which provide, directly or indirectly, all the waters guided into natural channels to form streams and rivers. The source of a stream may be the immediate run-off from rainfall, or sub-surface water from a spring, or the release of water held temporarily in lakes or ice.

The anatomy of a river

On their course to the sea, rivers develop a distinctive slope or *gradient*. The side-view of the entire gradient, known as its *long profile*, reveals a generally concave shape, steeper towards the source of a river and flatter towards the mouth. Throughout a river's course, material is constantly being eroded from some sections and deposited in others. Where the river beds are very irregular and full of holes, it is likely that erosion is taking place; where the beds are floored with alluvial material, deposition is taking place. Erosion occurs where the stream has an excess of energy. When its energy is decreased, by a fall in gradient or by an obstacle, such as the still waters of a lake, the stream is no longer competent to transport its debris and must start to deposit it.

A river is often described as passing

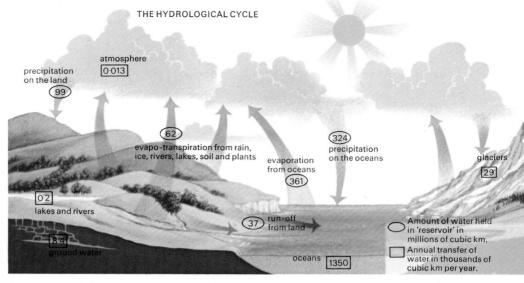

atmosphere **0·013**

precipitation on the land **99**

evapo-transpiration from rain, ice, rivers, lakes, soil and plants **62**

evaporation from oceans **361**

precipitation on the oceans **324**

glaciers **29**

lakes and rivers **0·2**

run-off from land **37**

ground water **8·4**

oceans **1350**

◯ Amount of water held in 'reservoir' in millions of cubic km.

▢ Annual transfer of water in thousands of cubic km per year.

Colorific!

Above: The natural cycle of water from land to ocean, up to the atmosphere and back to land again is known as the *Hydrological cycle.* The sun's heat provides the energy by which water is evaporated from the surface of land and sea and transpired from vegetation. Precipitation falls as rain or snow; some is absorbed by the soil and plants, some is held as ice or seeps into the ground. What is left runs off the surface to enter the complex network of lakes, streams and rivers.

Left: Rushing water, large boulders and pot holes (worn into the bed rock by the constant rocking of boulders) are typical of a youthful mountain stream.

Spectrum

Right: An aerial view of the Rakaia river near Windwhistle gorge in New Zealand. It shows several features of a mature river adjusting to changes in base level. In the foreground, several raised terraces have been created as the river has cut down into the land surface uplifted by earth movements. The present river is developing a new flood-plain with deposition on inside bends, erosion on the outer-side. In the distance, interlacing of distributaries, known as *braiding*, is in evidence where the river leaves its gorge.

Below: In a straight channel, frictional drag is greatest along the bed and banks, so the river current is fastest towards mid-channel and close to the surface. Straight uniform channels are unstable and meanders soon develop.

Below right: In curved or meandering channels, erosion develops at the outside of bends where the velocity is highest, and deposition occurs on the innerside of bends where the current is slackest.

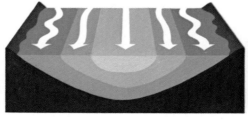

Above: The colourful
Agua Azul (meaning blue
water) cascades down a
series of steps on its
way through the
Mexican jungle. A
resistant band of rock
acts as a temporary base
level for a stream until
it is cut through by
waterfalls, cascades
and rapids.

Left: A stream is
likely to encounter
rocks of varying
resistance in its
course. The variations
predispose the stream
to change its direction
and so to develop a
winding course,
creating a series of
interlocking spurs.

Below: An incised
'goose-neck' meander
cut by the river Saar
flowing through Bavaria
in south-west Germany.

through successive stages of development, from youth to maturity and on to old age. Because of the erosive energy of youthful streams, the upper course of a river is characterized by steep-sided, V-shaped valleys and gorges, through which the water rushes and tumbles over many rapids and waterfalls. Running water by itself has very little erosive power. River erosion is the cumulative effect of a great variety of processes including *corrosion*, the solvent and chemical activities of river water on the materials with which it comes into contact, and *hydraulic action*, which loosens and removes bed and bank material.

Once armed with loosened debris, running water becomes very destructive. *Corrasion* (not to be confused with corrosion) is the process by which the river bed is worn away by the boulders, pebbles, sand and silt being carried along in the stream. *Attrition* is a mechanism in river erosion whereby the transported materials or *load* are themselves broken down into smaller pieces by the continuous battering they receive as they move downstream.

A river's load can be transported in four different ways; by *traction* where the load is rolled along the stream bed; by *saltation* where the particles are moved in a series of short jumps; by being held up in *suspension*; and in *solution*, dissolved in the water. As the velocity of the river slackens, the larger boulders and pebbles come to rest, leaving only the material in suspension and solution to continue its journey downstream.

In any inspection of a natural river, the nature of the bed and land adjacent may indicate erosion or deposition although the river itself may appear to be incapable of either. But if the same river is looked at in flood, the large and apparently immovable boulders are being bounced along the bed, and material is being deposited in the lower reaches. In this way an estimated 8,000 million tonnes of eroded rock waste are transported from all parts of the world to the sea every year. This represents an annual loss corresponding to 77 tonnes per sq km (200 tons per sq mile).

Erosion cuts into steeper sections of the river profile and deposition occurs on the gentler sections. Consequently, there is a tendency to reduce the differences in gradient and so form a smooth profile which irons out any irregularities such as small lakes, waterfalls and rapids, often produced when a river course crosses resistant rock bands. The deepening of the river valleys by erosive processes is limited by sea level, which acts as the lowest point or *base level* for erosion. All rivers attempts to smooth out their long profiles from source to mouth. When a river attains this condition it is said to be at a state of equilibrium or *grade* and the profile is known as a *graded profile*.

Rivers in maturity
When rivers reach middle age or maturity, sideways or *lateral erosion* becomes more important. Broad valleys with gentle slopes are produced and the rivers tend to meander. A *meander* (named after the classical River Meander of Troy) is the name given when a river follows the natural gradient of the land and forms semi-circular bends with geometrically perfect curves.

93

Aerofilms

William MacQuitty

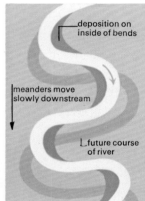
deposition on inside of bends

meanders move slowly downstream

future course of river

Left: This dry river valley in the Gilgit region of Kashmir contains a steeply sided alluvial cone. The cone was formed by the stream as it deposited its load when it left the mountain tract of its course.

Above: The valley of Glendaruel in Scotland. As a river develops its meanders, it deposits material on the inner sides of bends. The area of deposits is enlarged as the meanders move downstream. Eventually, this migration leads to the formation of a flood-plain which widens as the meanders swing freely from one valley side to the other, smoothing out headlands or bluffs as they go.

It was once thought that chance irregularities in a river's curve were the cause of meanders, but if this were so there would be odd meanders here and there, whereas meanders always conform to a pattern. Laboratory experiments have shown that even those rivers developing on a uniform slope of uniform sediment are always found to modify their channels by erosion and deposition so that a series of symmetrical bends develops.

Braiding is another feature of a mature river valley. This occurs when a river which is laden with debris emerges from a ravine onto a bordering plain. The velocity of the river is suddenly checked by the abrupt change of gradient and much of its sediment load is dropped. The large volume of debris thus deposited obstructs the flow of the river which divides into *distributaries* which continually separate and unite.

Meandering rivers develop their flood plains by depositing silt and alluvium as they migrate seawards. Further deposits known as *overbank deposits* are left on the flood plain by flood waters each time the river overflows its banks. The flow of the water which floods onto the banks is not controlled by the main current since it is outside the river channel. As the flood slows down, it drops the coarsest part of its load, gradually building up a low embankment or *levee* on either side of the river. As the levee develops so too does the river bed. Silt, carried down by flood waters too small to overtop the levees, is deposited on the river bed as the flood subsides. If, however, the flood waters do breach the levees the consequences can be disastrous.

J. Allan Cash

erosion of banks on outside of bends

river about to break through

FORMATION OF NATURAL LEVEES

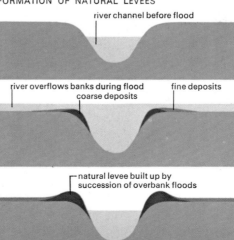
river channel before flood

river overflows banks during flood
coarse deposits   fine deposits

natural levee built up by succession of overbank floods

Above: An ox-bow lake and sloughs (areas of dead water) formed on a flood plain by a meandering river in Alberta, Canada.

Right: How an ox-bow lake is formed. As a river develops its winding course, each bend is enlarged and the meanders migrate downstream in a serpentine fashion. Meanders continue to swell in broad loops with gradually narrowing necks. In times of flood, the neck is gradually cut off and a deserted channel or ox-bow lake is formed.

Left: Natural levees, often many metres high, are built up from the sediment deposited by a succession of overbank river floods.

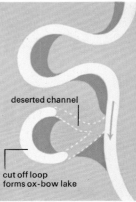
deserted channel

cut off loop forms ox-bow lake

Above: Braided channels in the Matanuska River in Alaska. Braiding occurs when a river emerges from its energetic mountain stage laden with debris on to a bordering plain and is slowed down. In the above example, the complex interlacing network of channels are separated by shoals of sand and islands of shingle.

Right: The junction of the Amazon and Negro rivers in South America. The Negro is stained black with sediment and the Amazon is muddy. Their silt loads are so heavy that the waters do not mix until several kilometres downstream. This is known as *encontro das aguas* or meeting of the waters.

Left: The fan-shaped Maggia Delta protruding into Lake Lugano in Switzerland provides an ideal setting for the town of Lugano. The main distributary of the river has been channelled into a canal to combat flooding.

Below: A section taken through the sediments of a fan-shaped or *arcuate* delta. The foreset beds are built up outwards into the sea or lake by successive loads of sediment tipped in that direction. The marked cross-bedding of layers of silt is notable. Finer sediments are deposited further out to sea to form the bottom-set beds. The veneer of top-set beds form the seaward continuation of the river's floodplain.

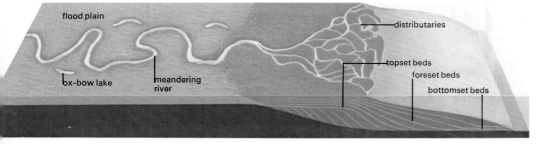

The effect of base level change

Rivers are rarely allowed to achieve a state of equilibrium or grade. More often they are interrupted by changes of base level, caused either by a change in the sea level or by earth movements which have uplifted or lowered the earth's surface. If a region is depressed by earth movements, its surface is brought nearer to base level, and because the work to be done by erosion is diminished, the stages of the cycle then in progress are passed through more quickly.

On the other hand, if a river that has already established a flood plain is rejuvenated—that is, the base level is lowered—the river will cut through the alluvium onto the rocks below in an attempt to re-grade its course. The margins of the original valley floor are then left as *terraces* above the level of the rejuvenated river. Subsequent rejuvenation would result in a second pair of terraces left on the valley sides. A *knick-point* results where the regraded profile meets the old profile. It is characterized by cascades and waterfalls and may often be difficult to distinguish from a break in the long profile caused by resistant rock bands.

If at the time of rejuvenation a stream was freely meandering on a floor of alluvium underlain by more resistant formations, the deepening channel would soon be etched into the underlying rocks with a winding form inherited from the original meanders. In England the 'hair pin' gorge of the River Wear, Durham, is a familiar example of such an *incised* meander.

Activity in old age

In old age, the wide, heavily-laden river glides sluggishly over a very broad, almost level plain. Its main work is deposition. Most of the sediment load of a river is carried out to sea or to a lake where the velocity is checked and, provided that deposition is at a greater rate than removal by currents, much of the load is deposited as an alluvial tract called a *delta*.

There are three basic types of delta formation. If the river water is denser than the sea or lake because of its load of sediment, it flows along the bottom and forms an *elongated* delta. If the river water has the same density as the sea or lake, it spreads out in the shape of a fan and an *arcuate* delta, like that of the River Nile, is formed. Finally, if the river water is less dense, it makes a few confined channels for itself and a *bird's foot* delta, like that of the Mississippi, is formed. Deltas can grow with great rapidity. For example, the delta below Astrakhan in the Soviet Union, where the Volga meets the Caspian Sea, was at one time growing at the rate of 1.6 km (1 mile) every five or six years.

Deposition does not only occur in the lower parts of a river course. Many youthful mountain rivers descend steeply to neighbouring lowlands where they drop their suspended load to form *alluvial fans* (so called because of their shape) or, in special cases, steep sided *alluvial cones*. Where closely spaced streams discharge from a mountain region their deposits may eventually unite to form a continuous plain or *piedmont alluvial plain*. For example, the Indo-Gangetic Plain in India extends from the delta of the Indus to that of the Ganges-Brahmaputra.

River Systems

On their journey to the sea, individual streams and rivers merge together to form a characteristic network or design, which is referred to as the *pattern of drainage* of a river system. In most areas, this pattern is one of considerable complexity, and in fact drainage patterns vary greatly from one kind of terrain to another: they are influenced by the slopes over which the rivers flow, the differences in rock hardness and structure that the streams meet during their course, and the recent history of earth movements in the drainage area.

Patterns and texture of drainage

In areas of uniform layers of sedimentary rocks, such as clays, drainage patterns emerge which resemble the branching of a tree. The *dendritic* patterns (from the Greek word 'dendron', meaning a tree) resemble the branching of trees. In scarplands and other areas of gently dipping rocks where branches of smaller streams tend to join the larger streams or rivers at right angles, a lattice-shaped or *trellised* pattern is more likely. *Radial* or *concentric* drainage patterns, in which the channels radiate in all directions from a central area, develop on the slopes of volcanoes or conical-shaped hills.

The relative spacing between the streams of a river's network is aptly described as *drainage texture*. Fine-textured drainage indicates a closer network of stream channels than coarse-textured drainage. Drainage texture is influenced by many factors, including climate: for example, areas which receive all their rain in short, sharp thunderstorms often develop a fine-textured network. Texture is also affected by rock structure: drainage lines are more numerous over highly impermeable surfaces such as clays which do not allow water to soak into them than over permeable rock like chalk or limestone.

The Bad Lands topography in parts of the western United States illustrates one set of conditions which leads to the development of fine texture—impermeable clays, sparse vegetation and rain falling in violent thunderstorms. Coarse drainage texture is well displayed on the sand and gravel outwash plains in front of glaciers.

In 1945, a useful method of measuring drainage texture was suggested by R. E. Horton, an American hydrologist. He developed several numerical measures so that objective comparisons could be made between the texture of different drainage networks. For example, he defined *drainage density* as the value of the sum total of the stream lengths in the system divided by the total area drained by the system under investigation. In this way the texture of several drainage systems may be compared.

Horton also devised a system of listing streams in an order of rank. A stream with no branches or *tributaries* joining it was called a *first-order* stream. Where such streams join they form a *second-order* stream. It is possible for a second-order stream to receive another first-order tributary without being promoted to the next (third) order, but where two second-order streams join up then a *third-order* stream begins, and so on. The complexity

Aerofilms

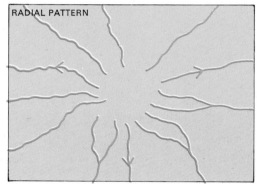

RADIAL PATTERN

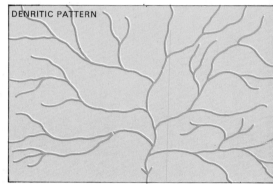

DENRITIC PATTERN

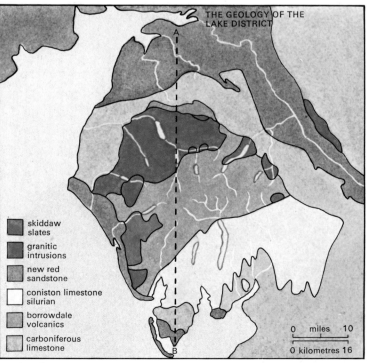

THE GEOLOGY OF THE LAKE DISTRICT

- skiddaw slates
- granitic intrusions
- new red sandstone
- coniston limestone silurian
- borrowdale volcanics
- carboniferous limestone

0 miles 10
0 kilometres 16

red sandstone
carboniferous limestone
borrowdale volcanics
coniston limestone
A
skiddaw slate
B

Left: Map and geological section of the English Lake District, showing a radial pattern of superimposed drainage. The area consists of folded early Palaeozoic rocks enclosed by a frame of limestone and sandstone, which were themselves once covered by later layers. In the Tertiary period the region was uplifted into a dome and the first streams were consequents that flowed radially down the slopes of the rising dome. These cut their valleys deeply into the underlying rocks. Today there is little evidence left of the younger rocks, but the drainage pattern of the vanished cover still substantially remains— it has been *superimposed* on the older rocks. Note how the rivers radiate from a central area.

Right: A spectacular aerial view of the Colorado river system as it cuts through the Kaibab plateau near the Arizona-Utah border. It shows the typical coarse-textured drainage of a mature river flowing through an arid area. The junction of the Colorado tributary is indicated by a circle. The dark mass of water is Lake Powell on the Colorado, upstream from the Grand Canyon. The lone peak to the east of the picture, south of the Colorado, is the Navajo mountain.

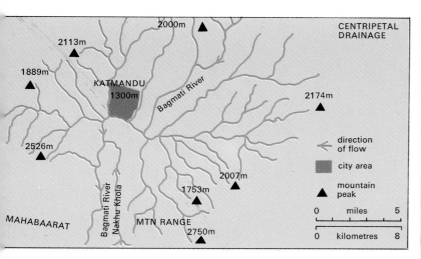

CENTRIPETAL DRAINAGE

2000m

2113m

1889m

KATMANDU
1300m

Bagmati River

2526m

2174m

Bagmati River
Nakhu Khola

2007m

1753m

MAHABAARAT

MTN RANGE

2750m

direction
of flow

city area

mountain
peak

0   miles   5

0   kilometres   8

Anthony Howarth/Susan Griggs

Left: Aerial view of the Colorado delta, often known as the 'burning tree' delta. The tributary streams join at various angles and resemble the twigs of a tree. This example shows how numerous branching systems, if allowed to develop freely in uniform layers of material, will take on a dendritic pattern.

Above: The Katmandu valley in Nepal has a remarkable example of *centripetal drainage*, in which streams flow towards a central depression. Along the single line of exit the Bagmati flows southwards towards the Ganges, while just a few miles east the Nakhu Khola flows in the opposite direction.

Right: Aerial view of the dry river beds near Lake Turkana in Kenya. These form a pinnate-type of drainage pattern. This is a special form of dendritic drainage in which the tributaries join the main river at acute angles, an effect produced by the unusually steep slopes on which the tributaries have developed.

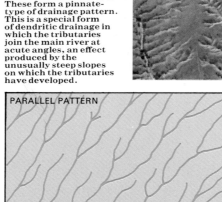

TRELLISED PATTERN

PARALLEL PATTERN

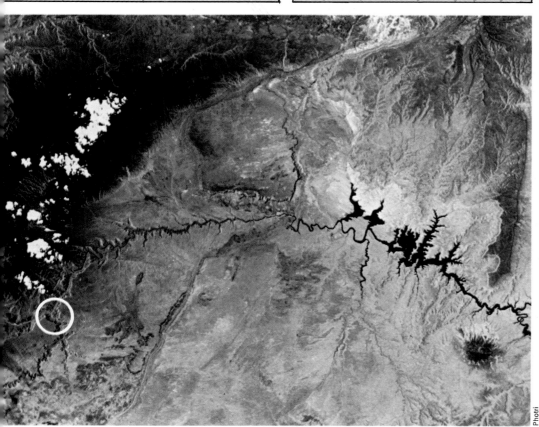

Photri

of different drainage systems can be measured by determining which have the highest order streams.

The origins of river systems

Names given to drainage systems often relate to the effect of structure and topography on their development.

A newly formed land surface is immediately exposed to weathering and erosion. In regions of sufficient rainfall, streams are created by the run-off of rain. Thus the streams and rivers whose original downhill course was determined by the initial slopes of the land are termed *consequent streams*, because their flow is a consequence of the pre-determined slopes. The final pattern of drainage to emerge then depends on the nature and structure of the rocks over which the consequent stream flows. If the rocks are uniformly resistant, a dendritic pattern will form. The branching drainage system developing from consequent streams is known as *insequent* or *lateral consequent*.

However, it is more common that an area consists of alternating strata of hard and soft rocks. As the consequent stream cuts its way down to the sea, it behaves in a different way as it passes over differing rock beds. Narrow valleys will be carved through the more resistant rocks, which will stand up as ridges, and the stream will wear away the clays and softer rocks to produce broad valleys.

In this situation, the tributaries feeding the main consequent stream are much more likely to take advantage of the weaker bands and to make rapid upstream or *headward erosion* along these. These tributaries are then known as *subsequent streams*. A typical trellised drainage pattern then develops, with the consequent rivers flowing parallel to the gentle dip slope of the rock and the subsequent tributaries flowing at right angles to this.

The valley of a subsequent stream steadily widens between the ridges formed by the bands of more resistant rock on either side. As the valley is broadened, the gentler slope will become steeper or gentler to approximate the angle of dip of

FORMATION OF INVERTED RELIEF

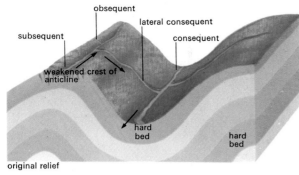

original relief

→ direction of flow

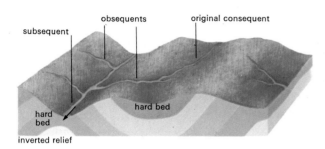

inverted relief

Left: The main stages in the development of inverted relief. On the original land surface (top), a consequent stream follows the hollow of the syncline. It is fed by a lateral consequent stream, and subsequent and obsequent streams are eroding the weakened peak of the anticline. At a later stage (bottom left), the pattern has been reversed and the relief is inverted. The subsequent stream has cut deeper than the consequent, which now acts as just one of several obsequent streams flowing into the lower stream valley.

Right: How a river system is superimposed over a landscape. In the initial stage (top), a river has established its course over horizontal beds of rock laid down unconformably over folded beds of varying resistance. After a period of down-cutting (bottom), the river has encountered the underlying rock but has maintained its original pattern. Where it has reached the buried anticline of resistant rock, it has eroded a narrow gorge.

FORMATION OF SUPERIMPOSED DRAINAGE

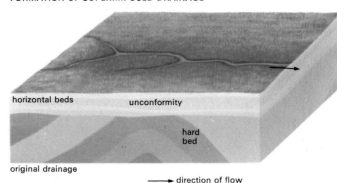

original drainage

→ direction of flow

superimposed drainage

the underlying hard rock. Gradually, run-off from these slopes will form new streams, called *secondary consequents* or *dip streams*, as they flow down the dip slopes to meet the subsequent.

These new streams are sometimes called *resequent streams* since they appear to be consequent in direction, but they are of a later generation, forming only when the original incline down which the consequents flow is broken up into dip slopes. Shorter streams will also flow in the opposite direction down the steeper escarpment slope of resistant rock to join the subsequent stream, and are known as anti-dip or *obsequent* streams.

Inverted relief

The original surface of the land on which some drainage systems develop take the form of a series of synclines (dips) and anticlines (rises). If, for some reason, the erosive powers of rivers wear away the anticlines at a greater rate than the synclines, then the synclines eventually form the mountains and the anticlines will form the valleys. This phenomenon, where the topography is 'opposite' to the structure, is known as *inverted relief*, although it is in fact the more usual case in areas of folded rocks. For example, Snowdon, the highest mountain in Wales, has developed from a synclinal structure.

During the first stage in the development of inverted relief, the main consequent stream follows the natural hollow of the syncline. However, the peak of the anticline is often so weakened or even cracked by folding that the hard bed capping the structure is easily breached near the crest of the anticline. Subsequent streams will easily develop here, whilst obsequent streams will begin to flow down the inward-facing scarps. If the arrangement of the hard and soft beds on the anticline is suitable, erosion of the anticline by the subsequent streams may be much faster than erosion by the consequent streams in the synclinal valley. The relief now becomes inverted.

After erosion has continued for a period of time, the subsequent streams may cut

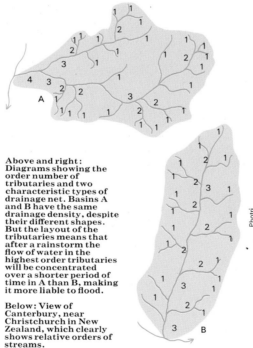

Above and right: Diagrams showing the order number of tributaries and two characteristic types of drainage net. Basins A and B have the same drainage density, despite their different shapes. But the layout of the tributaries means that after a rainstorm the flow of water in the highest order tributaries will be concentrated over a shorter period of time in A than B, making it more liable to flood.

Below: View of Canterbury, near Christchurch in New Zealand, which clearly shows relative orders of streams.

Above: NASA satellite picture of the Amazon tributaries in western Brazil. The smaller river Tarauaca flows into the Jurua, which meanders across the flat Amazon basin. An example of how drainage systems simplify in time, myriads of streams have been gradually superseded by a few main drainage lines.

Below right: The Brecon Beacons in south Wales. The streams on the right, which drain into the sea at Newport, are cutting into the watershed by headward erosion, thus lengthening their valley upstream. They will eventually capture the streams on the left, which drain to a different river and meet the sea at Cardiff.

Photri

G. R. Roberts

Below: How a river is captured. In the first stage, the streams have formed a trellised drainage pattern over gently dipping hard and soft beds. The detail shows a powerful subsequent stream making headward erosion through soft rock about to capture its neighbouring consequent stream.

RIVER CAPTURE

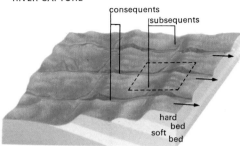

trellised pattern

→ direction of flow

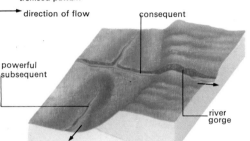

detail of trellised pattern

after capture

Above: Capture is complete. The powerful subsequent has pirated the headwaters of its neighbouring consequent and has continued its headward erosion to capture the next stream. The sharp bend where the two streams meet is known as the elbow of capture. Below the elbow, the course of the captured stream soon

diminishes and a wind gap develops where the stream used to flow.

Right: The junction at which the Ouse has captured the river Nidd in Yorkshire. The Ouse, a major consequent aided by active subsequents, has acquired a large drainage area at the expense of other rivers.

Right: The River Thames flowing through the Pool of London below Tower Bridge. Before the last Ice Age and the subsequent reflooding of the North Sea, Britain was joined to the Continent and the Thames was a tributary of the Rhine. Once the English Channel formed, the Thames gained its own outlet to the sea.

Picturepoint

Aerofilms

down as far as a lower hard bed of rock. Its downward path is then checked, but the original consequents may erode relatively easily through the remains of the upper hard bed and underlying soft beds. Ultimately a pattern very like the original develops, but as the streams are not direct descendants of the original consequents, they are more properly described as secondary consequents.

Watersheds

The ridge of high land separating two neighbouring streams or river systems is known as a divide or *watershed*. As early as 1877, the American geologist G. K. Gilbert discovered that, in the later stages of the fluvial cycle, watersheds between streams of similar size are uniformly spaced and stream gradients are roughly equal on opposite sides of the watersheds.

However, Gilbert found that this was not true in the earlier stages of the cycle. A stream flowing down the steeper slope on one side of an unequally inclined ridge erodes its valley more rapidly than one flowing down the other, more gentle slope. As a result the watershed gradually recedes or migrates towards the side with the gentler slope. The dividing ridge quickly takes on a characteristic ruggedness, varying in height. This concept came to be known as the *Law of Unequal Slopes*. Sometimes the crest is lowered until it develops into a depression or *col* in the divide which often becomes useful as a pass for roads built across mountain ranges.

River capture

A strange phenomenon which has come to light in the study of drainage systems is that of *river capture*. This interesting example of natural piracy takes place when a major consequent river acquires a vigorous subsequent tributary which is etching its way by headward erosion back along a very weak outcrop of rock, wearing back its watershed as its goes. Eventually the subsequent stream may break through the divide and intercept an adjacent river system whose upper tributaries or *headwaters* are captured and

Aerofilms

99

G. R. Roberts

Above: An incised meander in the Macdonnell Ranges, Australia, about 125 km from Alice Springs. A deeply cut meander like this indicates that the river course is *antecedent* to (older than) the earth movement that uplifted the area. The river cut deeper as it was raised to a greater height.

Right: Ethiopia, the river Yonder and the Lali-Bela. The ridge of rock between the two streams is a clear example of a watershed.

Below: The Shenandoah is a famous example of a subsequent river valley. In a folded landscape, a subsequent river usually carves out a broad deep valley because it flows over weak rocks, becoming a powerful stream. The Shenandoah is one of the Appalachian rivers in the eastern United States. These have been interpreted as distinctive examples of superimposed drainage. Powerful subsequent streams cut their way through the Cretaceous rock cover onto the Palaeozoic rocks beneath, dissecting the Appalachians into long mountain ridges.

Georg Gerster/John Hillelson

Picturepoint

diverted along the course of the subsequent stream. The *beheaded* stream is left as a *misfit* since the reduced volume of water is no longer appropriate to the valley through which it flows. If river capture is predominant in a region, a pattern commonly occurs in which tributaries join the main river in backward looping or 'boathook' bends, providing a *barbed* drainage system.

Most river capture is largely explained by differences in rock resistance. However, in areas of permeable rocks there is the possibility of underground diversion preceding and aiding surface capture. Active erosion at the head of a lower but vigorous stream may cause it to approach close to a higher level valley and gradually sap more and more of the upper stream's ground water supply. Tower Creek in Yellowstone National Park, USA, is an interesting example of the underground diversion of drainage.

A river's course can also be diverted or deranged by the imposition of a barrier in its path. Although *stream derangement* has several of the features attributable to river capture, including barbed tributaries, it is the result of an entirely different mechanism. Glaciation is the chief cause of stream derangement. An example of this is to be found in North America where the present course of the Upper Missouri River is largely the result of the advancement during the Pleistocene Ice Age of the ice-sheets across the pre-glacial course of the Missouri. At that time it had its outlet to the north in the Hudson Bay in Canada. The glacial advance caused the Upper Missouri to abandon this route and establish a new course, roughly following the glacial boundary, to the Mississippi flowing south to the Gulf of Mexico.

Superimposed drainage
Some river systems have managed to maintain their original patterns despite obstacles erected during the geologic history of the area. Much of Britain, for instance, was originally covered by chalk and Jurassic rocks, lying unconformably above more ancient Palaeozoic rocks. As the land emerged from the sea during the late Cretaceous period, rivers were formed consequent to this surface.

As the valleys deepened, stripping away much of the younger cover, the rivers cut into the older, more resistant rocks, many with structural features which resulted in barriers across the river courses. In highland Britain, although the chalk cover has disappeared, the rivers remain carved into spectacular valleys through older rock while maintaining a close approximation to their original courses. This type of drainage pattern, in which a river system has been let down over an older landscape, is referred to as *superimposed* or *epigenetic* drainage.

If a stream continues through its erosive cycle whilst mountain uplift and folding are in progress it is said to be an *antecedent stream*, for the river is older than the earth movements. The resulting features of this antecedent drainage pattern will depend on the rate of the earth's uplift compared with the rate of the river's downcutting. Antecedence has been used to explain the nature of some of the rivers flowing across the Himalayas, notably the Arun and Tista, which flow against the structure of the mountains through impassable gorges.

The Rhine, on its way through western Europe from its source in the Swiss Alps to the North Sea, links up with a number of other rivers – among them, the Sieg, the Wupper, the Ruhr and the Lippe.

Robert Estall

Lakes

Lakes are a familiar sight in most landscapes, but they are notoriously difficult features to define except in the most general terms. Broadly speaking, *lakes* are bodies of water enclosed by land, occupying hollows on the earth's surface. They form when the floor of a hollow is relatively impermeable, preventing the water from seeping into the ground, or when the floor lies below the *water table*—the highest level at which the pores of underlying rock are saturated with water.

Despite this basic common feature, lakes have a huge variety of different characteristics. They may be very large or very small, deep or shallow, natural or man-made, freshwater or salty, and even permanent or seasonal. They vary in size from the small ponds known by different names in different parts of the world—for example, *tarns* in England, *lochans* in Scotland, *étangs* in France, and *billabongs* in Australia—to the large features frequently referred to as *inland seas* and in some cases given the name 'sea'. In fact, the Caspian Sea in central Asia is the largest lake in the world, with a total area of 371,800 km² (143,550 sq miles).

Larger lakes often exhibit characteristics very similar to those of seas or oceans, though usually on a smaller scale. For example, winds blowing over large lakes can generate waves of sufficient size to result in erosion processes similar to those at the sea coast. Another similarity between seas and lakes is the creation of

Above: A lake is a perfect example of a complete 'system', in which the inputs and outputs of material and energy are readily identified. Once the hollow has been formed, water can be supplied by inflowing rivers, underground water, melting ice and precipitation. Sediment and decaying organic material accumulate on the floor. Lake water is lost to evaporation and to outflowing rivers, which may drain the lake completely by eroding through the lake wall.

Right: Rivers issuing from glaciers may deposit sand and gravel around and on top of residual blocks of ice. When the block melts, the sediments will collapse, forming a surface depression. If this fills with water it is called a *kettle lake*.

Below right: Ribbon lakes often receive fast-flowing tributary streams which deposit alluvial fans on the valley floor. In time the fans may spread out and divide the lake in two, as happened at Interlaken in Switzerland.

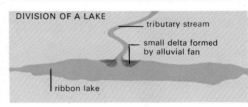

FORMATION OF KETTLE LAKE

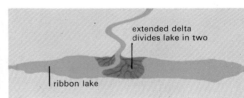

DIVISION OF A LAKE

Left: An aerial view of the Dead Sea between Israel and Jordan. The Dead Sea formed in the basin of the Great Rift Valley—its floor lies over 800 metres below the surface of the Mediterranean to the west. Its high concentration of salt brought in by rivers results from rapid evaporation of the water.

Right: Crater Lake in Oregon (USA) occupies a giant caldera formed by the collapse of a volcanic crater about 8,000 years ago. The lake is 9 km in diameter, 600 m deep and the steep inner walls stand a further 600 m high. Wizard Island in the centre of the lake is the exposed summit of a volcanic cone pushed up by later activity.

Photri

Natural Science Photos

deltas where rivers flow into them, and lakes even have a type of tidal movement known as a *seiche*. Although seiches usually involve rises and falls in lake level of only a few centimetres they occur on a much shorter time-cycle than oceanic tides and may produce over 20 high 'tides' per day.

Although the water in lakes is usually described as fresh, under certain circumstances lake water can have a higher salt concentration than sea water. Thus in semi-arid parts of the world, rather than being drained by an outflowing river, lakes frequently lose water by large-scale evaporation from their surfaces, leading to the build-up of salts in lake water. The Great Salt Lake in Utah, USA, and the Dead Sea between Israel and Jordan, for example, both have salt concentrations six to seven times that of sea-water.

Creation of lakes

The most convenient way to classify lakes is to explain how the hollows containing them first originated, although it is common for a single lake to be due to more than one cause. However, apart from those produced artificially, all these hollows can be said to be manifestations of the unstable land surface and climate of the earth.

Firstly, a significant number of lakes are formed as a result of crustal or *tectonic* movement, volcanic activity, or changes in relative sea-level. Tectonic activity involves subsidence of the earth's crust, a mechanism that was responsible for the creation of Lough Neagh in Northern Ireland and Lake Victoria in East Africa, or down-faulting of a block of land, as occurred in an area of central Asia to produce the deepest lake in the world, Lake Baykal, 1,940 metres (6,365 ft) deep. The best known down-faulted blocks occur in the rift valleys that extend in a linear belt from Jordan to East Africa.

Craters are frequently created by volcanic eruptions and under suitable circumstances these hollows may be filled with water after volcanic activity has ceased. One of the best known and largest examples of this type is the characteristically circular Crater Lake in Oregon, USA, with a diameter of 9 km (6 miles). On a smaller scale the numerous *Maaren* of the Eifel district of Germany are crater lakes between 500 metres and 1 km (1,600 to 3,200 feet) in diameter. Occasionally a lava flow or accumulation of other volcanic material may block a valley and so form a lake. One example of this is Lake Kivu in East Africa, which originally drained northwards to the Nile but, following the eruption of the Birunga volcanic field, has since overflowed southwards to Lake Tanganyika.

If relative sea-level falls, either by a rise in land-level or fall in sea-level, or both, numerous lakes will be left in hollows on the former sea floor. This happened on several occasions during the Ice Ages, for at various times sea-level fell due to the abstraction of ocean water to form ice, and land-level rose as ice sheets that had depressed the land surface by their weight melted.

Hollows scooped out of the land

A second group of processes responsible for lake formation involves erosion of various kinds. Moving bodies of ice are probably the most important of these erosion agents, leaving a variety of

Above: Loch Einich in Scotland is a ribbon lake, lying on the floor of a glacial trough with typically steep, smoothly curving sides. Lakes are very common in glaciated areas as glacial erosion and deposition leave behind an irregular surface, with an abundance of hollows in which water can collect.

Left: Loch Ness, home of Nessie, a prehistoric 'monster' supposed to have survived the extinction of the dinosaurs 65 M.Y. ago. Towards the end of the last Ice Age about 12,000 years ago, Loch Ness was joined to the sea. Subsequent uplift of the land resulted from the melting of ice which had depressed the surface of Scotland by its weight. Any 'monsters' in the loch would have been trapped as Loch Ness was cut off from the sea.

Below: 'Bottomless lakes' carved out of gypsum in New Mexico (USA). Certain rocks—such as gypsum, rock salt and especially limestone—dissolve under the action of acidic water. Hollows are created that may become lakes if they lie below the water table or if the underground outlet of running water becomes clogged with inwashed clay. Lakes also form above collapsed caverns.

Aerofilms

H. Steenmans/ZEFA

Jerome Wyckoff

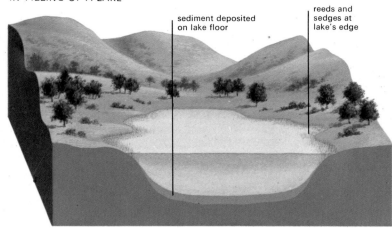

sediment deposited
on lake floor

reeds and
sedges at
lake's edge

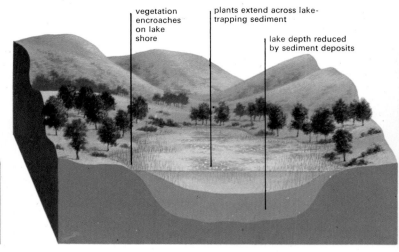

vegetation
encroaches
on lake
shore

plants extend across lake-
trapping sediment

lake depth reduced
by sediment deposits

Michael Freeman/Bruce Coleman

Photri

Left: An ox-bow lake in the forests of the Amazon Basin. The lake was left behind when the River Jutat cut through the narrow neck of a looping meander and changed its course. Ox-bow lakes soon disappear unless fed by a fresh supply of water. Already the trees and other vegetation have quickly colonized the ends of the loop, disguising the original course of the meander.

Right: Lakes Maurepas (below the river) and Pontchertrain were created partly by levee deposits from the Mississippi river and partly by the coastal deposits from the Gulf of Mexico (top right corner).

Below: The Parallel Roads of Glen Roy in Scotland gained their name from a legend that they were the hunting tracks used by giants. In fact they mark the former shorelines of an old lake, formed about 10,000 years ago by glaciers that blocked the mouth of the valley and trapped the waters of melting ice. The highest level of the lake has thus been recorded at 350 m.

attractive lakes in formerly glaciated areas. They form, for example, in deep, rounded hollows, known as *cirques* or *corries*, that have a rock lip or in deepened basins in troughs scoured out by glaciers. These are termed *ribbon lakes*, of which the Finger Lakes of New York State and the lakes of the Italian Alps—Maggiore, Como and Garda—are good examples.

In lowland areas, glacial erosion has often produced a very irregular topography that becomes a landscape of lakes and rocky outcrops. Topography of this type is found in parts of the Canadian Shield, north-west Scotland, as well as in Finland.

Another type of erosion that produces lakes is solution, by which rock material is dissolved in acidic water. In limestone areas this process may form steep-sided hollows known as *swallow holes* up to 30 metres (100 ft) deep which can fill up with water if they either lie below the water table or become clogged with inwashed clay. Lough Derg on the River Shannon in Ireland is thought to be due to the expansion and deepening of the limestone bed of the river by surface solution.

Deflation, the erosive action of the wind in desert regions, can also produce hollows of substantial size. If the hollows are eroded down to a level below that of the water table, they become shallow salt lakes or swamps. Many oases in the Sahara originated in this way.

There are rare examples of lakes that

Barnabys

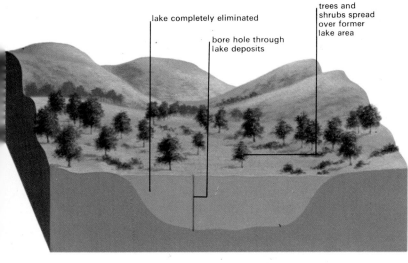

lake completely eliminated

bore hole through lake deposits

trees and shrubs spread over former lake area

Left: How a lake is filled by sedimentation and vegetation growth. In the initial stage the lake is clear of vegetation, but rivers flowing through carry sediment loads that are largely trapped by the calmer waters of the lake. Coarser deposits form deltas and beaches around the shores and finer deposits collect on the floor, gradually filling up the basin. When the depth is reduced to 1-2 m, plants may extend across the lake, greatly accelerating silting by trapping sediment. Eventually the lake becomes a swamp, a marsh and then firm ground on which trees and shrubs grow. Bores taken through old lake deposits reveal evidence of past environments.

Right: A salt lake on Santiago Island in the Galapagos Group, East Pacific. Salts left behind in the dry season are used commercially.

Below: Lake Tekapo in New Zealand is silting up. Where rivers flow into lakes, their velocities are checked and the sediment being transported is deposited in the form of deltas, as here where the muddy waters enter the lake.

Bottom: The Hoover Dam was built across the Colorado River in 1935, creating the 190 km long Lake Mead. The variation in lake level—shown by the light zone above the lake surface—is partly due to climatic factors and partly to human control of the water allowed to escape. The Colorado River deposits 700,000 tonnes of sediment in Lake Mead every year and if left to itself the lake will become completely infilled by 2250 AD.

Heather Angel

G. R. Roberts

Photri

have developed in the impact craters of large meteorites. The largest positively assigned to this origin is Lake Bosumtwi which occupies the Ashanti Crater in Ghana and is about 10 km (6 miles) wide.

Barrier lakes

A third group of processes which form lakes involves various types of deposition. Glacial deposits are often laid down in irregular sheets, in which the numerous hollows may fill up with water. Two other lake types associated with glacial deposits are those formed behind a barrier of terminal moraine and *kettle lakes*, formed in hollows produced by the melting of blocks of ice.

River deposits also form lakes. Common examples occur where river deposits seal up both ends of abandoned meander loops, thus forming *ox-bow lakes*, while the building of natural levees on both sides of river channels can prevent flood waters from flowing back into the river channel, creating flood plain lakes. In coastal locations this action produces delta *lagoons*, though these are often partly sealed by marine deposits.

Vegetation growth and animal activity can create barriers for lakes, but man is by far the most effective dam constructor. The growing demands for water have led to the large-scale impounding (blocking off) of rivers or enlargement of previously existing lakes. In the United States alone over 40,000 km² (15,000 sq miles) is now covered with artificially impounded water, an area larger than Belgium.

Elimination of lakes

One feature common to all lakes is their transient existence. Not only can their level change from time to time but eventually all lakes tend to be eliminated altogether. Lakes have been observed to drain temporarily after earth tremors, while the tilting of blocks of the earth's crust may lead to a more permanent elimination. Where lakes owe their existence to the position of the water table above the floor of a basin, it is clear that a fall in the water table will result in a drop in the level of the lake and in some cases to its complete disappearance.

Climatic change can produce changes in lake levels. For example, during the Ice Ages, evaporation rates were much lower in many presently semi-arid areas and a number of so-called *pluvial lakes* existed. The largest of these was Lake Bonneville in Utah which covered an area of 50,000 km² (20,000 sq miles) and was over 300 metres (1,000 ft) deep in places. The Great Salt Lake is a present day remnant of it. Similarly, most desert lakes or *playas* are particularly transient features. They may form during an occasional heavy shower but due to rapid evaporation they quickly disappear.

Just as lakes can be formed by a fall in relative sea-level, they can be destroyed by a relative rise of sea-level. This must have happened many times at the end of the Ice Ages as ice masses melted and returned water to the oceans. The best known example is probably the Baltic Sea which at one time towards the end of the last Ice Age was a fresh water body known as Ancylus Lake. As sea-level rose its threshold was overtopped and it became an arm of the sea.

Lakes may also disappear if the dams impounding them are broken through or removed. Ice-dammed lakes, for example, are drained if the water is able to escape under the ice or if the ice melts.

Lakes are of great importance to man. They not only provide natural reservoirs of water, but also help to regulate the flow of rivers, thus preventing excessive flooding and intermittent flow. However, outlet rivers supplied by the overflow from the lake tend to erode down through the barrier holding back the lake waters and may eventually drain the lake.

Another slow process by which lakes eventually disappear is sedimentation or *silting up*. If none of the previously described processes leads to elimination of a lake, then gradual sedimentation on the lake floor and vegetation growth will eventually fill it in, although this may take thousands of years.

One interesting aspect of lakes that have been filled by sediment and vegetation is that they can yield considerable information regarding the geomorphological, vegetational and climatic histories of surrounding areas. Radiocarbon dating of the bottom deposits gives a date for the creation of the lake and in glaciated areas gives a clear indication of when the area was deglaciated. Analysis of the pollen present throughout the core allows scientists to work out the vegetational history of the area and together with the study of beetles and other insects present is valuable in deciphering the climatic changes since the lake was created.

Limestone Terrain

Of all the major rock types, limestones produce one of the most distinctive types of terrain. A variety of features associated with limestone outcrops are recognizable throughout the world; some of these have been known for centuries by local names and as a result words from many different languages make up the current vocabulary describing limestone features. Many such words are either Slovene or Serbo-Croat, borrowed from the limestone terrain in Yugoslavia, an area composed of rugged mountains, the Dinaric Alps, and the low plateau of Istra. This region is known as the *Karst*, a term which is now commonly used by geologists to mean limestone terrain.

Natural waters, whether in the soil or in a stream, are actively erosive or *aggressive* when they first come into contact with the limestone of karst areas. All limestones, including both marble and chalk, are largely composed of calcite (calcium carbonate), one of the most common and readily dissolved minerals. As water percolates through the soil it picks up a considerable amount of carbon dioxide from the high percentage found in soil air. Calcium carbonate reacts with carbon dioxide and water to form the very soluble salt, calcium bicarbonate, which may be carried away in solution.

Limestones are mainly dissolved in two ways. Firstly, water percolating through the soil cover gradually lowers the overall land surface. In humid, mid-latitude areas, the rate at which the groundsurface is lowered may be as much as 50 to 100 mm (2-4 in) in a thousand years. Secondly, water which has converged into surface streams over non-limestone rocks concentrates solutional activity at the point where the river passes on to a limestone outcrop.

The other important feature of limestones is the fact that they are well-jointed. *Joints* are fractures in which little or no movement parallel to the walls of the fracture has taken place. Vertical joints originated due to contraction following the drying out of the limestone when it was first deposited. If the joints are horizontal, they mark changes in the character of the sediment or pauses during its deposition, and are termed *bedding joints* or *bedding planes*.

Joints allow water to find a path through the limestone. Some features of karst areas are due essentially to jointing and are very similar to comparable landforms in other well-jointed rocks which are non-soluble. For example,

Sonia Halliday

Above: The most striking feature of any limestone country is the general lack of any surface water. This dry, steep-sided gorge in Cappadocia, Turkey, was carved into massive, horizontally-jointed limestone. The cracks and bedding planes provided passages for water which dissolved the rock, creating large cavities. Debris at the foot of the cliffs suggests the gorge may be a collapsed cavern; alternatively it may be the steep-sided valley of a now vanished river.

Right: Calcite and aragonite may be deposited in layers of colourful crystals along the joints in limestone.

Below: This section reveals several underground features of well-jointed limestone. A surface stream running off impermeable rock disappears down a swallow hole and opens up a series of vertical shafts, chambers and narrow passages along the joints, before it reappears. Frequently, dripping water will form stalactites, stalagmites and pillars of limestone.

Ardea

UNDERGROUND FEATURES OF LIMESTONE

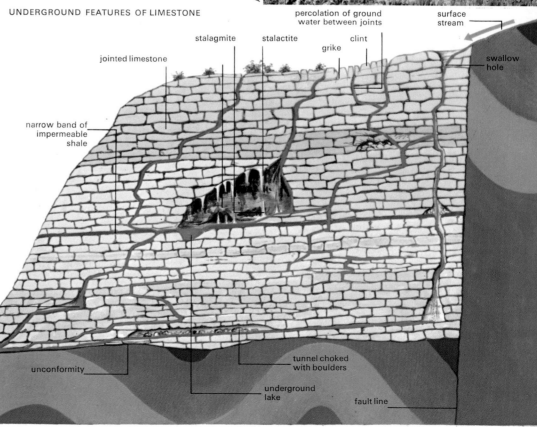

stalagmite — stalactite — percolation of ground water between joints — surface stream

jointed limestone — grike — clint — swallow hole

narrow band of impermeable shale

underground waterfall

resurgent stream

impermeable rock

unconformity

tunnel choked with boulders

underground lake

fault line

106

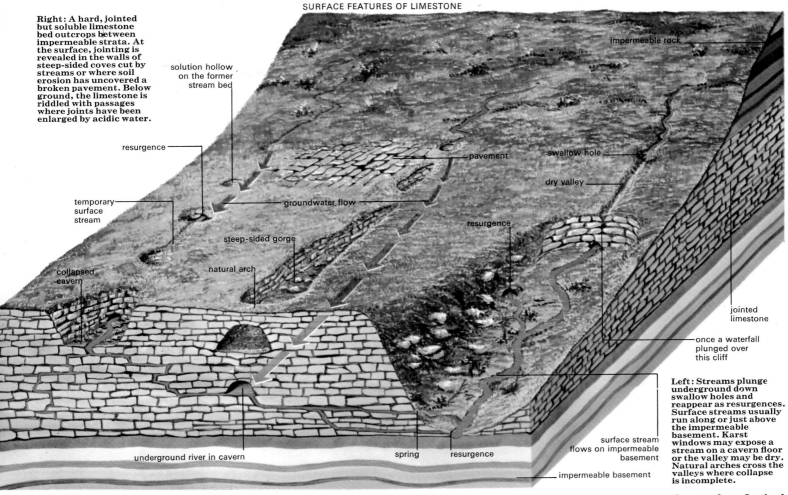

Right: A hard, jointed but soluble limestone bed outcrops between impermeable strata. At the surface, jointing is revealed in the walls of steep-sided coves cut by streams or where soil erosion has uncovered a broken pavement. Below ground, the limestone is riddled with passages where joints have been enlarged by acidic water.

solution hollow on the former stream bed

resurgence

temporary surface stream

groundwater flow

steep-sided gorge

natural arch

collapsed cavern

underground river in cavern

resurgence

spring

resurgence

impermeable rock

swallow hole

dry valley

jointed limestone

once a waterfall plunged over this cliff

surface stream flows on impermeable basement

impermeable basement

Left: Streams plunge underground down swallow holes and reappear as resurgences. Surface streams usually run along or just above the impermeable basement. Karst windows may expose a stream on a cavern floor or the valley may be dry. Natural arches cross the valleys where collapse is incomplete.

Heather Angel

J. L. Mason/Ardea

Institute of Geological Sciences

Above: At Hutton Roof Crag in North Yorkshire, a well-drained upland limestone pavement (or lapiés surface), bare of soil, has been eroded. As shown in the detail (above left) solution has worked along the roughly rectangular pattern of joints to hollow out the deep grooves called grykes between the masses of limestone clints. The largest clints are about 1 m across and the grykes may be over 0.5 m deep.

Left: A dry valley in Somerset, England. Theories vary as to the origin of such features. Some authorities view them as the product of cavern collapse; others as relics of a colder climate, when streams eroded the frozen, and thus impermeable, rock.

gorges cut into the rock are often flanked by sharp sides and steep cliffs that follow the outline of the jointing pattern. If a limestone is less well-jointed, like the porous chalk outcrops, smoother outlines develop in the landscape. Chalk is a soft, white type of fine-grained limestone. Because of its purity—chalk is composed almost entirely of calcium carbonate—it is highly soluble and easily eroded, giving rise to the gently rolling scenery found in the hills of eastern and southern England and the hills of Picardy and Artois in France.

It is the combination of these properties of limestone, being both soluble and well-jointed, that explains the distinctiveness of karst areas. For example, a surface stream may disappear at the junction of major joints, creating the limestone feature known as a *sink* or *swallow hole*. In England, a well-known example of a swallow hole is Gaping Ghyll, a deep opening in the Carboniferous Limestone in the Yorkshire Pennines. If a disappearing stream continues to erode its bed upstream from a swallow hole, the valley ends abruptly in a horseshoe-shaped cliff above the opening. This is termed a *blind valley*. The valley of the River Reka in Yugoslavia ends in this way.

Underground cave systems

Once underground, the stream continues to eat along the joints, enlarging caverns in the limestone. In horizontally-bedded strata, caves are made up of a series of vertical drops or *pitches* linked by horizontal *passages*. In mountain karsts, the total depth of caves is considerable. Near Lyon in eastern France, for example, the Gouffre Jean Bernard is estimated to 107 be 1,200 m (4,000 ft) deep.

Just below the surface, beneath a soil cover, solution slowly etches out the joint pattern. Due to deforestation and the consequent soil erosion in many areas in the Middle Ages, roughly rectangular blocks known as *limestone pavements* or as a *lapiés surface* are now revealed as a feature of well-jointed limestones. In north-west Yorkshire, the pavement is called a *clint* and the solution-enlarged joint is termed a *gryke*. The German word *karren* is widely used to describe grykes and solutional gutters on bare limestone outcrops.

Where major joints intersect, solutional activity may tend to concentrate and develop a funnel-shaped surface cavity, now widely described by the Slovene word *doline*. Dolines may be as much as 100 m (330 ft) in diameter. If the base intersects an underground drainage system, the doline sides may collapse to form a circle of sheer cliffs, termed a *shaft doline*. Such a doline, broadened to afford a view of the underground river emerging from one cave then disappearing into another, is called a *karst window*.

However, shaft dolines and karst windows are not common. Cave systems often have no noticeable effect on landforms developed above them on the surface, although some authorities suggest that a number of valleys in karst areas have formed by caverns collapsing.

Dry valleys

Drainage patterns, however, are markedly affected by cave systems; in many cases entire valleys are now streamless because all precipitation finds its way into underground fissures, voids or caves before it can concentrate as a surface stream. Such *dry valleys* can therefore be attributed to a lowering of the groundwater levels, as solution progressively enlarged joints which were once very narrow.

Dry valleys are also partly explained by climatic changes during the Quaternary and post-glacial periods of the last two million years. For instance, during the Quaternary period, the Karst in Yugoslavia was under the strong meteorological influences of the sub-Polar front and the ice cap of the Alps. Cyclones from the sea brought great quantities of moisture to the Karst mountains, much of it falling as snow, and the enormous floods of summer melts exceeded the capacity of the cave systems to lead all the water underground. This abundant surface flow over the permeable limestone cut out valleys, which today are dry.

Dry valleys and a lack of surface drainage are characteristic of most chalk country. One explanation suggested for the formation of streamless valleys in the highly porous English chalk areas is that they were cut when the ground was permanently frozen, which meant that the limestone was temporarily impermeable.

Climate is an important factor when present-day comparisons are made between the main karst areas of the world. Because solutional processes are governed by the amount of effective precipitation that falls, and by temperature, limestone terrains are not the same in different climatic zones. For example, in arctic or alpine areas, the main agent is the large volume of snowmelt which runs over bare rock surfaces in late spring and summer. Karren are therefore distinctive characteristics of such regions.

S. Schmidt/Bavaria

Left: The Karst region of Yugoslavia slopes down from the Dinaric Alps to the Dalmatian coast on the Adriatic Sea. This barren, rocky land is the most distinctive and closely studied of all limestone areas and many of the names given to local features are now used to describe limestone terrains found elsewhere.

Right: A polje, a large steep-sided depression, in the Montenegro hills. Poljes appear to be almost exclusively Yugoslavian features. They are of considerable agricultural importance in this bare, barren area as their alluvial floors often provide the only cultivable land available. Thus settlements often develop on the perimeter.

Below: A section through a typical Yugoslavian karst area. The landscape is dominated by the large polje, bounded by limestone hills. The origin of poljes is problematic: they may be due to erosion, or to earth movements such as faulting. Poljes often flood in winter to form large temporary lakes.

Barnaby's

THE YUGOSLAVIAN KARST REGION

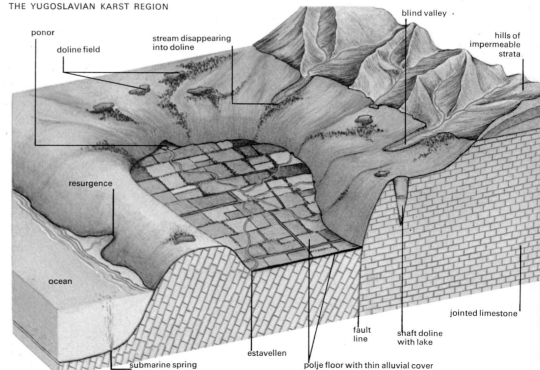

ponor

doline field

stream disappearing into doline

blind valley

hills of impermeable strata

resurgence

ocean

estavellen

submarine spring

polje floor with thin alluvial cover

fault line

shaft doline with lake

jointed limestone

Below: Cockpit country in central Jamaica is the classic area for cone karst—a landscape of limestone peaks which looks rather like an egg box. Cockpit karst is restricted to limestones with widely spaced joints in tropical regions, other examples being found in Cuba, Vietnam, New Guinea and Indonesia.

Right: Tower karst in Kwangsi province, China. These precipitous peaks were probably formed when dolines and other holes coalesced to produce wide plains with hums (isolated hills). The tower karst landscape has been the inspiration for the spectacular background scenery of many Chinese drawings and paintings.

William MacQuitty

A. L. Waltham

Above: White Horse Hill above Uffington in Berkshire. The large figure of a horse, thought to date from the Iron Age, was sculpted on the scarp slope by removing the turf to show the white chalk subsoil. Chalk is highly porous and its gentle topography is characteristically streamless.

Below: A steep gorge cut by the fast-flowing River Cunningham in Somerset Island in the Canadian Arctic. The underlying permafrost renders the limestone impermeable and prevents the surface stream from percolating into the rock. Usually rivers on a limestone surface are only found in areas of permafrost.

D. I. Smith

Terence Spencer/Colorific!

In contrast, warmer karst areas are dominated by large depressions known as *poljes*, from the Serbo-Croat word for field. A polje, however, is a very unusual type of field. It is the very flat floor of a large, isolated karst depression, cut across the bedrock and bounded by steep slopes on all sides. Poljes, which are often several kilometres long, experience seasonal flooding. Winter run-off from the surrounding hills is too great to be drained off by the existing cave systems. So a large temporary lake forms. Swallow holes at the edge of poljes are called *ponors*. Some underground systems act as springs in winter when water is plentiful and as swallow holes in summer. These seasonally fluctuating features are termed *estavellen*.

Poljes have not developed in cooler environments, although the *turloughs* of County Clare in western Ireland are very similar. The slopes of the perimeter of high land around the turloughs are gently inclined, whereas in humid, tropical regions the contrast between polje floor and the surrounding hills is more accentuated. The major reason for this is the increased acidity of water in warm, moist areas, caused by the swift decay of dead vegetation on the ground. Highly acidic water subjects the limestones to rapid erosion.

In karst country in the humid tropics where the hills have become isolated in a flat plain, the distinctive *tower karst* country is developed. The junction of the polje floor with the karst tower is very abrupt and there is often solutional undercutting of the tower. Rock falls at such points have been recorded in recent years in Malaya. Another distinctive feature of tropical karst is the enlargement of adjacent dolines until any flat land between them is eliminated. The higher land is reduced to a series of isolated peaks or *cone karst*. The classic example of cone karst is the Cockpit country of Jamaica.

Much of the calcium carbonate dissolved from limestones remains in solution until the drainage waters reach the ocean. But in certain circumstances, deposition of calcium carbonate may occur in sufficient quantities to create new landforms. Deposition seems to happen more in warmer climates and at points where water is slow-moving or running as a thin film over rock. Precipitated calcium carbonate is called *travertine* and occasionally forms *waterfall screens*, which look like petrified waterfalls. Within the tropical belt the best-known limestone terrain, the coral atolls, are formed by the abstraction of calcium carbonate from sea water by coral polyps.

There is always an impermeable basement to any limestone block which will halt the downward percolation of ground water. Within the limestone strata, thin impermeable layers like shale, volcanic ash or marl act as the floor of an extensive cave passage system and of the outlet of a spring or resurgent stream—until the layers are eventually breached. In a *covered karst*, a non-soluble or impermeable stratum remains above an underlying limestone mass. If the cover is relatively thin and the limestone strata beneath undergoes extensive solution, they may collapse, creating dolines in the cover rock itself.

109

Glacial Erosion

About ten per cent of the earth's land surface is covered in ice. As recently as 70,000 to 10,000 years ago, during the last major advance of the Pleistocene Ice Age, almost 30 per cent of the earth was blanketed by ice and snow, profoundly affecting the landscape of many areas. Today, the erosional effects of ice are reshaping such spectacular scenery as the mountains and valleys of the European Alps.

The ice which feeds the world's vast ice sheets and glaciers primarily forms through prolonged accumulation of snow. However, fresh snow is light and easily disturbed and, before it is converted into heavier, more tightly compacted ice, various processes have to take place. The change is mostly due to the compression of snow by the weight of successive additions from direct snowfalls and from avalanches down surrounding slopes.

In some areas summer temperatures and the increasing pressure of successive layers of snowfall cause some of the ice particles to melt. The *meltwater* produced then trickles down through the snow and refreezes, so that the compressed snow is further compacted. In this state, the snow is a porous mass of small, rounded granules known as *firn* or *névé*. The continued pressure of overlying snow concentrates the trapped air into gas bubbles under very high pressure, and the particles become even more closely locked together. When the ice finally forms a solid state composed of interlocking ice crystals, it is termed *glacier ice*.

Types of glacier

Broadly speaking, there are two types of glacier: valley glaciers and continental glaciers. By far the most extensive are *continental glaciers*, vast areas of ice spreading out under their own weight. The larger spreads, such as those covering Antarctica and Greenland, are usually called *ice sheets*, while smaller areas of ice, such as those in Iceland and Norway, are known as *ice caps*.

The largest European ice cap is in Iceland, covers about 19,500 km² (7,500 sq miles) and is about 230 m (750 feet) thick. This is relatively unimpressive, however, when compared with the Antarctic ice sheet which extends over 13,000,000 km² (5,000,000 sq miles), and the Greenland ice sheet, which covers an area 10 times the size of England and Wales—and in places is 3,000 m (10,000 ft) thick.

Much of Greenland is permanently covered in ice and, except for the southwest of the island (where the ice terminates before reaching the sea), the ice sheet spills through the coastal mountains and descends in the form of outlet glaciers.

Valley glaciers are slow-moving rivers of ice which flow downwards from higher to lower land along the easiest route, namely valleys. They can be divided into three sections, starting with the source or *zone of accumulation* where accumulated snow is transformed into glacier ice.

Moving out of the basin, the mass of ice

D. J. Drewry

Above: Small glaciers on mountain sides may erode a bowl-shaped *cirque*. This ice-filled cirque in Antarctica lies above the 200 km-long Beardmore Glacier, one of the world's largest.

GLACIATED LANDSCAPE

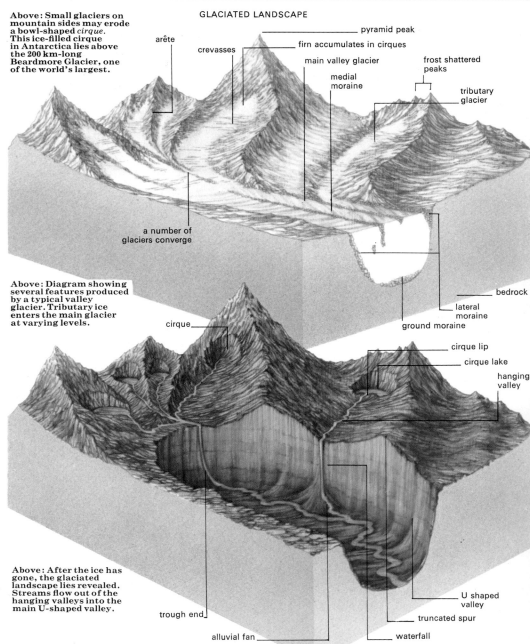

arête
crevasses
pyramid peak
firn accumulates in cirques
main valley glacier
medial moraine
frost shattered peaks
tributary glacier
a number of glaciers converge
bedrock
lateral moraine
ground moraine

Above: Diagram showing several features produced by a typical valley glacier. Tributary ice enters the main glacier at varying levels.

cirque
cirque lip
cirque lake
hanging valley

Above: After the ice has gone, the glaciated landscape lies revealed. Streams flow out of the hanging valleys into the main U-shaped valley.

trough end
alluvial fan
waterfall
truncated spur
U shaped valley

enters its zone of transit. As it flows downwards, its surface begins to split and crack, probably due to movement within the ice mass itself, to form openings or *crevasses*.

Crevasses also occur along the margins of the glacier, due to the difference in the rate of movement of ice in the middle of the glacier and along the valley wall. Other features of this stage are steep ridges called *seracs*, and *ice falls*, masses of ridges and crevasses, caused by a change in gradient of the glacier bed. The Khumbu ice fall in Nepal, for example, is badly crevassed, proving an obstacle to climbers using the southern approach to Mt. Everest.

During its downward journey, the glacier acts on, and wears away, the underlying rock. In addition, rock fragments detached from the valley walls by the action of frost, fall on to the glacier and are carried along by it. Debris transported and deposited by glaciers is termed *moraine*.

Finally, the ice mass moves beyond the *snow line* (the lower limit of permanent snow) into an area of decline or *zone of ablation*. Here the glacier is subject to the effects of evaporation and melting which contributes to this decline.

The processes of glacial erosion

Glacial erosion forms the first part of a continuous chain of glacial activity, which ends with transportation of debris to its place of deposition. Various factors contribute to the degree and rate of erosion: the strength, hardness and pattern of joints and fractures in the underlying rock, the thickness and speed of the glacier, and the concentration and characteristics of the rock fragments within the base or *sole* of the ice.

Three key processes are involved in glacial erosion. *Abrasion* refers to the scraping or scratching action on the glacier bed of rock fragments held in the lowest levels of ice. *Crushing* involves the grinding or breaking-down of bedrock by the weight and pressure of ice and debris, while *plucking* is the direct incorporation of crushed or abraded material into the glacier base. The processes of crushing and plucking are sometimes collectively known as *quarrying*. A fourth, less crucial process involves erosion by meltwater beneath the ice, concentrated into channels or cavities. Such fluvial erosion may constitute an important method of entirely removing loose material from a glacier basin.

Abrasion at bed level is principally controlled by the pressure of overlying ice. As the ice thickness increases, so the pressures at the base of the glacier also increase, resulting in accelerating rates of abrasion. It appears, however, that beyond a certain ice load rates of abrasion begin to decline and may be eliminated altogether.

Crushing of bedrock to produce rock fragments and boulders is also dependent upon the weight of the load of ice. Here too, however, it is thought that as ice thickness increases so the degree of crushing will reach a peak and then decline.

The action of plucking requires that ice comes into direct contact with loosened materials. These materials are then incorporated into the mass of ice in two ways: fragments may be picked up and encased in the viscous flow of the ice; or

Above: A glaciated valley in the Southern Alps of New Zealand. Glaciers flowing through mountainous country carve out deep, straight, U-shaped valleys by concentrating erosion at the bed and sides. After the glaciers have melted, these valleys provide some of the most impressive scenery of alpine areas. Peaks above the smoothed valley are fretted with spires and jagged pinnacles formed by the action of frost and ice.

Below: Mt Blanc, the highest peak in the European Alps, lies in a sea of moving ice spread over 100 km². Various parts of glaciers move at different rates and this view shows how the centre of a glacier flows faster than the sides.

Left: Geiranger Fjord in Norway was scooped out by very thick glaciers flowing swiftly out of the former Scandinavian ice sheet. These powerful outlet glaciers were able to erode very deep, steep-sided valleys, even below sea level. When the ice retreated and sea level rose, the great trenches were flooded to form fjords.

Below: Sutherland Falls in the Southern Alps (NZ) where much of the landscape was once covered by ice and valley glaciers. Less powerful tributary glaciers often left a valley perched above the deeper trunk channel. Such *hanging valleys* may have lakes in the overdeepened basins, from which waterfalls tumble.

111

a mixture of water and rock debris may amalgamate by being frozen on to the glacier sole.

The type and extent of these processes depends particularly on temperatures at the glacier bed. The temperatures at the sole of *wet-based* or temperate glaciers and ice caps are at the *pressure melting point* (the lower melting point of ice when under great pressure) due to the sheer weight of overlying ice and warmer mean annual temperatures at their surface. A thin layer of water may consequently exist on the bed, causing the ice mass to move faster. For example, most valley glaciers in the Alps, in Scandinavia, in parts of the Rocky Mountains and in Iceland are wet-based. The whole range of erosional processes—abrasion, quarrying and melt-water beneath the ice—are vigorous in these glaciers.

Dry-based or cold ice masses, on the other hand, are characterized by temperatures at their base below the pressure melting point. In other words, they are frozen to the rock and no water can exist at the bed. Such conditions occur over large areas of the Antarctic and Greenland ice sheets and in some valley glaciers in high latitudes. Naturally the action of meltwater is completely suppressed here, and although plucking of materials appears to be somewhat enhanced under cold conditions, in general erosion is less effective.

Landforms produced by erosion

A great variety of distinctive landforms are created by glacial erosion. On a small scale, scratches known as *striations* are produced mainly by abrasion. Rock

Norman Myers/Bruce Coleman

Left: Glaciers on the Greenland coast descend to the ocean, carving deep valleys, often below sea level. High on the mountain sides, exposed rock has been shattered under the severe glacial climate. Many highland areas of maritime Europe would have looked similar to this some 50,000 years ago.

Right: An aerial view of ice-scraped plains in Jameson Land, north-east Greenland. Vast lowland areas of Canada and Eurasia were once covered by enormous ice sheets thousands of metres thick and similar to those still present in Antarctica and Greenland. Erosion by such ice has scoured the rock surface, producing a gnarled, hummocky and now barren terrain.

Right: Vestfjella in Antarctica are present-day *nunataks*. This is the Eskimo name given to isolated protruberances of land which look like islands in a sea of ice. They occur when ice sheets develop, drowning the former landscape, leaving only the highest mountain tops above the surface of the ice sheet. There they may be etched and fretted by the frost.

Below: The head of a glacier may be a deepened cirque in which accumulated snow is converted to ice. A deep vertical crack or *bergschrund* develops in the ice where the moving ice-mass pulls away from the cirque wall. The detail shows how frost-shattered rock falls into the bergschrund and is carried away by the ice.

D. J. Drewry

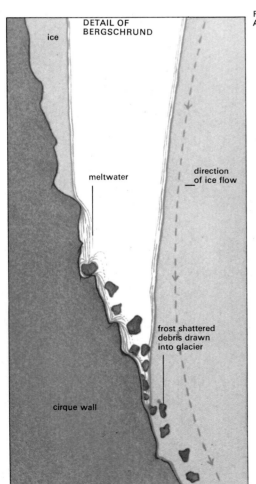

DETAIL OF BERGSCHRUND

ice

meltwater

direction of ice flow

frost shattered debris drawn into glacier

cirque wall

PROFILE OF A GLACIER

frost shattering

bergschrund

section shown in detail (left)

cirque

cirque lip

ZONE OF ACCUMULATION (snowfall)

rotational movement of glacier ice

crevasses at ice fall

ground morraine

rockstep

Institute of Geological Sciences

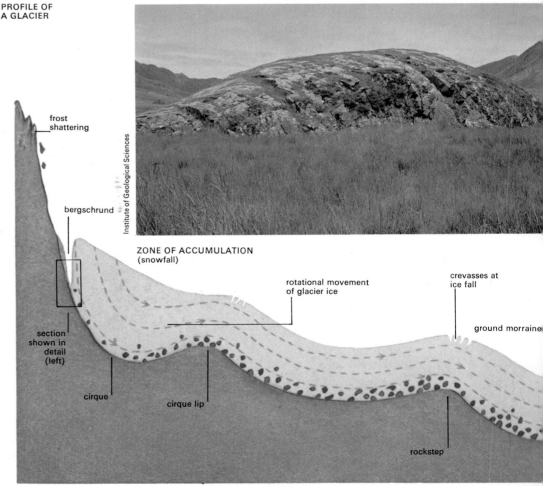

fragments, held tightly in the glacier base, are dragged across the bedrock cutting linear scratches of varying depth (from a few millimetres to a metre or more) and up to 100 m (330 ft) long. *Gouges*, crescent-shaped cracks, and *chattermarks*, close series of gouges, also originate from boulders coming into contact with the bed and causing it to fracture.

On a larger scale, ice may mould hummocks, mounds and small hills of hard rock into asymmetric, streamlined landforms. Such features, termed *roches mountonnées* or *whalebacks*, are found widely in glaciated regions such as Scotland, north Wales and Scandinavia.

In mountainous regions, such as the Alps and Rockies, hollows or *cirques* (known as *cwms* in Wales and *corries* in Scotland) are found above and at the heads of many glaciated valleys. These deep bowl-shaped rock depressions, with a steep backwall and a flatter floor, frequently contain a small lake or tarn once the ice has melted. Many cirques have diameters up to 1-2 km (0.6-1.2 miles), with cliffs up to 1,000 m (3,300 ft) in height.

Glacial valleys are distinguished by their generally straight, deeply hollowed appearance and constitute one of the most spectacular elements of glacially sculptured highlands. In cross-section their shape is broadly that of a 'U' contrasting strongly with the 'V' shape of valleys produced by fluvial erosion. Nevertheless most glacial troughs have evolved due to the modification of former river valleys occupied by temperate glaciers during glacial episodes.

Tributary glacial valleys are frequently left as *hanging valleys* above a main glacial trough since glaciers, unlike rivers, do not combine to erode to a common base level. Each individual glacier acts as a semi-independent force, and the main, usually thicker glacier erodes its valley more deeply than the tributaries.

Fjords are valleys reaching to sea-level in mountainous coastal localities, created either by glacial erosion below sea level, or by the submergence of glacial troughs as the sea level rises. They usually have excessively deepened basins and precipitous sides, the result of vigorous erosion due to considerable ice thickness and high ice velocity. The Skelton Inlet in Antarctica (at present still ice-covered) has a maximum water depth of 1,933 m (6,350 ft) and a full vertical elevation range of 4,500 m (14,750 ft). Other equally impressive fjords occur in western Norway, Greenland and Scotland (where they are known as sea-lochs), and on the north-west coast of North America, in Chile and in South Island, New Zealand.

Some elements of mountainous glacial landscape are the combined result of a variety of erosional processes. *Arêtes*, for instance, are the knife-edged, serrated ridges that separate glacial valleys or cirques. Pointed pyramidal peaks or *horns*, such as the Matterhorn and Weisshorn in the Alps, form as a result of erosional retreat of a series of cirques around a central mountain massif.

In contrast to highland regions, the topography produced by glacial erosion in lowland areas is less marked and exhibits quite different characteristics, which are related to ice sheet activity rather than that of valley glaciers. Frequent among landforms here are ice-scoured plains made up of numbers of rounded rock-knobs and hollows, often termed *knock and lochan topography* in southern Scotland. In some locations ice has imprinted a dominant grain or lineation on the scoured terrain, which mirrors the overall direction of ice flow and is called *fluting*. Large tracts of the Scandinavian and the Canadian shields display this kind of landscape. On a greater scale, extensive basins may be formed by glacial erosion, especially near the margins of former ice sheets. A key element governing the glacial processes which produce these types of landform is the condition of the bedrock, and the relief of undulating lowland regions, exposed when the ice melts, may closely reflect varying degrees of abrasion and quarrying of weak and resistant strata.

D. J. Drewry

Right: Formation of a roche moutonnée. The ice sheets covering upland areas in the last Ice Age shaped the underlying hard rocks into streamlined features reflecting the movement of the ice. Rock is scraped away on the up-glacier side, while loosened material on the down-glacier flank is plucked away.

Left: A roche moutonnée in Caernarvonshire, Wales.

Right: A *crag and tail* is produced where a mass of resistant rock lies in the path of an oncoming glacier or ice-sheet. The 'crag' protects the softer rocks in its lee from erosion and the movement of the glacier over the top leaves a gently sloping 'tail'.

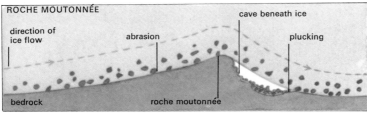

ROCHE MOUTONNÉE

direction of ice flow · abrasion · cave beneath ice · plucking

bedrock · roche moutonnée

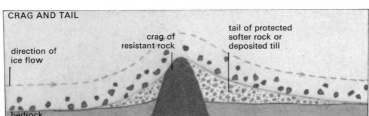

CRAG AND TAIL

direction of ice flow · crag of resistant rock · tail of protected softer rock or deposited till

bedrock

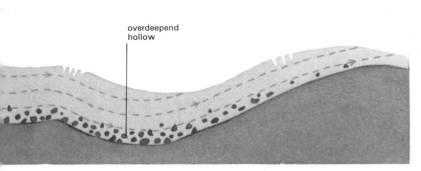

ZONE OF ABLATION (evaporation and melting)

overdeepend hollow

Left: The long profile of a glacier reveals the usually low gradient of the ice as it flows from high relief to lower ground. Unlike water, ice can flow uphill under the right circumstances and carve out *overdeepened* hollows. The early stages of the glacier, where ice forms faster than it melts, is known as the *zone of accumulation*. The *zone of ablation* begins when the glacier loses more ice to evaporation and melting than it gains.

Right: The entrance to an ice cave in Norway. In such caves or tunnels in the ice, scientists can view the bed of a glacier and study how moving ice erodes the underlying rocks. Stones held in the glacier base are scraped over bare rock surfaces.

Ardea

113

Glacial Deposits

During the last two million years, over 30 million square kilometres (11,500,000 sq miles) of northern Europe, North America and Asia were periodically covered by great ice sheets. The melting of the ice left large expanses of these continents covered by a veneer of glacial sediments, varying from a few centimetres to more than 400 metres (1,300 ft) thick.

On land, glacial sediments are now of great economic importance. They constitute some of the world's most fertile agricultural land and are a major source of sand and gravel for building aggregate (material added to cement to make concrete). On the deep-sea floor, glacial debris produced by the melting of icebergs, covering vast areas, has lain relatively undisturbed since deposition and thus provides crucial clues to the recent glacial history of the earth.

Glacial deposition forms the final part of a train of glacial processes beginning with the incorporation of soil and rock into a glacier as it erodes the land. These materials are then transported and often modified by moving ice and water before their final deposition in a range of environments, often producing distinctive landforms.

Glacial sediments are classified into two main groups: 'till' and sorted deposits. *Till* is a random mixture of rock particles, including at times both tiny clay particles and massive boulders (hence the alternative name, *boulder clay*); it is deposited directly by the glacier. Stratified or *sorted deposits*, on the other hand, require the action of water or wind to sort their particles according to size and weight. Once deposited, sediment is also altered by chemical processes, which adds to the distinction between younger and older material.

Till and moraine

Deposits of till produced by the ice are generally described as *moraine*, a term which is also applied to all debris transported by a glacier.

Till can be transported by ice in various ways. If it is carried at or near a glacier's surface, elongated lines of sediment may form, either at the sides of a glacier in the ablation or melting zone (*lateral moraine*), or where laterals from tributary glaciers coalesce in the centre of a main glacier (*medial moraine*). If sediments are carried at the bed of a glacier, they may form closely stacked layers with occasional lumps of other materials. The thickness of these basal layers is about one per cent of the glacier's depth and the concentration of debris decreases upwards from the base. As it is carried along, till is often modified as pebbles are broken, scratched, smoothed and frequently changed in shape. Only a very small percentage of material survives such destructive processes for more than about 30 km (20 miles)—and then only in a ground-up form. Granite and metamorphic rocks, for instance, may be reduced to fine sand over long distances, while shales persist only as clay-sized particles. However, very large boulders may be transported many kilometres by ice and, when deposited, stand out as *erratics*, rocks or rock fragments foreign to their new geological

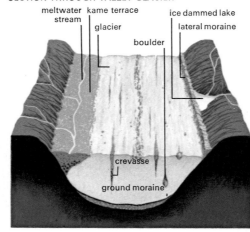

meltwater stream · kame terrace · glacier · boulder · ice dammed lake · lateral moraine · crevasse · ground moraine

Above: Far from being rivers of pure ice, glaciers are typically 'dirty'. Vast amounts of material are picked up and carried as moraine in the sides, base and body of glaciers. Debris is also supplied by meltwater streams, which may flow alongside a glacier, adding to the deposits of lateral moraine.

Below: When the ice has melted, a variety of glacial deposits decorate the landscape. *Kame terraces*, laid down by streams which flowed along the margins of valley glaciers, and other lateral moraines are subject to stream erosion. Former ice-crevasse fillings and erratics are strewn over the valley floor.

DEPOSITS LEFT AFTER ICE HAS MELTED

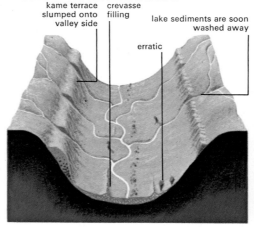

kame terrace slumped onto valley side · crevasse filling · lake sediments are soon washed away · erratic

Aerofilms

Above: Small glaciers have withdrawn from the precipitous flanks of the Breithorn-Monte Rosa massif in the Swiss Alps, leaving behind long moraine ridges of rock debris. These impressive lateral moraines, lying parallel to the sides of the former glacier, are being rapidly lost to landslides and mountain torrents.

Below: A trail of loose rock fragments stretches along the centre of this glacier in Greenland. Such linear ridges are called *medial moraines* and originate from the union of lateral moraines when two adjacent glaciers come together. They are best developed in the lower reaches of melting glaciers.

D. J. Drewry

setting.

Till carried at the base of a glacier is often deposited in horizontal sheets. Sediments close to the glacier sole are continuously transported by the force of the moving ice until this force becomes insufficient to carry the debris with it. The immobile till is then described as *lodged*. Basal till is also deposited by *melting-out*, which occurs when the lower layers of a glacier melt, leaving their sediment on the bed.

Till can also originate from sediments carried on the surface of a glacier. As the surface melts, a thick deposit is produced on top of the glacier, heavily charged with meltwater; this is known as *flow-till*.

Landforms produced by till

By far the most predominant form taken by till, after the ice masses have disappeared, is that of a shapeless sheet of boulder clay, such as those found in eastern England, northern Germany or parts of the eastern USA. Such sheets are usually the product of lodgement and sometimes carry a superficial layer of flow or melt-out till. Within spreads of till, however, a variety of other forms occur, related to special conditions on the glacier bed during deposition.

D. H. Teuffen/ZEFA

Left: High up on the right bank of the Glacier du Collon in the Swiss Alps, a close-up shows lateral moraine, formed by material incorporated into the glacier from rock-falls on the valley side. Here the glacier (on the left) has shrunk back, revealing the moraine, subsequently gullied by rain waters.

Below: Tottering pillars of earth in the Val d' Hérens, Switzerland. The constituents of a thick layer of *till* (a mixture of clay, rock fragments and boulders carried and then deposited by ice sheets and glaciers) have been exposed to view by heavy rainfall. The larger boulders have protected the earth spires from rain erosion.

Picturepoint

Left: The *sandar* plains of southern Iceland consist of large amounts of sediment and debris carried away by streams and rivers of melting snow and ice from glaciers and ice caps. These pro-glacial rivers have built up spectacular spreads of sand and gravel stretching over many tens of square kilometres.

Below: A floating tongue of ice near Scoresby Sund, Greenland. In severely glaciated areas such as Greenland and Antarctica glaciers may reach the sea and start to float. Icebergs break off from the edges and drift out into open sea, often for great distances. When they melt, debris and moraine carried in and on the ice is deposited on the sea floor.

Bavaria

Drumlins are streamlined mounds of till, commonly appearing in clusters. They may have rock cores and often occur behind moraines formed at the front of an ice sheet. The drumlins which extend over much of Northern Ireland, are one of the largest groups in the world. They vary considerably in size, ranging from a few metres in length and height, to over 1.5 km (1 mile) long and 60 m (200 feet) high. It seems probable that drumlins originated as masses of debris lodged beneath the glacier and subsequently streamlined by moving ice. Other moulded till forms such as *flutes* (ridges parallel to the former direction of ice flow) are produced by similar processes.

Both basal and surface till are often continuously deposited at the front of a glacier or ice sheet. While the ice front remains fairly stationary, materials falling down the front or carried along by meltwater build up a ridge of debris or *terminal moraine* along the margin of an ice sheet or at the end or *snout* of a glacier. Only terminal moraines from the last or furthest glacial advance usually remain, but those left after the retreat of powerfully erosive glaciers can be most spectacular. The largest terminal moraine in Britain is the Cromer Ridge near the coast of Norfolk, which is 8 km (5 miles) wide, 24 m (15 miles) long, and over 90 m (300 ft) high.

Sorted sediments

Sorted deposits, often with well-developed layering or *bedding*, have very different characteristics from till. They accumulate either close to an ice mass (where they are termed *ice-contact* deposits) or at a greater distance beyond the ice front

D. J. Drewry

Courtesy Institute of Geological Sciences

E. A. Francis

J. Allan Cash

(*pro-glacial* deposits).

Some of the most important groups of sorted sediments are those deposited by glacial meltwater. Where these are of the ice-contact variety, a distinctive morphology and sediment texture may be produced. *Eskers* are long, narrow ridges which snake sinuously up and down over gently undulating terrain, often reaching several hundred kilometres in length and hundreds of metres in height. In some cases they are made up of mounds joined by low ridges, in others of complex networks of criss-crossing ridges. The sediments forming eskers are sorted pebbles and cobbles, often with little sand or silt. Crude stratification is present with cross-bedding and structures such as ripples and dunes.

Eskers are primarily formed by streams tunnelling beneath, within or on a glacier, carrying sediment which sinks to ground level when the ice melts. Observations have indicated that some eskers may also be produced from sediments carried by melt-water streams flowing into pro-glacial lakes. Some of the best developed eskers are to be found in the lake country of Finland and other examples occur in central Ireland and parts of northern Canada.

Other ice-contact deposits include *kame terraces* which are laid down mainly by streams flowing in a trough between valley glaciers and their valley walls. As the ice retreats, deposits are left on hillsides, which sometimes slump down into the valley.

Meltwater deposits

Pro-glacial sediments, washed out of an ice mass by meltwater, are deposited beyond the ice front and form fan-shaped spreads of sediment called *outwash*. Where confined in a narrow valley, outwash deposits are called *valley trains*. The condition of meltwater and debris issuing from a glacier determines the nature of the sediments in these trains. Close to the glacier, they may be coarse but decrease in size down the valley.

Where sedimentation is not confined by a valley, outwash fans may coalesce to produce broad alluvial expanses or *outwash plains*. Much of the south coast of Iceland is made up of outwash material, called *sandar*. In New Zealand, the Canterbury Plains on the east-central side of South Island constitute an outwash plain of over 10,000 km² (4,000 sq miles) left by sediment-laden meltwaters from glaciers in the Southern Alps.

D. J. Drewry

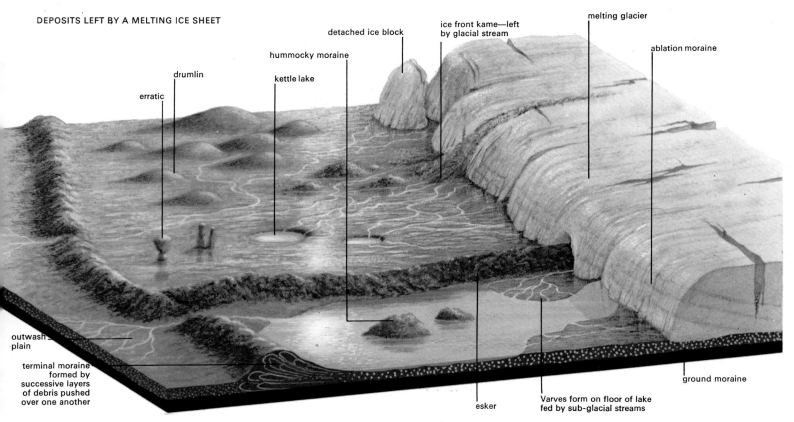

erratic — drumlin — hummocky moraine — kettle lake — detached ice block — ice front kame—left by glacial stream — melting glacier — ablation moraine

outwash plain

terminal moraine formed by successive layers of debris pushed over one another

esker — Varves form on floor of lake fed by sub-glacial streams — ground moraine

Right: An aerial view of an *esker* lying between lakes in the Canadian tundra near Hudson Bay. Eskers are long, sinuous ridges of sediment formed by water flowing in tunnels near the bed of a glacier. When the ice disappears they are left as long piles of sorted debris, snaking across barren ice-scoured terrain.

Below: A glacier will often deposit a girdle of rock and debris at its front or *snout*. Such curved ridges are called *terminal moraines* and their size depends on how long the glacier snout remains stationary. The terminal moraine of the Roslin Glacier in East Greenland, shown here, is large and marks the furthest advance of the ice in recent years.

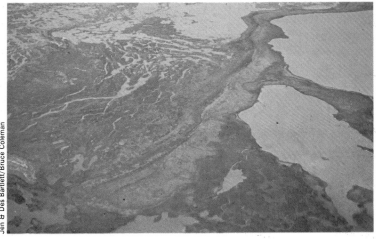

Jen & Des Bartlett/Bruce Coleman

Above: Several of the depositional features left behind by a retreating ice sheet or glacier. The ridge of terminal moraine marks the furthest advance of the ice front and has formed a natural dam for a lake fed by meltwater. A blanket of ground moraine covers the whole glaciated area. On the lake floor, annual deposits of varves are also being laid down. The shapes of the winding esker and streamlined drumlins reveal the direction of the former ice-flow. Kettle lakes form in hollows left by large, detached melting blocks of ice. Beyond the ice front, streams spread out over a broad outwash plain.

Where glacial meltwaters are blocked by rock-bars, moraines or other obstructions, pro-glacial lakes may form and sediments in these are termed *glacio-lacustrine* (that is, deposited in glacial lakes). As streams enter the lakes, their speed is checked and part of their load is deposited, creating deltas.

Glacial chronology

Within lakes, finer materials also settle, forming *varves*, distinctive banded deposits. Each varve consists of two layers, one coarse and light in colour, the other darker and finer. During the summer thaw, the flow of water is able to carry and deposit the coarser material, while in winter, when water movement diminishes due to freezing, the finer particles settle; thus each varve represents one year's deposit. Exceptionally well-preserved varves found in southern Sweden were investigated late in the nineteenth century by Baron de Geer. His pioneering and painstaking work of counting varve 'couplets' gave some of the earliest accurate dates to the fluctuations and overall retreat of ice in Europe.

During the Pleistocene Ice Age, strong winds were generated by the climatic conditions. Fine materials (silt and clay constituents) were picked up and carried over many hundreds of kilometres, eventually to be deposited as *loess*. This is a porous, crumbly silt deposit, usually without bedding, coloured yellow, orange or brown due to staining by iron minerals. Loess occurs in sheets many metres thick, particularly in central North America, eastern and central Europe, and China, and it is highly fertile. The loess zone of Europe is one of its most important agricultural areas.

Glacial deposits at sea

The most extensive area of glacial deposition is to be found, not on land, but on the sea-floor. Glaciers descending from coastal mountains may reach the sea and float out if the water is sufficiently deep. The edges of continental ice sheets may also terminate as a thick shelf of ice over the sea. In both cases chunks of ice may regularly break off at the edges to form *icebergs*. These are then carried by currents and wind into the open sea where they eventually melt away.

Any sediments carried by these icebergs will then be deposited as a mantle on the sea-floor. These glacial sediments contrast strongly with normal marine deposits because of the greater size of particles, their lack of fossils and the often distinctive scratches, cracks, grooves and polish on individual grains. Extensive accumulations of such deposits in the Southern Ocean today completely girdle the ice-covered Antarctic continent and date back 25 million years. In the Northern Hemisphere they cover the floor of many sea areas, testifying to the presence, in the not-too-distant past, of ice sheets on adjacent land.

117

Frozen Landscapes

In many of the cold regions of the world, the land is free from glaciers and ice sheets but temperatures are low enough to result in distinctive processes and landscape features. In 1909 the term *periglacial* (literally meaning 'around the ice') was introduced into geomorphology to describe the climate and associated features found on the margins of past and present ice sheets. The term periglaciation is now used to include all cold climate phenomena except those directly related to ice itself or glacial meltwater.

At present about 20 per cent of the world's land area is periglaciated. In the southern hemisphere, periglaciation occurs in those parts of the Antarctic not covered in ice, on the tops of the South American Andes and mountains in New Zealand, Australia and New Guinea. But the main periglaciated areas are in the northern hemisphere, where they are associated with the freezing peaks of many mountain ranges, Arctic Canada and Greenland, and the cold tundra of high latitudes. Tundra areas are barren, treeless plains where the average temperature of the warmest month never reaches above 10°C. They stretch across Alaska, northern Canada and parts of northern Europe and Asia, including vast tracts of Siberia. Something like 50 per cent of the total area of the USSR may be underlain by permanently frozen ground.

Frozen ground

There are two main types of frozen ground: seasonally frozen and permanently frozen ground, known as *permafrost*. Seasonally frozen ground is the zone near the surface where annual freezing and thawing takes place. It varies in thickness from a few millimetres to some four metres (up to 13 ft).

Below seasonally frozen ground and towards the poles lies the permafrost, which can be hundreds of metres thick. One exceptional figure of 1,500 m (almost one mile) was recorded in Siberia but there have been few other records of permafrost extending deeper than 500 m (1,650 ft). The maximum depth will vary with different rock types, but is largely determined by the heat-flow from the

Left: Aerial view of the thawing Canadian tundra. Snow geese are migrating over a scene typical of much of northern Canada and USSR in spring. Much of the snow and ground has melted but the water is unable to drain through the underlying permafrost. In some places, lakes and swamps have formed; in others, the saturated soil forms a very muddy, active surface layer.

Below: A drilling rig on the oil-rich North Slope of Alaska. The tundra surface presents an unstable foundation on which to build as it melts in summer. Beds of gravel have been spread over the ground where roads and buildings are laid out in an attempt to insulate the surface from seasonal warming.

Jen & Des Bartlett/Bruce Coleman

Robert Harding

Below: Permafrost is the perpetually frozen layer of the earth's crust, found where ground temperatures remain below freezing for a period of years. A section taken through Siberia (right) shows the relative thickness of permafrost and the active layer (the surface layer above the permafrost subject to annual freeze and thaw). The active layer is thinnest above the continuous permafrost and thickest above the discontinuous permafrost. Further south only the surface layer freezes.

PERMAFROST UNDER SIBERIA

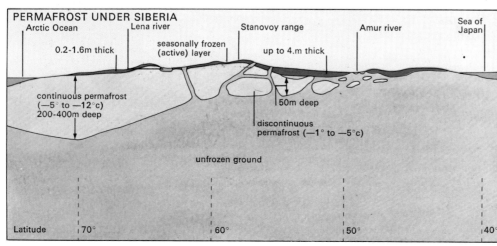

Arctic Ocean — Lena river — Stanovoy range — Amur river — Sea of Japan

0.2-1.6m thick

seasonally frozen (active) layer

up to 4.m thick

continuous permafrost (—5° to —12°c) 200-400m deep

50m deep

discontinuous permafrost (—1° to —5°c)

unfrozen ground

Latitude 70° 60° 50° 40°

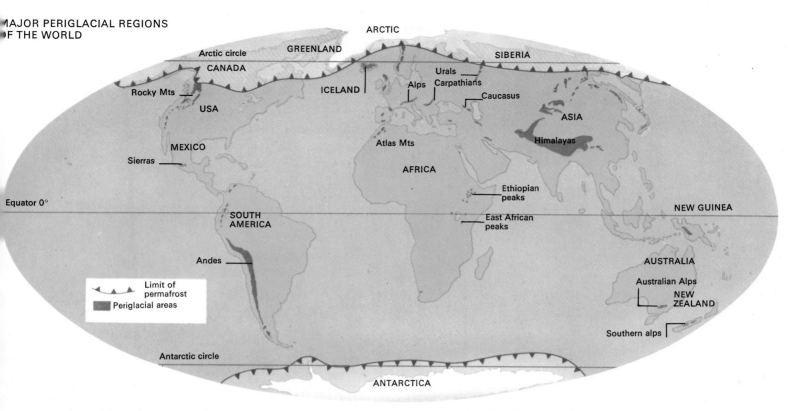

ARCTIC
GREENLAND
Arctic circle
CANADA
SIBERIA
Rocky Mts
ICELAND
Urals
Carpathians
Alps
Caucasus
USA
ASIA
MEXICO
Himalayas
Atlas Mts
Sierras
AFRICA
Equator 0°
Ethiopian
peaks
NEW GUINEA
SOUTH
AMERICA
East African
peaks
AUSTRALIA
Andes
Australian Alps
NEW
ZEALAND
Antarctic circle
Southern alps
ANTARCTICA

Limit of
permafrost
Periglacial areas

Above: Most of the world's periglacial regions are found in the high latitudes above the line marking the limit of continuous and discontinuous permafrost. Periglacial processes also occur in lower latitudes on high, cold mountains (even in the tropics) and in places where the ground freezes sporadically.

Right: This quarry face of an involuted till layer overlying chalk displays the severe disruption which periglacial action can cause in freezing ground.

Institute of Geological Sciences

Dr. Rendel Williams

Picturepoint

Left: Frost shattered boulders near the summit of Glyder Fawr (1000 m) in Snowdonia, Wales. Rock shattering is an important periglacial process which occurs in cold areas throughout the world. Water penetrates lines of weakness such as joints, then freezes and expands, thus widening the crevices in the rock.

Above: This ice-wedge cast in a gravel pit in East Anglia is a relic of former periglaciation. When a cooling surface contracts, cracks form which fill with water in spring. During winter freezing, an expanding ice wedge further opens the crack. Later, in a warmer climate, stones and debris fall into the crack as the ice melts.

earth's warm interior.

In summer, when the seasonally frozen layer melts it becomes very fluid. The water in this layer—known as the *active layer* if it is underlain by permafrost—is unable to drain through the frozen ground and creates a very muddy surface layer which may gradually begin to flow downhill. This slow, viscous flow is known as *solifluction* and often takes place in the form of huge soil tongues called *solifluction lobes* which are distinctive features of many hillsides in tundra areas.

In winter, when this active layer refreezes, two other related processes may come into play. These are known as *frost heave* and *frost thrust*. The surface of the ground freezes first and the frost gradually penetrates downwards towards the deeper permafrost. For a time the intervening layer remains unfrozen. But it becomes subjected to considerable pressure as when water freezes it increases in volume by about nine per cent. Thus as the ground gradually freezes, it expands by thrusting horizontally and heaving vertically between the solid permafrost and rigid surface layer. The tremendous pressure is most easily released by upward heaving of the surface, producing contortions known as *involutions* in the soil layers. The rigid surface becomes considerably disrupted and objects such as stones, trees, fence posts and even telegraph poles have been seen to be completely heaved out of the ground.

On a smaller scale, surface displacement occurs when thin spikes of ice grow in the active layer as it freezes in winter. These spikes of *needle ice* consist of ice crystals which usually range from one to three centimetres (up to one inch) long, but can significantly alter the landscape; they can lift soil particles and stones above the surface and, if this occurs on a slope, when the crystals melt the material will fall and roll downhill.

A further example of the powerful action of freezing and thawing is *frost shattering*, one of the most intense forms of rock fragmentation on earth. When water freezes in cracks, joints or other

119

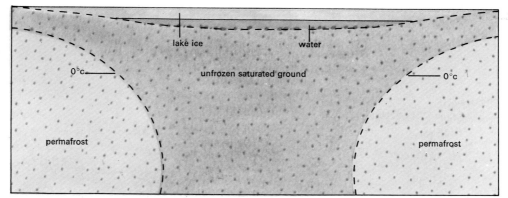
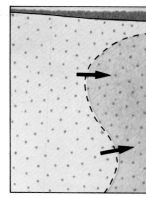

Right: How a closed system or Mackenzie type of pingo may be formed. (1) A broad, shallow lake overlies frost-free ground. (2) The climate may get colder, or the lake may drain or be filled with sediment or vegetation. The lake water and sediments then freeze and the area of permafrost spreads, trapping the saturated unfrozen ground. (3) Eventual freezing and expanding of entrapped ground water exerts sufficient upward force to create a dome on the surface. (4) Any unfrozen water is expelled upwards from the saturated ground beginning to freeze and becomes concentrated below the pingo. It too eventually freezes as permafrost completely envelopes the area.

lines of weakness in rock, its nine per cent increase in volume exerts considerable pressures. The expanding ice acts like a wedge driven into the rock, and this *ice* or *frost wedging* results in splitting and shattering of the rock.

Frost shattering varies greatly with rock type. Sedimentary and other relatively soft, porous rocks have a great water-holding capacity and are usually well-bedded. Consequently, such rocks are generally more susceptible to frost wedging than igneous or metamorphic rocks. However the cleaveage planes in metamorphic rocks such as slate and schist provide lines of weakness where frost shattering may occur, producing flat, angular slabs of rock.

A variety of features resulting from the melting of ground ice in permafrost areas resemble those found in limestone karst areas. These include such features as caverns, disappearing streams and troughs, known collectively as *thermokarst*. However, rather than being the work of chemical processes, thermokarst is created when the permafrost is disrupted by large-scale climatic changes or by local environmental disturbance.

For example, in the early 1920s forest was cleared from land near Fairbanks, Alaska (USA), to prepare the area for agricultural purposes. The area had been underlain by vertical wedges of ice and, when the vegetation was removed, the ice wedges began to thaw, causing the soil to collapse into them. An extensive pattern of depressions and thermokarst mounds developed, varying from 3 to 15 m (10-50 ft) in diameter and up to 2.5 m (8 ft) high, creating an undulating topography quite unsuitable for its intended agricultural use.

Perhaps the most spectacular features of periglaciated areas are *pingos*, an Eskimo word describing scattered, isolated hills. The term was introduced into geomorphology in 1938 to describe the conspicuous domes with radially cracked summits that are particularly common in the continuous permafrost zone. They can be over 50 m (165 ft) high and up to 600 m (2,000 ft) in diameter.

There are two types of pingo: closed and open system types. The closed system has been best examined in the Mackenzie River delta area of Canada where 98 per cent of the 1,380 pingos mapped occur in fairly level, poorly-drained sites such as former lake basins.

The open type of pingo is best developed in East Greenland and most common on slopes rather than on level areas. It appears to be associated with artesian springs which provide a continual supply of ground water under presure. As this water approaches the surface it freezes, and the expanding ice exerts considerable upward pressure on the ground above.

Patterned ground

One of the most striking and controversial features of a periglacial landscape is the unusual geometric patterning found in the soil. The most common shapes are circles, polygons (many-sided forms) and stripes so perfectly arranged as to appear deliberately laid out; yet these patterns occur naturally in the cold terrain. The circles are stony areas measuring from a half to three metres (18 in to 10 ft) across, often with vegetation growing around their margins. In some the stones are smaller in the centre of the circle than towards the edge.

The polygons are usually larger, sometimes reaching over 10 m (33 ft) in diameter. They are delineated by vegetated furrows or lines of stones enclosing areas of finer debris. Polygons are best developed on fairly level areas. Where the ground steepens, stripes form—these are thought to be the downslope extension of polygons; an intermediate form is the extended polygon or net.

Patterned ground has been the subject of considerable debate in geomorphology; its origin remains unclear, although some polygons seem to result from ice wedging.

Wind, water and snow

Violent winds sweep over the cold, exposed periglacial terrain, leaving a trail of wind-scoured features and transported sediments. In fact, wind action is one of the most important processes at work, capable of sand-blasting the rocks to produce sharp-edged, polished stones, termed *ventifacts* or *dreikanter*. The thick deposits known as *loess* are fine-grained sediments swept up and carried sometimes great distances by the wind from bare areas of glacial and outwash deposits.

River flow in the periglacial zone is characteristically irregular. Water will cease to flow altogether during prolonged periods of sub-zero temperatures, but during the spring thaw powerful torrents rush over the river beds causing considerable erosion and movement of debris. Similarly, coastlines in periglaciated areas are usually frozen up during winter, but in summer intense shattering of coastal rocks may take place as each tidal

Dr. D. Drewry

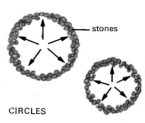

Below: Perhaps the most striking, and puzzling, features of periglacial areas are the patterns found in the ground. These stone circles on Devon Is. in Arctic Canada are well sorted, with a border of stones surrounding the finer material in the centre. The diameter of the near circle (shown by the red gloves) is about 1 m.

stones

CIRCLES

Dr. C. Embleton

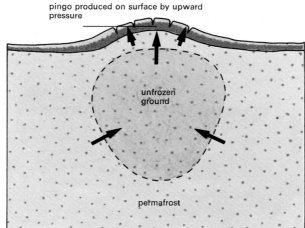

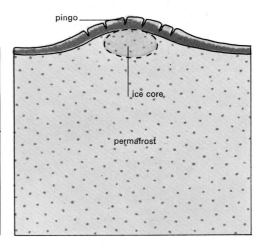

lake ice and sediments frozen to lake bed

unfrozen ground reduced by permafrost encroaching from all sides

pingo produced on surface by upward pressure

unfrozen ground

permafrost

pingo

ice core

permafrost

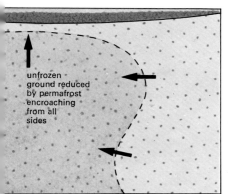

Left: Isolated mounds, known by the Eskimo name *pingos*, in the Mackenzie delta area of Arctic Canada. These surface 'blisters' form on the sites of former floodplain lakes and overlie areas where the pressure of freezing and expanding ice has heaved up the ground. Summer meltwater may collect as lakes in the cracks and hollows on the summits of the domes.

Above right: Blocks of frost-shattered dolomite near Platteville in Wisconsin, USA. Toppled by former periglacial conditions, these rocks slid downhill to their present resting place.

Right: These rounded tongues of earth, known as solifluction lobes, on Baffin Is, Canada, are water-logged surface deposits which flow slowly downhill when activated by summer thawing. The rounded stones suggest that the lobe material is reworked glacial till.

fine sediment | POLYGONS

Above left and left: Scientists are still debating how such remarkably perfect geometric shapes can form in patterned soil. One possible reason is that fine material has a greater water-holding capacity than stones. Areas of fine water-saturated sediments or mud expand on freezing, thrusting embedded stones outwards and upwards, but draw back more effectively during thawing because of their greater cohesion. Continued freezing and thawing may produce patches of fine material separated by narrow bands of stones, which appear as circles or polygons on level ground as shown in the diagram (above left) and as stripes on slopes. The polygons on Spitzbergen (left) are well sorted, with stone bands bordering patches of fine debris. Small plants and flowers typical of tundra areas are growing in the fine soil.

rise fills cracks with sea-water which freezes when exposed to air at low tide.

Erosion also occurs in areas apparently protected by a blanket of snow. Beneath patches of snow continual thawing by day and freezing by night leads to bedrock weathering, with the loosened particles being washed out by meltwater. Snow-patch erosion or *nivation* thus tends to create large, distinctive hillside hollows that may eventually become cirques.

Man in periglacial areas

Man faces considerable problems as he penetrates further into periglacial areas in order to exploit their mineral reserves. The difficulties stem largely from the presence of permafrost and its susceptibility to melting when disturbed by human activities. When the ground is frozen it has great bearing strength but when thawed it turns into mud with no strength at all. Consequently it is impossible to build centrally-heated dwellings directly onto the permafrost. A common solution is to raise the buildings off the ground by using stilts or piles so that air can circulate between the heated building and the permafrost. However, the piles are open to attack by frost heaving and must be lubricated and placed sufficiently deep to prevent this happening. Where roads and airport runways are constructed, the ground is insulated by spreading a gravel blanket about one metre (3 ft) thick over the ground.

The provision of services, particularly water and sewers, to polar settlements creates many problems. In summer there are few difficulties, but in winter water is in short supply and chunks of ice must be melted down. A number of the larger settlements have piped-in water supplies but the problem is in preventing freezing.

Sewage is often hauled by bucket or wagon and dumped on the river ice to be carried away with the spring break-up. Some settlements have heated sewage-disposal systems but it is not possible to put the pipes underground since the heat would disrupt the permafrost. This is also true of the pipelines constructed in such cold, remote areas as Alaska to carry the relatively warm oil from polar oil fields to more temperate latitudes. Buried pipes can be fairly effectively insulated. An alternative is to construct the pipelines above ground on piles, but this is expensive and may inhibit the migration of such animals as caribou to their traditional breeding grounds.

The Ice Age

There have been several ice ages in the earth's history, periods when for one reason or another ice caps and glaciers became much more extensive than usual and large areas of the earth's surface were dominated by glacial and periglacial processes. The evidence of these ice ages is there to be seen in the rocks and, although the further one goes back in time the fainter the evidence becomes, we can be certain that there was an ice age in the late Pre-Cambrian period some 700 million years ago; another in the Carboniferous, about 300 million years ago; and a third, known as the *Pleistocene Ice Age*, which began only two million years ago and is probably still going on.

A variety of theories have been put forward about the causes of the latest Ice Age—some suggest extra-terrestrial explanations such as variations in the heat radiated by the sun. A recent theory suggests that the positions of the drifting continents relative to the pole may account for the earlier ice ages as well as for climatic changes which affected both hemispheres. Ice caps form more easily on land than on oceans, and during the Carboniferous ice age extensive ice sheets swept over much of Gondwanaland, the massive continent then located over the South Pole.

Some scientists have stressed the increase in cold, high elevations on which glaciers could develop during the mountain-building activity in the late Tertiary period. Others argue that intensive volcanic activity may have ejected great clouds of dust and ash into the upper atmosphere which shielded the earth's surface from the sun's rays. However, critics of both theories have pointed out there have been periods of mountain-building and great volcanic activity in the past which were not followed by ice ages. The conflict of opinion and lack of real evidence means that what actually caused the ice ages remains at present a matter of pure speculation.

The Pleistocene Ice Age

The events of the Pleistocene had a profound effect on the landscape and its soils, on the distribution of land and sea and thus on the migration and settlement patterns of our ancestors. For example, London is built on a series of river terraces formed during the Pleistocene as a result of climatic and sea-level changes. Without them the Thames valley would be an arm of the sea and the Romans would never have chosen the site of London as a crossing place.

All the great harbours of the world, such as New York, Vancouver, Sydney and Wellington owe their existence to the melting of the Pleistocene ice caps which raised the sea to its present level. Long before man was settling the land and developing his farming methods, the Ice Age was moulding it and controlling the ways in which he might use it.

But it would be wrong to think of the Ice Age as one long freeze-up. In fact it consisted of a series of alternate cold and warm periods, probably seven cold with six warmer ones separating them. During the cold periods the climate was a good deal colder everywhere than at present,

Courtesy Director, Institute of Geological Sciences

Above: An artist's reconstruction of a glacial landscape during the Pleistocene Ice Age shows the edge of a great ice-sheet, with cold, barren terrain in its immediate vicinity. Vegetation in the poor soil consisted of mosses and small arctic-alpine plants. Among the animals to withstand the intense cold were hairy mammoths.

Right: The areas of permanent present-day ice are shown with the maximum extent of Pleistocene ice sheets in the northern hemisphere. (The ice may have reached its furthest limit in different areas during different glacial periods.) Most of the increased volume was due to the growth of large ice sheets over N.W. Europe and N. America.

Below: About three times more of the earth's surface was covered by ice in the Pleistocene than at present. The impact was less dramatic in the southern hemisphere where there are fewer high latitude land masses on which ice sheets could grow. But the Antarctic ice sheet (below) grew thicker, there were ice caps in New Zealand and thick ice on the Andes.

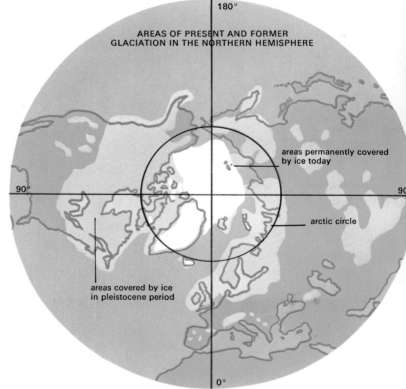

AREAS OF PRESENT AND FORMER GLACIATION IN THE NORTHERN HEMISPHERE

180°

90°

90°

0°

areas permanently covered by ice today

arctic circle

areas covered by ice in pleistocene period

Bavaria

climate colder/warmer than present	British standard stages	Probable equivalents elsewhere
	Holocene Flandarian 10,000 yrs ago	Post-glacial
	Devensian	● Weichsel ● Würm ● Wisconsin
	Ipswichian	● Eem ○ Sangamon
	Wolstonian	● Saale ○ Illinoian ○ Riss
	Hoxnian	● Holstein ○ Yarmouth
	Anglian	● Elster ○ Kansan ○ Mindel
	Cromerian	○ Aftonian
	Beestonian	● North European ○ Alpine ○ North American
	Pastonian	
	Baventian	
	Antian	
	Thurnian	
	Ludhamian	
	Waltonian 2 million yrs ago	

PLEISTOCENE

LIMITS OF THE ICE ADVANCE

— Devensian

Wolstonian

Anglian

Left: The record of climatic change in Britain during the last 2 million years. The Pleistocene was not a period of continuous glaciation. There were lengthy periods, the *interglacials*, when the climate became as warm or warmer than today's. (Shorter cold and warm episodes termed *stadials* and *interstadials* also occurred.) The stages have different names in other parts of the world, where the ice may have advanced at different times. Attempts have been made to roughly equate them, but correlation becomes more uncertain further back in time. The map shows the limits of ice advances in England and Wales during the Pleistocene.

Above: The severity of past climates in parts of Britain which escaped glaciation during the last ice advance is demonstrated by fossil periglacial features. These fossil polygons (on level ground) and stripes (on slopes) occur in East Anglia. Fossil pingos are found in Wales and elsewhere in Europe.

Right: The entrance to part of the South Pole Station in the frozen Antarctic wastes. About 89 per cent of ice on earth today is in the Antarctic ice-sheet. Considerable research is being carried out on the glaciology of the polar ice sheet, as well as the biology, geology and geomorphology of areas not covered by ice.

Below right: There is clear evidence of ice ages prior to the Pleistocene. Outcrops of *tillite* (consolidated till) on top of Table Mountain near Cape Town are relics of the Carboniferous ice sheet which covered parts of Gondwanaland.

but only during the last three was it actually glacial in northern latitudes. (In Britain, these are known as the Anglian, Wolstonian and Devensian stages.)

At such times the polar ice extended far beyond its present limits, in Europe reaching as far south as southern England, the Netherlands and south Germany. In North America, the ice reached a line running roughly from Seattle in the west to Long Island in the east, and passing well south of the Great Lakes. During the last major advance, 15,000 to 20,000 years ago, ice covered about 30 per cent of the earth.

However, the ice advanced only during the coldest of the cold periods. In the intervening ones, known as *interglacial periods*, the climate was as warm as, or even warmer than, the present day. For example, during the last interglacial in Britain (the Ipswichian), elephants, rhinoceros and hippopotami wandered as far north as Yorkshire, where their bones are sometimes found in caves or in river and raised beach deposits. So although in Britain the Pleistocene is thought of as an Ice Age, glacial conditions existed for only a very small part of that time. In more southerly countries they never existed at all—for what fell as snow in northern Europe, came down as rain further south. In Africa there is evidence of alternate wet and dry phases, known as *pluvials* and *interpluvials*, which may correspond with the glacial and inter-glacial periods in Europe.

Each time the ice advanced, animals and plants were forced to migrate south-wards. Later, as the ice retreated, they were able to move north again and re-colonize the land. Consequently their remains, preserved as fossils by natural burial, can be used to record the climatic changes which the area has undergone. These fossils include vertebrates, such as elephants and rhinoceros for the warm periods, and reindeer and mammoths for the cold. The distribution of invertebrates such as molluscs can be equally revealing. In a warm period molluscs of southern type migrate northwards, whereas in a cold period they move south again and their place is taken by more boreal (northern) species.

Trees too are good indicators of climate, and the course of an interglacial can often be plotted by tracing the changes in tree cover from arctic tundra to fully developed temperate forest and back again. The evidence is gained by studying the proportions of different kinds of pollen that are preserved, layer by layer, in the sediments of ponds or lakes. This has proved to be a most effective way of building up chronological sequences based on climatic change.

The periodic expansion of ice sheets during the Pleistocene inundated about 30 million square kilometres (over 11 million square miles) of northern Europe, North America and Asia, covering large areas with a veneer of glacial sediments. The most characteristic of these is the till, or boulder clay, deposited by the ice itself. Much can be learnt by studying these deposits. For example, an exposure of till on the Yorkshire coast of eastern England might yield erratics (far-travelled stones) of Shap granite, Permian Breccia, Carboniferous Limestone, Magnesian Limestone and even a battered Liassic ammonite. This would tell geologists that the ice which deposited the till came from

123

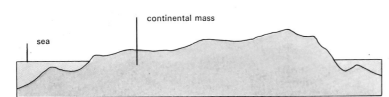

1. BEFORE ICE AGE

sea

continental mass

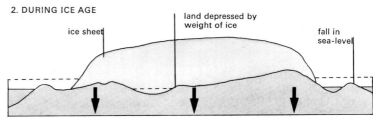

2. DURING ICE AGE

ice sheet

land depressed by weight of ice

fall in sea-level

Above: Eustatic (sea-level) and isostatic (land level) changes. Before a glacial period, land and sea-level are stable (1). When thick ice builds up on land, its weight depresses the crust. The seas also fall, as water is lost to form ice (2). When the climate warms, the ice melts and returns to the seas. But the land also rises as its burden is removed (3). Shorelines will be formed along the boundaries where the land meets the sea. If the land subsequently rises more than the sea, old beaches will be raised above the present shoreline (4). Canada and Scandinavia are still rising, although the ice melted several thousand years ago.

Below: Drowned drumlins in Strangford Lough, Northern Ireland. The drumlins, moulded by an Ice Age glacier, were flooded by a rise in sea-level when the ice melted. However, relative sea-level was once even higher, as shown by the raised beaches and cliffs in shadow on the right sides of the drumlins.

Aerofilms

Explorer

the Lake District in north-west England by way of the Vale of Eden, over the Pennines (ice can go uphill, unlike water) to Teesside, and so down the North Yorkshire coast. Such an assemblage is the 'trade-mark' of that particular till; it serves to identify it wherever it is seen, or to distinguish it from other tills which may contain different assemblages.

Almost as extensive as till are the sheets of outwash sand and gravel which spread out from the margin of an ice cap or glacier. The bulk of our present resources of sand and gravel, so vital to the building and heavy construction industries, originated from this water-sorted debris during the Pleistocene. In dry weather a third kind of deposit may become important. Strong winds, blowing over the outwash plains, pick up the silt (sand is too heavy, and clay is usually bonded by moisture) and carry it in the form of dust storms, perhaps for many miles, before re-depositing it as an even spread of loess, blanketing the landscape. Many of the superficial deposits known as *brickearth* on British geological maps are actually thin beds of loess. Much thicker deposits extend from France right across Europe into the USSR—in fact all along the line of the Pleistocene glacial limit.

Changes in sea level

The impact of the Pleistocene Ice Age on the earth as a whole was not restricted to the deposits of glaciation and a changing pattern of plant and animal life in the immediate vicinity of fluctuating ice sheets. As the ice was retreating and advancing, so world sea-level was rising and falling. During a glacial period immense quantities of water are locked up in the form of ice. With less water left to fill the oceans, sea-level falls equally all over the world, leaving raised beaches and river terraces to mark its former height. In the warmer periods most of the ice melts again and sea-level rises, flooding the former land surface and its vegetation, which may later be identifiable as a buried forest.

These world-wide changes in sea-level, brought about by an actual rise or fall of the oceans, are termed *eustatic movements*. During the coldest part of the last glacial period (the Devensian in Britain) sea-level was at least 100 m (330 ft) lower than now, so the English Channel and much of the southern North Sea were dry land and other land bridges existed wherever there are now shallow epicontinental seas. On the other hand, if all the existing ice in the world (most of which is held in

Below: The fossil remains of small land animals are particularly useful in learning about past climatic changes. Snails have become accepted as helpful indicators of Pleistocene temperature fluctuations. This is the shell of an interglacial species, *Vallonia enniensis*, found in Ipswichian deposits in Britain.

Right: Mammal remains are often found in inter-glacial deposits. This excavation of a skull of a woolly rhinoceros was carried out about the turn of the century at Barrington in eastern England, with great care to retrieve the skull intact. Other cold climate mammals were mammoths, bison, reindeer, musk oxen and wolves.

B. W. Sparks

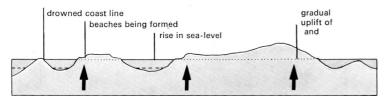

drowned coast line
beaches being formed
rise in sea-level
gradual uplift of and

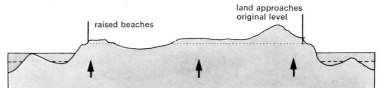

raised beaches
land approaches original level

Left: A string of icebergs 'calving' off from the Antarctic ice cap. Pleistocene glaciers in northern latitudes could spread over land, but Antarctic ice spilled into the deep water around the continent and icebergs drifted north to warmer latitudes where they melted. Only about 10% of an iceberg appears above water.

Below: The Dog Stone near Oban, west Scotland, is a raised, undercut sea-stack, eroded by the sea and left high above the present coastline by isostatic uplift of the land. Its name comes from a local tradition that the stack was used by a giant to tie up his dog, which wore a groove at the base by trying to get free.

Right: Blocks of ice dug or drilled from the Antarctic and Greenland ice-sheets reveal strata in the ice. Each layer represents a year's snowfall, and their age can be found by counting the number above a certain point. By measuring the amounts of oxygen isotope O^{18} in the ice, past temperatures can also be identified.

Dr Murray Gray

Dr. P. Schoeck/ZEFA

Sedgwick Museum

the two great continental ice sheets, Antarctica and Greenland) were to melt at once, the sea would rise a further 50 m (115 ft)—with catastrophic effect.

While the level of the sea was rising and falling during the Pleistocene, the land in the glaciated areas was rising and falling as well. This is because the continents behave, in the long term, as though they are 'floating' on the denser rock beneath. Extra weight such as thick ice depresses land masses and removal of it allows them to recover their original level. This adjustment, which happens only gradually, is the *isostatic effect.*

In a glaciated area there will thus be the interaction of two processes, one raising and lowering the land, and the other raising and lowering the surface of the sea. Where the shoreline eventually lies depends on many factors, but broadly speaking in the glacial centres isostasy is more effective than eustasy. In Scandinavia and northern Scotland, for instance, there is a series of raised beaches representing former shorelines, now elevated well above present sea-level. However, away from the glacial centres, for example in southern England and France, the eustatic effect is more important, and these areas are characterized by sub-

merged coastlines, drowned valleys and buried forests.

Increasing awareness of the history of the recent past provokes fascinating questions about the future. Will the polar ice caps melt, drowning major population centres? Or are we still in an ice age, and will another cold period eventually lead to the depopulation of the densely settled areas of the northern hemisphere?

The correct answer is that nobody knows. All that is certain is that the time elapsed since the end of the last glacial period (about 10,000 years) is less than the duration of most of the interglacials, so there is no real reason to assume that the Ice Age is over and done with.

Perhaps post-glacial time (the Holocene or Flandrian stage) is just another interglacial period. What is more, perhaps the mid-point of that interglacial is already past, for there was undoubtedly a time, around 4000BC, when the climate was slightly warmer than it is now. One consoling thought is that climatic change takes place very slowly. It has taken 10,000 years—about 400 generations—for the climate in southern England to change from arctic to temperate; so we need not really worry that another glaciation is imminent.

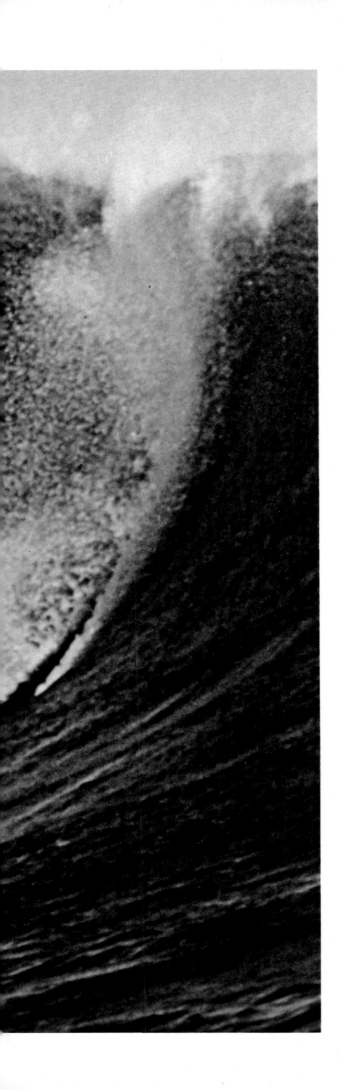

The Oceans

The Polynesians are believed to have used small wooden boards to surf among the Pacific Islands from New Zealand to Tahiti. They passed on the skill to the Hawaiians, who gave it to the rest of the world.

The Sea at Work

The seas make a constant assault on our coasts. Yet the pounding action of the waves is not only destructive, for while cliffs and other coastal landforms are being eroded, the resulting rock debris (often quickly reduced to fine material like sand) may be deposited by that same wave action elsewhere.

The power of waves

Most coastal changes occur under storm conditions, when the destructive powers of waves are at their greatest. The energy of a wave depends on its *length* (the distance from crest to crest), its *height* (the distance from trough to crest) and its swiftness or *celerity* (measured by the period of time between waves). Variation in any one of these characteristics will change the ability of a wave breaking on a coast to erode and move material.

However, the most important factor in the power of a wave is its height. Because this depends in part on wind speeds, the highest waves most commonly occur in storms, when gales whip the sea into a furious assault on the coast. The crash of storm waves on a cliff traps pockets of air in the rock cavities and compresses them. Then as waves fall back, the air expands explosively, throwing spray, pebbles and shattered rock high into the air. Further erosion is the result of the *corrasive* action of the debris hurled by waves against the coasts. The material itself is worn into smaller particles by the constant grinding or *attrition*.

The immense amount of damage that can be caused by storm waves was dramatically illustrated in January 1953 along the coasts of the North Sea. Under strong northerly winds and the high tide, a surge of water was forced into the southern part of the North Sea. The effect was devastating. In many places along the eastern coast of England, the beach was completely washed away by the sea, and once this protection was lost, the cliffs were exposed to rapid erosion. In some areas of Lincolnshire, low cliffs were cut back by more than 10 m (33 ft).

The sea can also change a shoreline considerably without actually eroding the cliffs or beach. On tropical coasts, for example, huge waves are generated by violent hurricanes. In 1960 Hurricane Donna in two days shifted an estimated 5,000,000 m³ (176,500,000 cubic ft) of sand from one part of the Florida coast to another. Under normal conditions it would take about 100 years to transport that amount. Although very little erosion —that is, breakdown of material—had occurred, at the end of the storm, each resort had an entirely new beach similar in all respects to the pre-storm beach.

Cliffs

Perhaps the clearest example of the erosive action of the sea is the way a cliff is undercut by wave action, and then eventually recedes as the unstable slope above collapses. Cliffs are undoubtedly the most striking landform to be seen along a coast, and although their height is entirely determined by the relief of the land, the sea can have dramatic effects. In England, for example, some parts of the Isle of Sheppey are retreating by more

Photri

Above: Waves breaking on the rocky shore of Oregon's Pacific coast. The cliffs are fairly low (about 10 m high) but their vertical faces indicate active erosion by waves. Weaknesses in the rock have been exploited to create an attractively varied coastline of capes and bays. Outcrops of more resistant rock have produced an intertidal island (centre right of the photograph) and a curving arch (bottom). Rock debris and driftwood are deposited at the cliff-base by the gentle swell waves.

Right: Waves tend to reach the shore at right angles. As they approach the coast, the waves 'feel' the sea bottom. The increased friction slows the waves as they bear down on the protruding headlands. Initially, the brunt of the sea's attack is borne by the headlands and the less disturbed conditions in the bay offer safer anchorage for shipping. However, since the sea-floor is uneven, waves will advance more quickly into the bays where the water is deepest and a wave front becomes curved as the water shallows. The bending, or *wave refraction*, increases until, at the moment of wave break, the front is almost parallel to the coastline.

Right: Aerial photograph of Sakonnet Point on Rhode Is. (USA) showing waves being refracted as they near the coast. In the lee of the offshore rocks the waves produce an interference pattern.

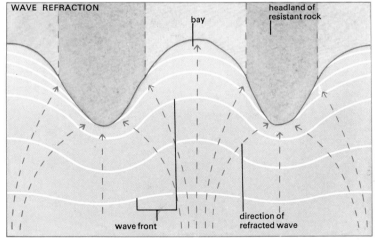

WAVE REFRACTION

headland of resistant rock

bay

wave front

direction of refracted wave

Dr. John S. Shelton

129

than three metres (10 feet) every year. On another part of the eastern coast of England, the cliffs are being eroded even further—as much as 10 metres (33 feet) a year.

Yet the sea can attack the cliffs only within a very restricted vertical range, in effect up to a level reached by the highest waves. Concentrated at the base of the cliff, the sea's erosive force obviously varies with the strength of the waves. In sheltered locations, for example, cliffs are eroded much more slowly than those on exposed coasts. However, the other major factor affecting the rate of erosion is the geology of the area. Cliffs composed of soft rocks, such as clays or glacial sands, can be attacked and the rock debris washed away very quickly.

Cliffs of harder rock such as granite offer much greater resistance to the pounding force of the sea, even along exposed shores such as Land's End at the tip of southwest England and the stormy Cape Horn of South America. Where harder rocks alternate with softer ones, the sea often carves out *bays* and *coves* in the less resistant rocks, leaving the harder ridges jutting into the sea as *headlands*. Straight shorelines are characteristic only of faulted coasts and those formed of rocks of generally uniform resistance to erosion. Along the English Channel, for example, the famous White Cliffs of Dover and the Seven Sisters coast near Eastbourne are composed of chalk of very even texture.

Marine erosion at the cliff-base occasionally creates unusual landforms. Most hard rocks have fault joints and other lines of weakness which are exploited by the sea, sometimes cutting *inlets* and *caves* deep into the cliffs. The explosive pressure of trapped air and surging water inside a cave may be sufficient to erode upwards through the roof to form an opening known as a *blowhole* from which clouds of spray may shoot upwards. Quite often, caves hollowed on both sides of a headland join up to form a natural arch. In time, when the top of the arch collapses, the remnant of the headland stands as a detached pillar, known as a *stack*. All tall, off-shore rock pinnacles are called stacks, irrespective of how they were formed. Many well-known examples occur around the coasts of Britain, such as the chalk pinnacles known as the Needles off the Isle of Wight, and the Old Man of Hoy, a 137 m (450 ft) high pillar of Old Red Sandstone, in the Orkney Islands of Scotland.

Beaches

A beach is a deceptively transient feature, a sloping accumulation of loose material —which may consist of boulders, *shingle* (coarse gravel), pebbles, sand, mud and shells—along the sea-shore. Movement of material both up and down and along the beach ensures that it is constantly changing. Beaches may be removed overnight by a violent storm, as occurred in 1953 along the Lincolnshire coast—but they usually build up again during long periods of calm weather. Often, a thin layer of material is moved nearly continuously, being deposited at one end of the beach, washed by *longshore drift* along the length of it, and carried out the other end.

The continuous interplay of waves and this loose material contributes to the

Dr. John S. Shelton

Picturepoint

Picturepoint

Left and right: The changing appearance of beaches from one season to another is familiar to people who live near sandy sea-shores. Usually a beach loses sand during storms when the waves are highest and most destructive, and regains it during calmer periods. These two photographs of the same part of Boomer Beach near La Jolla, California, show a dramatic gain and loss of sand. In summer (right) gentle swell waves carry material up to the shore, building up a soft sandy beach. In winter (left) storm waves wash away the easily-moved, fine material such as sand, carrying it out to sea, and expose the coarse fragments at the base of this beach.

Right: Waves thump against the protective sea-wall at Portmellon in Cornwall. In winter the south-western corner of England often suffers storm waves swept across the Atlantic Ocean. Such waves possess a large amount of energy and can bring major changes to shorelines in a very short time. It has been estimated that Atlantic storm waves pound exposed coasts with an average force of 10,000 kg per square metre (2,000 lb/sq ft).

Far right: Tidal mud-flats at Dawlish on Devon's south coast. In sheltered coastal areas such as this where waves are feeble, deposition dominates over erosion. Fine silt and sand are laid down by the sea and rivers add their alluvium. Salt-tolerant vegetation tends to colonize the flat ground and this helps to trap more silt. In tropical areas, mud-flats support mangrove swamps.

Below: This former island in the Scottish sea-loch Eriboll is joined to the mainland by a *tombolo*, a linking deposit of sand and shingle.

Dr. John S. Shelton

Picturepoint

Carl Purcell/Colorfic!

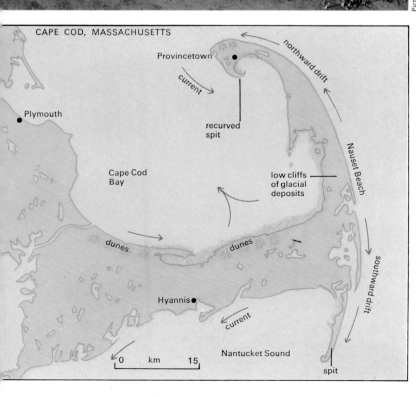

CAPE COD, MASSACHUSETTS

Plymouth

Provincetown

northward drift

current

recurved spit

Cape Cod Bay

low cliffs of glacial deposits

Nauset Beach

dunes

dunes

current

Hyannis

southward drift

current

spit

Nantucket Sound

0   km   15

Above: Miami Beach, the tourist and convention centre in south-eastern Florida (USA), is built on an offshore sand-bar. Separated from the mainland by shallow Biscayne Bay, the island was a mangrove swamp until developed and joined to Miami proper by causeways in 1912. The growth of coastal deposits such as bars and spits depends on sizeable longshore drift of material along an irregular coastline. Here the drift is from the south, as shown by the sand trapped on the near-side of the groynes, low walls or jetties built to protect the beach from further erosion.

Left and right: At Cape Cod on the coast of Massachusetts, the easily-eroded glacial debris is gradually drifting both north and south along Nauset Beach. Long bands of shingle and sand, known as *spits*, are extending the length of the beach. Spits are formed by *longshore drift*, which occurs when waves arrive obliquely at a beach (right). Material carried both up and along the beach by the swash is pulled straight down the slope by the backwash.

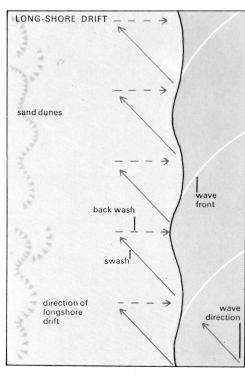

LONG-SHORE DRIFT

sand dunes

back wash

swash

direction of longshore drift

wave front

wave direction

great variety of beaches. Sand and shingle may be washed up from the sea-floor and a small amount of debris is provided by cliff erosion, but most of the material comes from sediment carried to the sea by rivers and then transported along by the waves and currents. The river Nile, for example, is responsible for nearly all the beach sediments in the south-east corner of the Mediterranean Sea. The remains of shells, corals and other organisms may be a further source of beach material.

It is often possible to trace the varied origins of material. For example, at Cap Griz Nez, near the French Channel port of Calais, the beach consists of huge boulders more than a metre (39 in) across, which have fallen from thick limestone bands in the cliff face. Flint cobbles the size of a fist are found on Chesil Beach in Dorset, having been eroded from the chalk on the Channel floor, then washed up by the waves.

Coarse sand is common in the beaches of Cornwall, having been eroded from the granite rocks inland, while extremely fine sands from the Old and New Red Sandstone areas provide a popular holiday beach at Weston super Mare on the Bristol Channel coast.

On all beaches, eroded material is gradually broken down into smaller pieces by the constant pounding of the sea. The surge or *swash* of waves pushes pebbles and sand up the beach, while the *backwash* (the return of seawater down a beach after a wave has broken) or underwater currents drag the material down the slope. Generally, the coarser the material, the steeper the beach slope will be. The steep profile of the shingle beach at Chesil Beach, for example, is partly due to the large size of the flints, whereas the beach at Weston-super-Mare slopes gently because of its fine sand. Where a mixture of sediment sizes occurs, as at many beaches of East Anglia, the coarser material tends to gather at the highest part, and there is usually a marked change in slope between this and the finer sediments towards the low water level.

The shape of a beach is also affected by

Aerofilms

Bruce Coleman

Above: The *cuspate foreland* at Dungeness on the English Channel is one of the best examples of this very unusual feature. Its origins are unclear but shingle has been added to the foreland in a sharply defined series of beach ridges. Many fine ridges were destroyed by the construction of the Nuclear Power Station.

CLIFF SCENERY

cave

bay

J. Rufus/Robert Harding

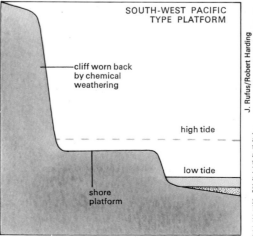

NORTH ATLANTIC TYPE PLATFORM

cliff

high tide

low tide

shore platform

undercutting leads to cliff collapse

beach material

SOUTH-WEST PACIFIC TYPE PLATFORM

cliff worn back by chemical weathering

high tide

low tide

shore platform

Above: Seastacks and a rocky shore platform project out to sea at a cove near Hartland Quay on the north coast of Devon. The gently inclined *platform* was built and extended as the cliffs were eroded back. Debris from the cliff face has fallen onto the platform, to be swept away by the waves. On coasts like this—

battered by strong storm waves—mechanical erosion by the sea picks out the weaknesses in the rock strata. Harder rocks resist destruction and many cliffed coasts end in a series of offshore rocks or *sea stacks* on which lighthouses are often built. Well-known examples include the Needles off the Isle of Wight.

Above and right: There are two basic types of shore platform. The North Atlantic type (above) has an inclined surface stretching from the cliff-base to beyond the low-water mark. It is typical of storm wave coasts, where erosion by the sea leads to undercutting of the cliff. The abrasive and quarrying action of the

waves is usually concentrated into joints and cracks in the rock, producing an irregular surface, as seen at Hartland Quay. The SW Pacific type (right) is characterized by a near-horizontal platform that ends abruptly at a low tide cliff. Here chemical weathering is important. The sea merely removes loosened material.

Above: These inspiring arches on the coast of the Algarve, Portugal, are known locally as the 'bridges of piety'. Natural arches are an attractive feature of many cliffed coasts. They are most likely to form where horizontally bedded rocks are cut by major vertical joints. Limestones and basalt are particularly suitable.

Right: A fountain of spray shoots out of a *blowhole* on Española or Hood Is. in the Galapagos. Blowholes occur where a chimney extends from the cliff top down to a sea cave. As waves enter the cave, usually at high tide, air is forced up the chimney, carrying water with it, usually with a great roaring noise.

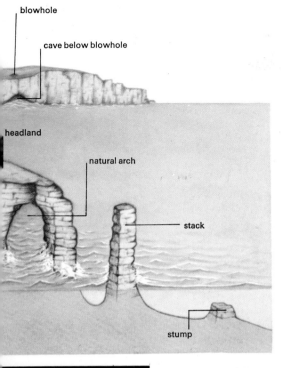

blowhole

cave below blowhole

headland

natural arch

stack

stump

variations in the movement of waves. Once the direction of prevailing waves or the swash and backwash change, the beach is modified, either by erosion or deposition. If the beach is battered by high waves, as often occurs in winter, the loose material raked from the beach is carried back to the sea, producing a more gentle slope (often separated from the beach beyond the level of wave attack by a small sand or shingle cliff). By contrast, when these steep waves are replaced by more gentle *swell waves* (those which are not driven by winds) material tends to be built up and the beach slope is increased. This produces the generally steeper, larger beaches of summer.

Waves tend to approach the shore at right angles. This is true even of a cape and bay coastline, for as the waves approach the shore, they first encounter the shallower water opposite the headlands, and are slowed down. Opposite the bays, however, the water usually remains deep, so that the waves advance more rapidly. As they too begin to 'feel bottom' they slow and a swinging effect, known as *wave refraction*, occurs by which the line of advance of the waves becomes generally parallel to the shore so that they break head-on.

In many places, however, waves are not fully refracted, and approach at an angle to the coast. This results in *longshore drift*: the movement of shingle and sand along a coastline. Where longshore drift is strong, an abrupt change in the direction of the coast or the entry of a river can produce a *spit*, a narrow ridge of sand, gravel and pebbles piled up by the waves.

Orford Ness on the Suffolk coast is a shingle spit which first sealed off the estuary of the River Alde and then extended southwards for several kilometres across the mouth of the River Butley. The town of Orford lies inland between the two rivers, but 750 years ago it was a port facing the open sea. The curiously shaped triangular beach known as a *cuspate foreland*, and found for example at Dungeness in Kent and at Cape Kennedy (Canaveral) in Florida, is the

result of material adjusting to a particular pattern of wave or current action.

Man has attempted to arrest the drift of material along some beaches by constructing barriers or *groynes*. While they may prove a temporary success, groynes all too frequently upset the natural relationship between beach supply, wave action and sediment transport, so that at the end of the protected zone serious erosion occurs. As an alternative to this a number of attempts have been made to artificially replenish beaches by dumping material of an appropriate size. For example, Portobello beach near Edinburgh—robbed of its sand by a long history of erosion—has received this treatment with some success and the technique has been quite widely adopted in California and Florida.

Shore platforms

Along rocky coasts, a level rock shelf or *shore platform* extends seawards from the cliff-base. Shore platforms show almost as much variety as beaches but two basic forms can be recognized. The first, typical of storm wave coasts where mechanical erosion is dominant, consists of an inclined surface stretching to low tide and below. The second consists of a near-horizontal platform that ends abruptly at what is called a *low tide cliff*. This form is typical of tropical and warm temperate areas, such as the New South Wales and Victoria coasts of Australia, where chemical weathering is important.

The surface form of the platform owes much to the waves and the underlying geology, but it also depends on the processes by which a platform is eroded. Alternating hard and soft sands in shore platforms are eroded at differing rates so that miniature scarps and vales are produced. Biological activity is often a notable feature of shore platforms and in warm seas becomes very important. A continuous sea-weed cover tends to protect the platform surface, but a variety of intertidal organisms cause erosion. Some creatures such as piddocks survive by drilling a hole into the platform surface, enlarging it as they grow. Others, like the sea urchin, excavate a shallow hollow or cave. On limestone rocks a number of animals, as for example the limpet, create a variety of hollows by exuding acids which eat into the rock. In these limestone areas, chemical solution is often an important weathering process. But, inevitably, it is slow and its effects may be overtaken by other, more powerful, erosive processes such as the pounding of storm waves.

Above: Some of the most striking features along a cliffed coast are those sculpted by the ceaseless battering of the sea. Caves occur quite commonly at weak points in the rock face; for once the sea has cut a hole in the rock, it enlarges it by compression and erosion. Collapse of the cave roof may produce a blowhole. If two caves develop on opposite sides of a headland, the waves may erode through their back walls to carve a natural arch. The sea will continue to erode the arch. When the roof of the arch gives way and debris is carried away by the waves, a large pillar or stack is left offshore. Further erosion may leave a stump, only revealed at low tide.

Below: Robin Hood's Bay in Yorkshire, created by the rapid erosion of cliffs of soft rock. In many such cases, the sea actually erodes very little material, but it encourages mass movement processes to operate on the cliff and then removes material that slumps onto the beach—as in happening in the foreground.

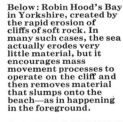

Heather Angel

Alphabet & Image

The Ocean Floor

Like the back of the moon, the floor of the ocean was almost entirely unknown until a few years ago. In the days of the great circum-global expedition of HMS *Challenger* in 1872-1876 the depth of the ocean was still being determined by line sounding. This was achieved by laboriously unwinding a line with a weight attached to the end until it touched the ocean bottom. As the ocean is commonly 5,000 m (3 miles) deep, this was very time consuming and required careful judgement.

During and after the First World War, echo sounding was introduced. At first it consisted of letting off a single sound pulse into the ocean and 'listening' for its echo from the bottom. Knowing the speed of sound in water and the time taken for the echo to return to the surface, the depth of water could then be determined.

Under the stimulus of the Second World War continuously recording deep-sea echo sounders were developed which synchronized the repeated firing of a sound pulse with a recording device, such as an electrically-activated 'pen' scanning a moving paper roll. These echo sounders produced a continuous profile of the ocean floor along the line of the ship's course.

Because of this invention we now have a comprehensive and detailed idea of the morphology of the floors of seas and oceans—comprehensive because it can be obtained automatically whenever a ship is under way; detailed because it can provide precision within 2 m (6 ft) or so in depths of 5,000 m (3 miles) of water. For maximum accuracy it is necessary to actually measure the temperature of the ocean water from top to bottom, because this, together with salinity (saltiness) and pressure, affects the precise speed of transmission of sound.

Other methods similar to echo sounding include *continuous seismic profiling*, which can also be obtained from a moving vessel. However, this method uses a more powerful and lower frequency sound source than echo sounding. This will not only reflect back off the immediate ocean floor, but also in part penetrate through it, to be reflected back by underlying sediment layers and rock surfaces. In this way more information is gained about the structure of the rocks beneath the sea bed.

The *sidescan sonar* is a further advance, as it can look obliquely sideways from a ship, instead of vertically downwards, and therefore cover a broad band across the ocean floor. It is particularly good at picking out the pattern of rock layers which outcrop on the sea floor.

Ocean floor provinces

From all this wealth of information we can conclude that the ocean floor has just as varied a 'landscape' as the surfaces of the continents. The floor is made up of a series of major 'provinces', each with its own special characteristics. Working outwards from the coast, the first is known as the *continental shelf*, followed by the *continental slope* and the *continental rise*, and then out on to the *abyssal plains* and *hills*. However, at destructive plate margins, where the oceanic crust is subducted below the continental crust at the foot of the continental slope, deep *ocean trenches* are

THE OCEAN FLOOR

mid-oceanic ridge

transform fault

flat-topped seamount (guyot)

seamount

volcanic island

ocean trench

Above: This idealized panorama of the ocean floor illustrates the major sea-floor features to be expected in any ocean basin. In order to show these features clearly, the vertical scale is greatly exaggerated and the features have been grouped closer together than they are actually found. The depths are shown as if they were illuminated, although in reality there is little light below 200 m and it is completely dark below 1,000 m in the oceans.

Right: Recent pillow lavas on the mid-Atlantic ridge. Where molten lava erupts underwater, the leading edges of the flow very quickly and solidify into these pillow-like masses. Sediment is often trapped between the pillows and this helps to date the period of eruption. Unfortunately, chemical reactions between the fresh lava and seawater often make the usual radioactive methods of age determination unreliable, but the oldest known sediments brought up from beneath the ocean floor are 165 million years old.

Lamont Doherty Geological Observatory

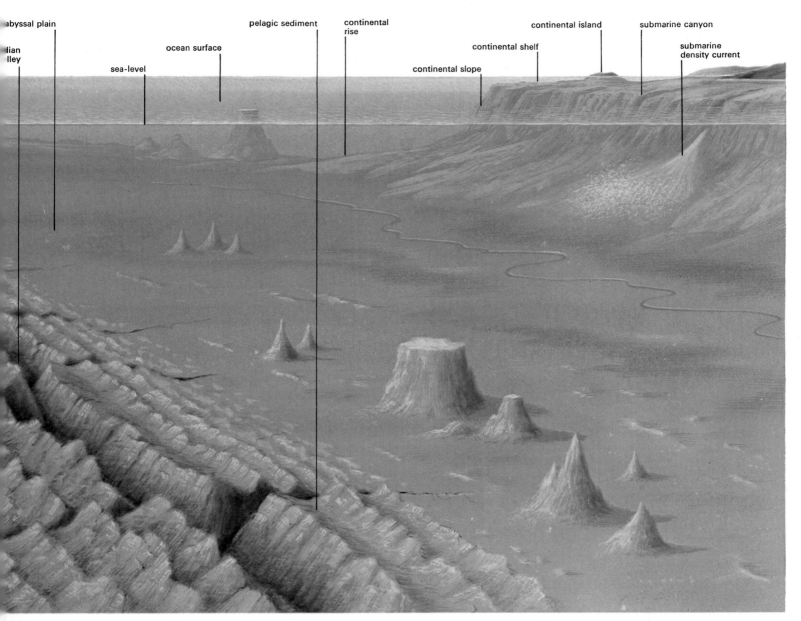

abyssal plain

dian lley

ocean surface

sea-level

pelagic sediment

continental rise

continental slope

continental shelf

continental island

submarine canyon

submarine density current

Left: In the ocean, as well as on land, rocks are often broken by large fractures or faults and form cliffs or escarpments. In this photograph, taken at a depth of 3,390 m (1,850 fathoms), boulders up to a metre across and other smaller angular blocks of rock can be seen at the bottom of a bare rock slope, on Palmer Ridge in the NE Atlantic. Samples of rock can often be obtained by dredging the sea floor.

Below: This picture shows ripples (about 20 cm from crest to crest) produced by currents passing over calcareous sands (rich in calcium carbonate) between outcrops of basaltic rock on top of a seamount, on the Carlsberg Ridge in the Indian Ocean. The photograph was taken 2,500 m down. Despite the conditions of darkness and great pressure, animals still thrive. A sea lily (or crinoid) is visible, its branched arms open to catch small organisms on which it feeds.

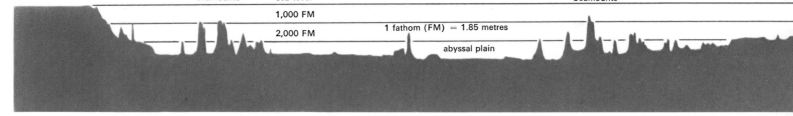

Kelvin seamounts   sea-level   Corner Seamounts

1,000 FM

2,000 FM   1 fathom (FM) = 1.85 metres

abyssal plain

Above: A cross-section of the bottom of the N Atlantic. The topographical profile shown is of the sea floor from Martha's Vineyard, Massachusetts (USA) to Gibraltar, 5,600 km away. An accurate picture of the undersea 'landscape' is given by modern devices such as this echo-sounding machine (left), which is producing a trace of the sea-floor off the Canary Islands in the Atlantic as the sounding ship moves over it. Each line records the echoes from one sound pulse.

developed instead of a continental rise. The final major province of the ocean floor comprises the flanks and crest of the *mid-oceanic ridges* or *rises*.

The *continental shelves* are the submerged edges of the continents. The water over them is usually no more than about 200 m (660 ft) deep. Because of its shallowness the sea bottom here is strongly affected by tidal and other currents which disturb and transport the sandy, clayey and shelly sediments produced by coastal erosion and by the growth of plants and animals in these shallow ocean waters. The width of the continental shelves varies in different parts of the oceans, from 2 km (1.25 miles) or less off the coast of Chile, to 320 km (200 miles) off Land's End in England, to over 1,200 km (750 miles) off the Arctic coast of Siberia.

At the seaward limit of the shelf there is usually an abrupt change in slope, and the sea bottom then descends steeply towards the deep ocean floor. This steep slope is known as the *continental slope*. It often declines at a rate of between 1 in 40 and 1 in 6 (the latter comparable with the steeper hillsides on land) from a depth of about 200 m (660 ft) to around 3,000 m (about 2 miles) deep. In parts of the ocean it is covered by a mantle, sometimes unstable, of clay and silty clay. Elsewhere it consists of the more or less cut-off edges of the layers of sediment making up the continental shelves. It is the continental slope, not the coastline, that marks the true boundary of each continent.

Many continental slopes are incised with vast steep-sided *submarine canyons* that cut back into the continental shelves —often nearly to the coast itself. Sometimes they occur directly off the mouths of major rivers: one, for example, has been discovered directly in front of the mouth of the River Congo in Africa. The canyons cut deep into the sea-floor, usually emerging somewhere near the foot of the continental slope, where there is often a fan-shaped sedimentary deposit on the deep-sea floor. These troughs are the result of submarine erosion by sediment en route more or less directly from the near-shore to the deep-sea floor.

At the base of the continental slope there is generally a more gently inclining province (sloping at a rate of 1 in 100 to 1 in 700) known as the *continental rise*, which takes the sea-floor down gradually to truly oceanic depths of 4,000 to over 5,000 m (16,500 ft). The rise is made up of sediments brought down by dense, heavy flows of sediment-laden water called *submarine density currents*, sometimes along submarine canyons from the adjacent continent, thereby building up the ocean floor above its normal level. The rise represents the coarser deposits of slowing density currents. Beyond it are the extensive *abyssal plains*.

The almost flat, featureless abyssal plains have been called 'the smoothest surfaces on earth'. Their actual inclinations are between 1 in 1,000 and 1 in 10,000. Beneath them is the irregular igneous basaltic crust. Over them are deposited the finer suspended debris which ultimately settle out from the larger density currents.

Mainly in the Pacific Ocean, beyond the influence of density currents, the ocean floor is composed of a series of gently moulded *abyssal hills*. The undulations reflect the original unevenness of the igneous basement. On these abyssal hills rain the slowly accumulating remains of planktonic (floating) plants and animals, which lived in the surface waters, but whose skeletons fall to the depths to form a fairly uniform blanket of sediment. In the narrower Atlantic Ocean, however, the abyssal plains stretch right out to the flanks of the *mid-oceanic ridge*.

The mid-oceanic ridge consists of a crestal region adjacent to the centre line along which new igneous crustal material (basalt) is being injected, and a flank region in which the crust very gradually subsides as it cools and is pushed away from the centre line. A slow-spreading ridge often has a characteristic median rift valley, as in the Atlantic, with peaks rising thousands of metres on either side of a fissure on average 50 km (30 miles) wide. Some points along the crest may actually project above sea-level as an island, such as Iceland, or as a sub-aerial volcano, such as Tristan da Cunha in the South Atlantic. Faster-spreading ridges, as in the south-east Pacific, generally lack such a central rift valley and have a lower profile.

The mid-oceanic ridges or rises are the site of formation of new ocean floor. Old ocean floor is consumed by underthrust-

Above and below: Echo sounders beam sound waves to the bottom and measure the time taken for the echo to be reflected back to the ship. A major advance came with seismic surveying, which uses more powerful low-frequency equipment to penetrate the sea floor and record underlying sediment layers and rock. By towing the array of devices, interference from ship-board noises can be avoided. These seismic reflection profiles (above) across the Bay of Biscay show that great thicknesses of sediment have accumulated under abyssal plain conditions. Multilayered profiles are often an indication that numerous episodes of deposition have occurred, by deep-sea density currents.

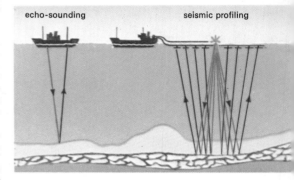

echo-sounding   seismic profiling

Seaphot

Above: A diver inspects the wreck of the sunken *Cooma* in the shallow waters of the continental shelf of Australia.

Right: The radiating feeding tracks on this abyssal plain (more than 5,500 m deep) indicates an animal buried in the soft calcareous *Globigerina* ooze. A sea lily can also be seen.

National Institute of Oceanography

Left: This NASA shot of the Atlantic coast off Cape Hatteras shows the extent of the continental shelf off the NE United States beneath the ocean waters. The line of puffy clouds marks the junction between the colder water covering the shelf and the warmer Gulf Stream waters further out. The shelf is an average 120 m deep.

Right: The very slow rates of sediment accumulation on the deep-sea floor may leave very resistant remains, such as whales' earbones and sharks' teeth, at or near the surface of sediment for very long periods. This now-extinct shark's tooth was dredged in the Pacific from a depth of over 4,000 m by HMS *Challenger* in 1874.

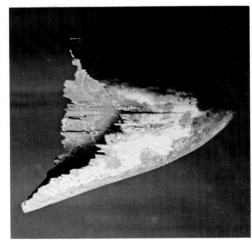

Alphabet & Image

ing, either beneath continents, or beneath other pieces of oceanic crust. At the point where the ocean floor is deflected downwards by crustal activity an *ocean trench* is formed. It is in these trenches that the greatest depths on the deep ocean floor are found. A depth of 11,033 m (36,198 ft) was recorded by echo sounding from the Marianas Trench off the Philippines.

Composition of the ocean floor

New ocean floor, freshly created at the mid-ocean ridges, is made of basaltic igneous rock. This may be either extruded onto the ocean floor as pillow lavas, or intruded as horizontal sills or vertical dykes into pre-existing sediments or igneous rocks. These rocks form the crest of the mid-ocean ridges. They also form the foundations of individual volcanoes or chains of volcanoes, and of their submerged counterparts, the volcanic *seamounts*. Seamounts are isolated peaks rising from the ocean floor, and are especially numerous in the Pacific Ocean. Here, in the Tonga Trench between Samoa and New Zealand, is the highest known seamount, its summit being some 8,690 m (28,500 ft) above the sea bed.

The original surface of the volcanic mid-oceanic ridge crest is very rugged. In time the depressions get filled in with *pelagic sediment* (mostly the skeletal remains of planktonic organisms) which is often re-deposited by slumping off the steep slopes of the surrounding volcanic rocks. The deposit in these so-called sediment 'ponds' is likely at first to be calcareous, because of the calcium carbonate content of the remains of the microscopic algae called *coccolithophores*, and the microscopic animals called *foraminifers*. In time the whole of the original surface will be blanketed by these deposits, known as *calcareous ooze*, and this is generally the case on the upper flanks of mid-ocean ridges.

At greater depths the ocean floor passes below the level (4,000 to 5,000 m) at which calcium carbonate dissolves. Here the sediment consists only of insoluble clay or the remains of siliceous (silica rich) organisms such as *diatoms* and *radiolarians*. Therefore drilling through those parts of the ocean floor covered by the oldest sediments will often reveal a sequence of non-calcareous, then calcareous sediments, then volcanic basalt rock.

From the shallowest water to the greatest depths, the ocean floor is almost universally colonized by animals of one kind or another. In soft sediment they live by burrowing into the sediment, on hard rock attached to the surface. Where currents run near the bottom it may be patterned by ripple marks, and near areas influenced by the past and present polar ice caps are found sand, silt and blocks of erratic rock, carried and eventually dropped by drifting icebergs. In fact the ocean floor is a veritable repository of the entire history of our planet.

JIM, an atmospheric diving suit (ADS) so massive that a man can safely take it into deep water and breathe air at ordinary atmospheric pressure.

Ocean Exploration

The voyage of the Greek explorer Pytheas beyond the Mediterranean Sea and along the Atlantic coast of Europe, around 325BC, is often considered as the start of ocean exploration. Perhaps its chief significance, indeed, lies in the fact that the voyage seems to have been deliberately undertaken and a written record of it was preserved. Others such as the Phoenicians had certainly been at least some of the way before.

The next milestones in ocean exploration are commonly taken to be the Spanish and Portuguese explorations of the Atlantic and Indian Oceans in the fifteenth century, culminating in the circumnavigation of the globe by Ferdinand Magellan's expedition in the early sixteenth century. But here again, others had explored these oceans before. The Vikings in the North Atlantic and the Polynesians in the Pacific had made remarkable journeys in small and often open boats in the first millenium AD. The record of these explorations is, however, contained only in the Nordic Sagas and oral traditions of the Polynesians. The Spanish and Portuguese on the other hand provided tangible and written testimony of their exploits to their royal sponsors, which we can still read today.

The centuries which followed saw a continuing and systematic exploration of the world's oceans by European navigators. The rewards were trade, wealth and colonies. By the eighteenth century, in the light of the developing interest in science, exploration was being deliberately sponsored to push back human knowledge of the limits of the oceans. In this spirit the English sea-captain James Cook made three major voyages mapping out the Southern Ocean which surrounds Antarctica and later, in the early nineteenth century, Sir James Clark Ross followed him southwards to explore the ice-rimmed margins of the 'last continent'. Previously Ross had been engaged in seeking a Northwest Passage from the Atlantic to the Pacific via the frozen seas of the Arctic region.

Perhaps the middle of the nineteenth century should be regarded as the end of the heroic age of ocean exploration. Certainly with the voyage of HMS *Challenger* around the world in 1872-1876, the systematic study of the world's oceans, in all their aspects, had begun in earnest.

The oceans of the world

We now know there are five major oceans —the Atlantic, the Pacific, the Indian, and the Arctic, with the southern extremities of the first three, around Antarctica, being gathered up as a fifth: the so-called Southern or Antarctic Ocean. Together with the adjacent seas, these make up 71 per cent of the surface of planet earth. They contain over 97 per cent of the water which occurs at the earth's surface.

The Pacific Ocean is the largest, measuring 15,500 km (9,600 miles) from Bering Strait in the north to Antarctica

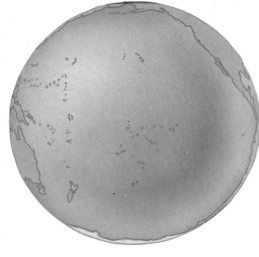

Above and below left: Planet earth or planet water? Looking down from a position directly over Tahiti in the Pacific, the earth appears to be almost totally covered in ocean. In contrast, this world map from about 1480, possibly known to Columbus, reflects man's long-standing ignorance of the vast oceans (and much of the continents) before the great voyages of discovery.

Below: It is not known when man first tried to explore the sea depths. The earliest record of a diving bell is by the Greek philosopher Aristotle (4th century BC). This 13th-century French painting shows Aristotle's pupil Alexander the Great in a glass barrel, in which he was reputed to have been lowered to the sea-floor. The king claimed he saw a great monster which took 3 days to pass.

M. Pucciarelli

Bildarchiv Preussischer Kulturbesitz

Michael Holford

Left: HMS *Challenger* under sail in the cold Antarctic Ocean. This 3-masted British Navy corvette, her guns replaced with scientific gear, sailed from the Thames in December, 1872, covering 110,844 km in a three and a half year around-the-world expedition. *Challenger*'s auxiliary steam engine enabled her to hold steady over the sea-floor during bottom soundings. The team of six scientists, led by Sir Wyville Thomson, also collected water and bottom samples, plants and animals, and observed sea temperatures and currents. The voyage was a turning point in the science of oceanography.

Right: The chemical laboratory aboard HMS *Challenger*.

Michael Holford

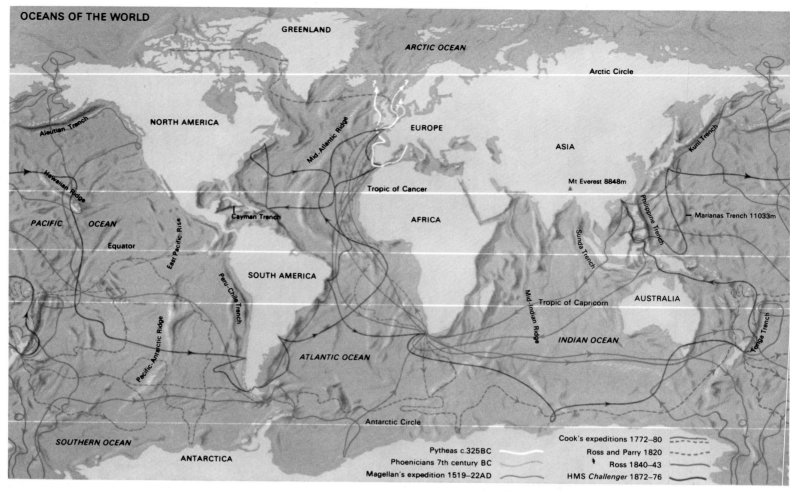

GREENLAND
ARCTIC OCEAN
Arctic Circle
NORTH AMERICA
Aleutian Trench
EUROPE
Mid-Atlantic Ridge
ASIA
Kuril Trench
Hawaiian Ridge
Mt Everest 8848m
Tropic of Cancer
PACIFIC   OCEAN
Cayman Trench
AFRICA
Philippine Trench
Marianas Trench 11033m
East Pacific Rise
Equator
Sunda Trench
SOUTH AMERICA
Peru-Chile Trench
Tropic of Capricorn
AUSTRALIA
Mid-Indian Ridge
Pacific-Antarctic Ridge
INDIAN OCEAN
Tonga Trench
ATLANTIC OCEAN
Antarctic Circle
SOUTHERN OCEAN
ANTARCTICA

Cook's expeditions 1772–80
Pytheas c.325BC   Ross and Parry 1820
Phoenicians 7th century BC   Ross 1840–43
Magellan's expedition 1519–22AD   HMS *Challenger* 1872–76

Above: If the world's oceans are drained of water, the varied 'landscape' of the sea-floor is revealed. The deepest trench is 25% further below sea-level than the highest land mountain is above it. The routes of some of the major sea voyages show man's increasing awareness of his watery planet.

Right: This corer is a hollow steel tube that is dropped into the sea-floor sediments. When withdrawn, it retrieves undisturbed samples of clay, ooze, volcanic ash and other bottom deposits.

Below: This probe is used to measure deep-sea temperatures and salinity (saltiness).

Seaphot

National Institute of Oceanography

in the south, and 17,550 km (10,905 miles) at its widest between Panama and Thailand. Altogether, the Pacific covers some 180 million km² (69.5 million sq miles). The other oceans are much smaller: the Atlantic covering 106 million km² (40 million sq miles) and the Indian Ocean 75 million km² (29 million sq miles). By comparison the North Sea covers a mere 600,000 km² (230,000 sq miles).

These figures begin to bring home to us the immensity of the unknown task that the early ocean explorers undertook when they started their endeavour. It also illustrates the uniqueness of planet earth in our solar system, where all the other planets lack water almost completely.

Below the surface

Knowing the extent of the ocean is, however, only half the story. The other major dimension of the oceans is their depth. The environment of deep water is quite alien and mysterious to man, but exploration of it has developed intensively in recent years.

The surface waters of the oceans are illuminated and heated by the sun's rays. They are therefore, at least in lower latitudes, both well-lit and warm. Gradually the sun's rays are absorbed as they penetrate the ocean water, and below about 100 m (330 ft) the water becomes increasingly cold and dark.

Moreover, at the surface the ocean water has only the pressure of the atmosphere above it, and the movement of the atmosphere to stir it. Pressure increases rapidly with depth owing to the weight of the overlying water. Water movement, especially wave motion, is largely reduced below a few tens of

Above: Jacques-Yves Cousteau in one of his submersible *Sea Fleas*. This Frenchman has perhaps done more than any other living man to excite the public imagination about life under the sea. He also perfected the aqualung, fed with compressed air, which has freed divers to explore the shallower sea depths.

Below: This unmanned, underwater, self-propelled television camera has been nick-named 'Snoopy' by its operators at the US Naval Undersea Center. By sending its pictures back to the surface vessel, Snoopy can be used over wide areas. Linked flash-units are needed at depths which lack natural light.

Right: The American nuclear submarine USS *Whale* surfaces at the North Pole in 1959. In the previous year, its sister submarine USS *Nautilus* made its epic voyage—the first crossing, underwater and under the ice, of the frozen Arctic Ocean by way of the North Pole. A new dimension was added to ocean exploration.

metres from the surface. To live at depth in the oceans, animals must be adapted to the pressure, the cold and the dark. Plants cannot live there at all. Because of their dependence on light energy for photosynthesis they are restricted to the top 100 m (330 ft) of the oceans' waters.

Most of the investigation into conditions in the ocean depths has been carried out remotely—by suspending instruments from lines operated overboard from surface ships. The number of devices available for this kind of exploration is enormous, but they generally fall into a smaller number of categories. There are thermometers, water-bottles and current meters for measuring the physical and chemical characteristics of the water; dredges, corers, heat probes and cameras for studying bottom sediments and bottom life; weighted lines for measuring the depth of the bottom.

Bottom depths were routinely measured by weighted line before the First World War. As small sampling or *coring tubes* were usually attached to the end of every sounding line, this had the incidental advantage that a small sample of the sea-bed was brought back on most occasions. Modern coring devices are very much larger, and heavily weighted. They are allowed to fall freely for the last few metres to the sea-floor by the action of a trigger mechanism and penetrations of up to 30 m (100 ft) can be made into soft sediment in this way. Steel chain-link dredges are used to break off sedimentary and igneous rocks and bring them back to the surface—a crude but effective way of bringing samples back to the surface from 3 to 5 km (2 or 3 miles) down. Cameras in pressure-sealed containers with linked

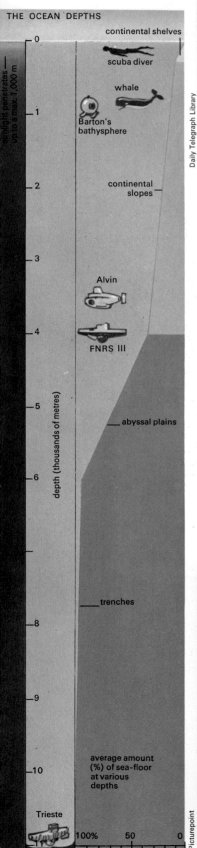

THE OCEAN DEPTHS

sunlight penetrates — up to a max. 1,000 m

depth (thousands of metres)

- 0 — continental shelves
- scuba diver
- whale
- Barton's bathysphere
- 1 —
- 2 — continental slopes
- 3 —
- Alvin
- 4 —
- FNRS III
- 5 — abyssal plains
- 6 —
- 7 — trenches
- 8 —
- 9 —
- 10 — average amount (%) of sea-floor at various depths

Trieste

100%   50   0

Picturepoint

Daily Telegraph Library

Keystone

Above: A bell and decompression chamber (left). Decompression presents a hindrance to divers, but is necessary to avoid decompression sickness ('the bends') caused by returning too rapidly to the surface from the ocean depths.

Left: A 'deep sea spacesuit', specially designed to withstand pressures at 300m. The suit is made of magnesium alloy. The diver breathes air at normal atmospheric pressure from a 20-hour supply of oxygen strapped to his back. There are four portholes for the diver to view the undersea world, and tools can be manipulated by lever-controlled fingers which protrude from the bulbous gloves.

Below: One of the most ambitious series of undersea experiments involves a carefully designed habitat in which 'aquanauts' can live for weeks at a time in shallow depths. This US-built *Sealab III* is a non-propelled craft from which divers can undertake salvage and construction work and scientists perform oceanographic and biological studies.

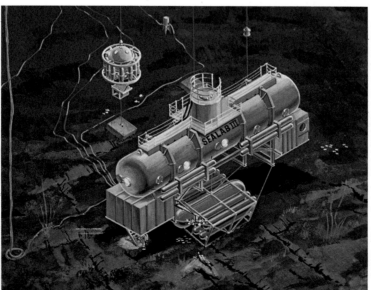

flash-units (there is no natural light in the deep sea) are used to take photographs either continuously or automatically by triggering with a weight suspended below the camera.

The temperature of the deeps is taken by special thermometers, called *reversing thermometers*, which break their mercury thread at the desired depth so that they can be read when returned to the surface. Water samples are often taken at the same time using *reversing water-bottles* such as the Nansen bottle. These are clamped in series on to the hydrographic (water measuring) wire carried on most research ships, lowered to the required depth and then triggered in rapid sequence by sending a mechanical messenger down the wire. Some instruments such as the *bathythermograph* are self-recording and continuously plot temperature (as measured by thermal sensors) against depth (as measured by pressure sensors) during lowering and raising.

Most meters used for measuring the strength and direction of ocean currents are also self-recording. They can be suspended in series at different depths beneath a stationary ship or, alternatively, fixed to a buoy and anchor system for weeks or occasionally months on end.

These routine and often tedious explorations of the oceans may not appear very glamorous, but they have probably contributed the most to our understanding of how the oceans work physically, chemically and biologically. We now have records made in this way that span more than a century of investigation, during which this last frontier of our planet has been well and truly probed.

The inconvenience of having to manipu-

Left: The *bathysphere* developed by Otis Barton. This iron diving bell, only 145 cm in diameter, was taken down to a depth of over 900 m off the coast of Bermuda by Barton and his fellow American, Dr William Beebe, in 1934. It was to be fifteen years before any other men would beat their record dive.

Above: The deepest descent ever achieved by man was made in this bathyscaphe (Greek for 'deep boat'). In 1960, the *Trieste*, manned by Piccard and Walsh, reached the ocean bed 10,917 m down in the Marianas Trench. The pressure was over one tonne per cm² (7.5 tons per sq inch) and the temperature a cold 3°C.

Right: The two-man submersible *Alvin* is built to survive pressure down to about 2,000 m. The *Alvin* has recently explored the Cayman Trough on the Caribbean floor for the Woods Hole Institution, but hit the headlines in 1966 by recovering the nuclear bomb lost by the US Air Force off the coast of Spain.

late instruments in deep water rather like a puppeteer has led many oceanographers to dream of actually venturing into the deep ocean to see conditions at first hand. Contingencies of war or prospect of financial rewards have gradually led to the development of submersibles that can operate in deep water. The problems faced are enormous, and the principal one is pressure. This increases rapidly with depth and any underwater vessel—which must (in order to support human beings) contain air at more or less atmospheric pressure—is liable to collapse or leak under the very great water pressures applied to it.

Over the continental shelves, water depths are only moderate, and in recent years, free-swimming divers using *SCUBA* (Self-Contained Underwater Breathing Apparatus) equipment have been able to dive routinely to 100 m (330 ft). By gradual pressurization and depressurization, and use of unusual combinations of gases for respiration, the extreme depth limit of this system has been trebled. This has been particularly useful in off-shore oil and gas field development, and in the exploration of submerged wrecks and cities, as for instance around the Mediterranean. This approach to diving has proved far more effective and flexible than the use of diving bells or heavy helmeted suits, although it is still not without its considerable dangers.

In these same fairly shallow depths, conventional submarines, with their re-inforced cigar-shaped steel hulls and buoyancy-modifying devices (enabling them to dive or surface at will) can operate easily. Most if not all of these vessels are, however, designed for military activities

and are not suitable for making underwater explorations. Nevertheless, some of the earliest successful measurements of gravity at sea were made in submarines. Also, in 1958 the first successful crossing of the Arctic Ocean was made underwater —and under the ice—by the United States nuclear submarine *Nautilus*. It actually surfaced between the ice floes near the North Pole itself. In many ways this was the last great geographical voyage of ocean exploration and was a remarkable combination of technological and navigational skill, with a blend of traditional audacity and good fortune.

Voyage to the greatest depths

Descending to very great depths, like rising to very great heights, has always been an especial dream and ambition for some human beings. Sometimes both ambitions have been held by the same man. Professor Auguste Piccard, a Swiss physicist, broke both the existing altitude record in a balloon (in 1931) and then the diving record (in 1953). Like Piccard, most divers attempting to descend deep into the ocean have agreed on the necessity for a spherical container to provide the main pressure vessel, as this shape is strongest under compression. The technical problems which arise thereafter concern the use of strong and flawless materials, the problem of creating portholes in such a vessel so that observations can be made through them, and the balancing of the thickness and thus the strength of the shell against its volume and buoyancy.

Several attempts were made earlier in this century to develop the technology of deep diving. In 1934, the Americans Dr

William Beebe and Otis Barton descended 923 m (3,028 ft) in their US-manufactured bathysphere. In August 1953, the French *FNRS 3* reached 2,112 m (6,930 ft) in the Mediterranean, only to have this record broken a month later by Auguste Piccard and his son Jacques, who descended 3,150 m (10,334 ft) to the Mediterranean sea-floor in the Italian-built bathyscaphe *Trieste*. The *FNRS 3* achieved 4,050 m (13,287 ft) in 1954 off the coast of West Africa, but the *Trieste*, purchased by the US Navy and piloted by Jacques Piccard and Lieutenant Donald Walsh, went on to establish an all-time record on January 23, 1960. They descended to 10,917 m (35,820 ft or 6.78 miles) in the Challenger Deep of the Marianas Trench, the deepest part of the deepest trench in the world.

Since that time emphasis has been placed on gaining greater flexibility and potential for observing and collecting from submersibles, rather than achieving record depths. Recent studies on the igneous rocks outcropping on the mid-Atlantic Ridge have been completed using submersibles at depths of around 2,000 m (6,560 ft).

In the Pacific, *Sealab III* has been used to maintain men at a depth of 200 m (650 ft) for a period of two months, making continuous observations of the sea-floor during that time. Scripps Institution of Oceanography in California operates a strange-looking vessel called *Flip* which can be up-ended to provide a very stable working laboratory extending to 100 m (330 ft) below the surface. We may expect continuing development of many other bizarre submersibles directed to economic exploitation or exploration of the sea-floor in the years to come.

143

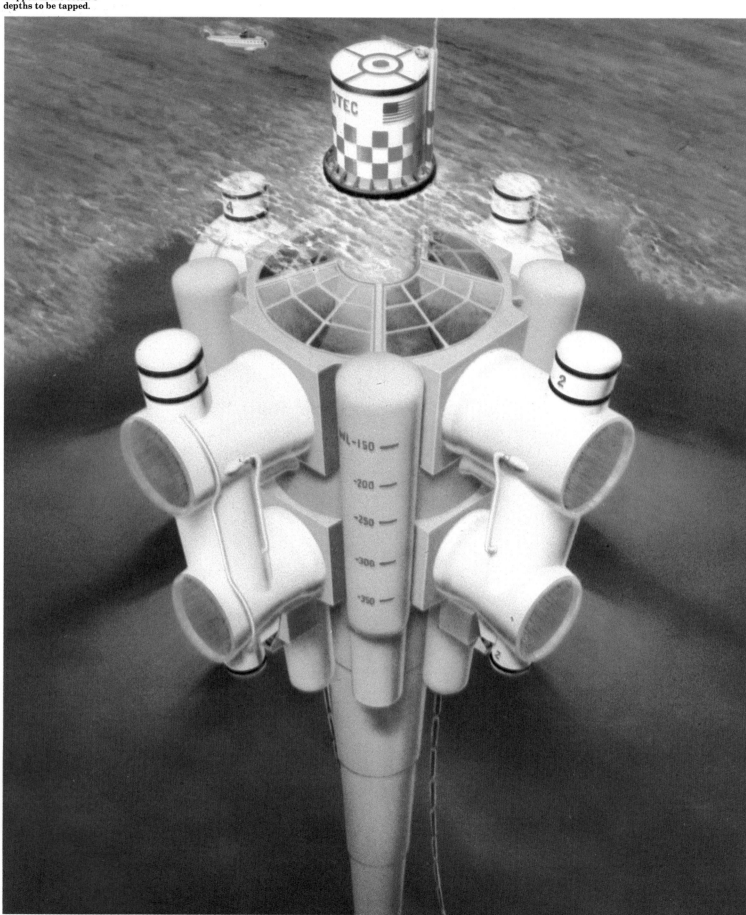

A design for a massive OTEC (Ocean Thermal Energy Conversion) plant. This would allow the huge stores of solar energy trapped in the ocean's depths to be tapped.

Index

Page numbers in *italics* indicate illustrations in addition to text matter on the subject.